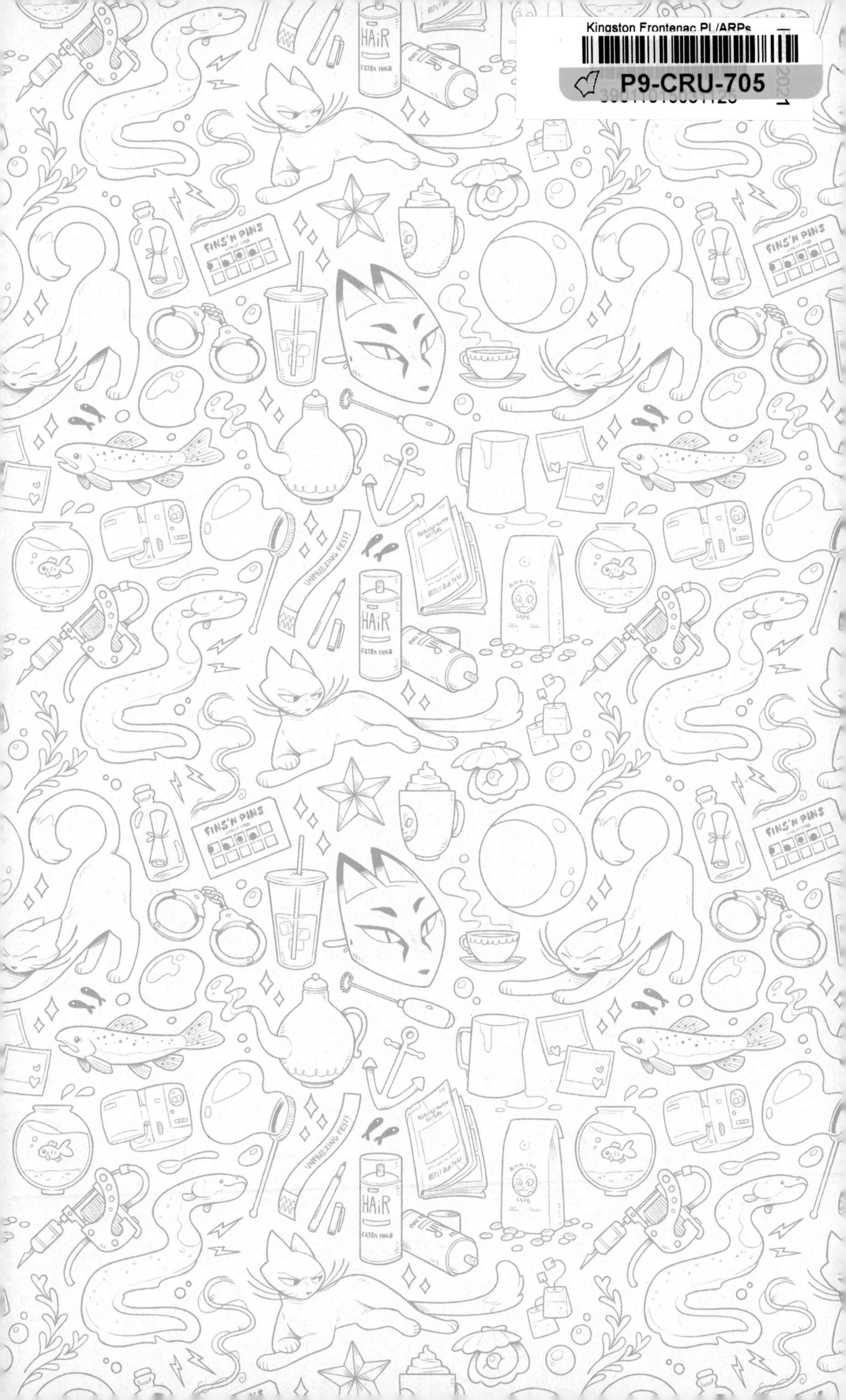
HAiR
EXTRA HOLD
FINS'N PINS
UNFREEZING FEST!
BLACK CAT
CAFE

MoonStruck

VOL 3:
TROUBLED WATERS

 IMAGE COMICS, INC. • **Todd McFarlane:** President • **Jim Valentino:** Vice President • **Marc Silvestri:** Chief Executive Officer • **Erik Larsen:** Chief Financial Officer • **Robert Kirkman:** Chief Operating Officer • **Eric Stephenson:** Publisher / Chief Creative Officer • **Shanna Matuszak:** Editorial Coordinator • **Marla Eizik:** Talent Liaison • **Nicole Lapalme:** Controller • **Leanna Caunter:** Accounting Analyst • **Sue Korpela:** Accounting & HR Manager • **Jeff Boison:** Director of Sales & Publishing Planning • **Dirk Wood:** Director of International Sales & Licensing • **Alex Cox:** Director of Direct Market & Specialty Sales • **Chloe Ramos-Peterson:** Book Market & Library Sales Manager • **Emilio Bautista:** Digital Sales Coordinator • **Kat Salazar:** Director of PR & Marketing • **Drew Fitzgerald:** Marketing Content Associate • **Heather Doornink:** Production Director • **Drew Gill:** Art Director • **Hilary DiLoreto:** Print Manager • **Tricia Ramos:** Traffic Manager • **Erika Schnatz:** Senior Production Artist • **Ryan Brewer:** Production Artist • **Deanna Phelps:** Production Artist • **IMAGECOMICS.COM**

Writer
GRACE ELLIS

Artist
SHAE BEAGLE

Pleasant Mountain Sisters Artist
CLAUDIA AGUIRRE

Colorist
CAITLIN QUIRK

Letterer
CLAYTON COWLES

Editor/Designer
LAURENN MCCUBBIN

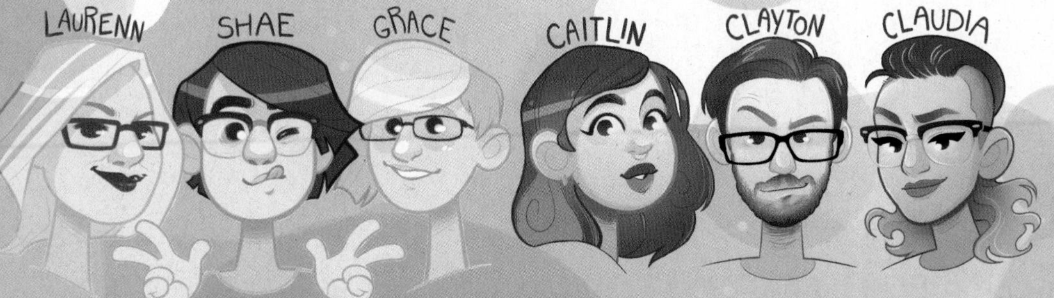
LAURENN
SHAE
GRACE
CAITLIN
CLAYTON
CLAUDIA

teammoonstruck@gmail.com • @teammoonstruck • #moonstruckcomic

CHAPTER ONE

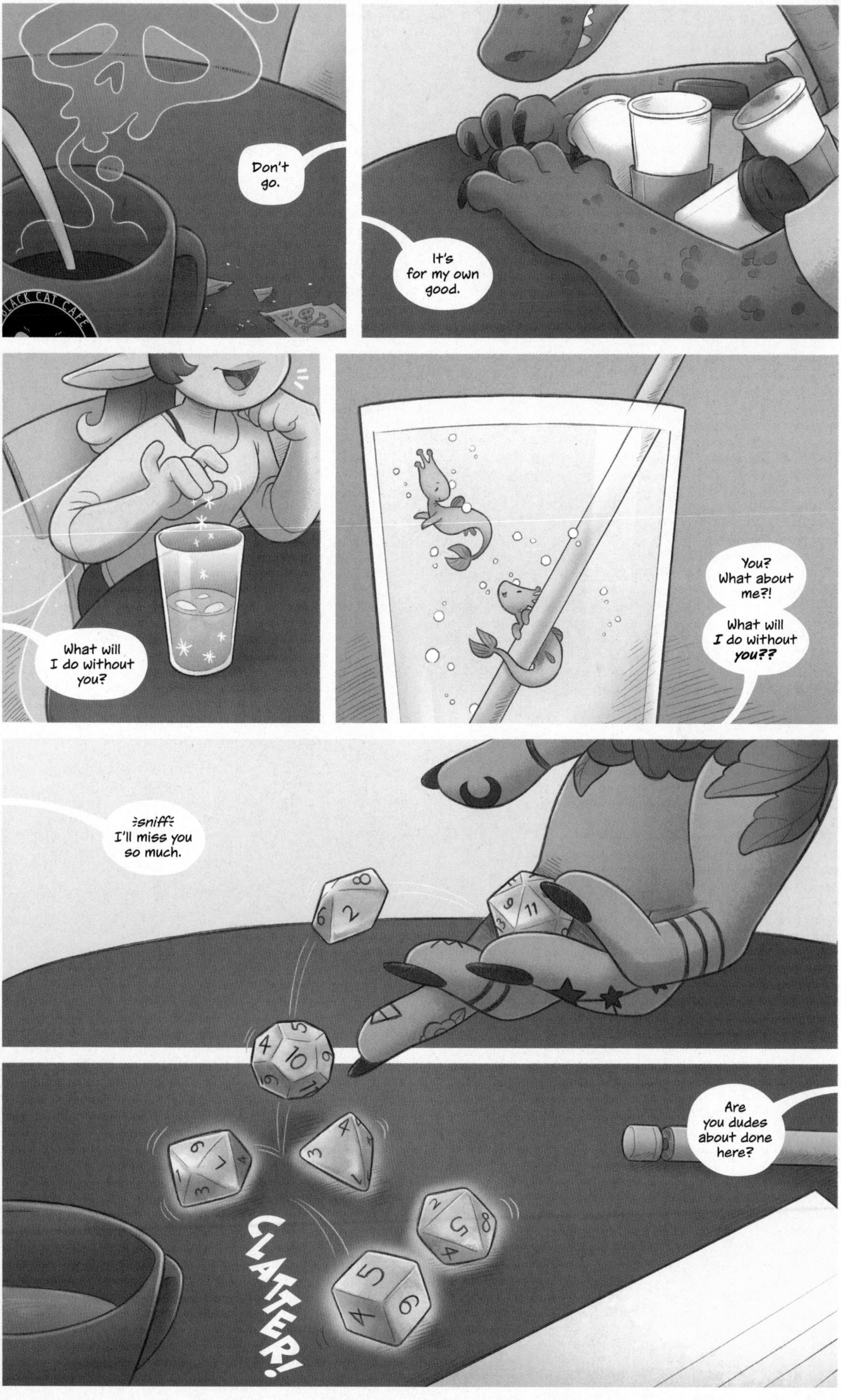
BLACK CAT CAFE
Don't go.
It's for my own good.
What will I do without you?
You? What about me?!
What will I do without ***you??***
sniff I'll miss you so much.
Are you dudes about done here?
CLATTER!

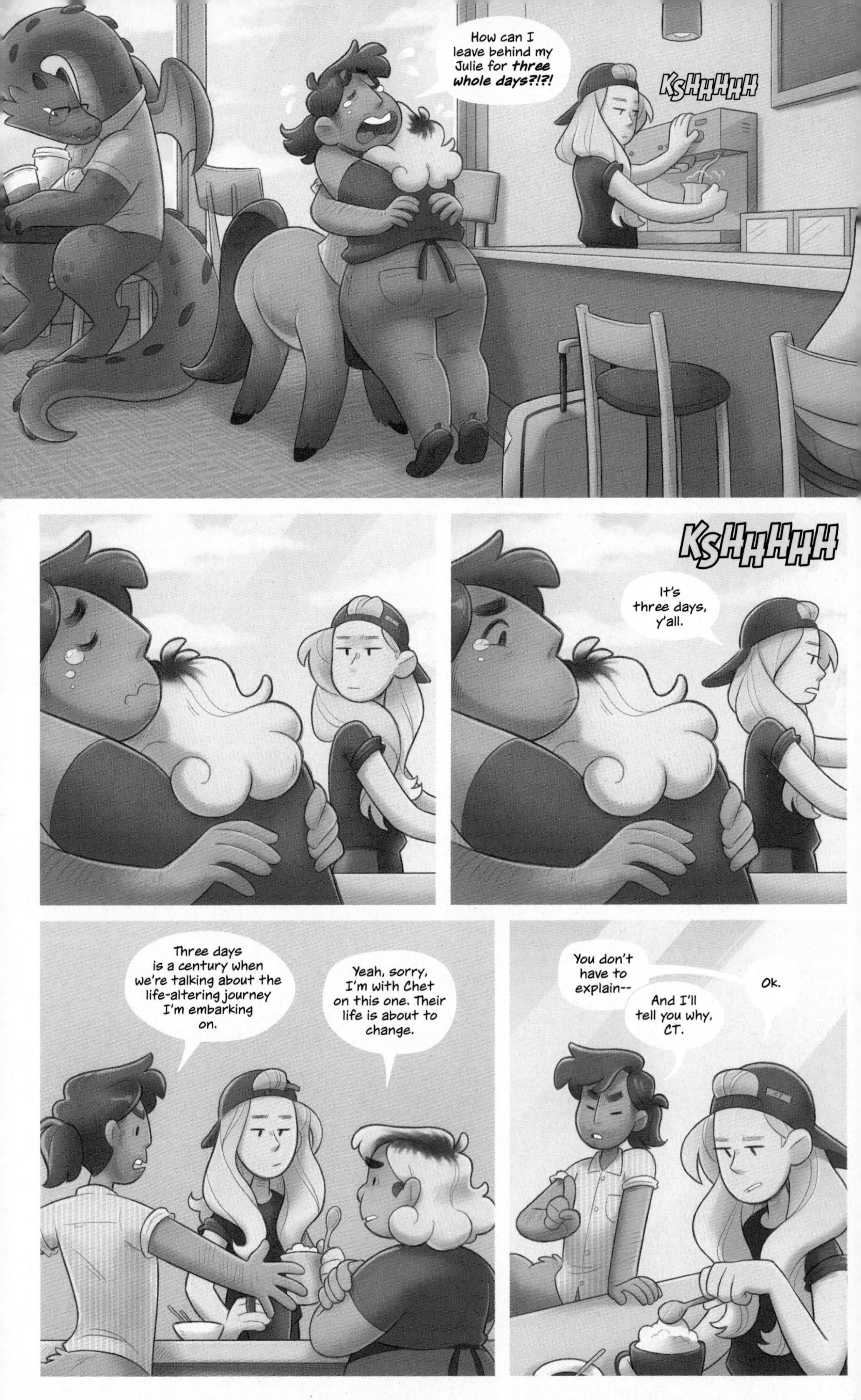
How can I leave behind my Julie for **three whole days?!?!**
KSHHHHH
KSHHHHH
It's three days, y'all.
Three days is a century when we're talking about the life-altering journey I'm embarking on.
Yeah, sorry, I'm with Chet on this one. Their life is about to change.
You don't have to explain--
Ok.
And I'll tell you why, CT.
CT

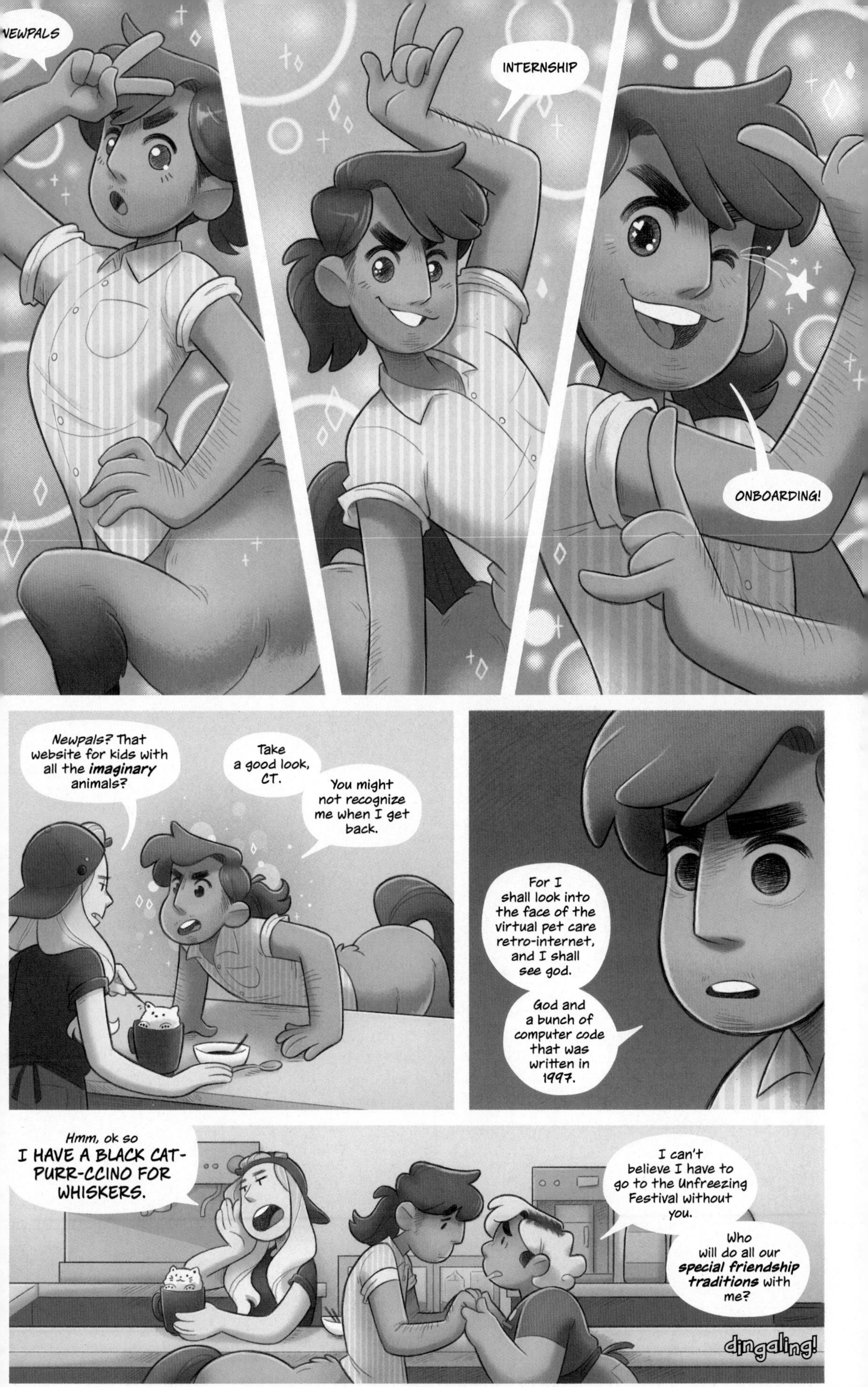
NEWPALS
INTERNSHIP
ONBOARDING!
Newpals? That website for kids with all the imaginary animals?
Take a good look, CT.
You might not recognize me when I get back.
For I shall look into the face of the virtual pet care retro-internet, and I shall see god.
God and a bunch of computer code that was written in 1997.
Hmm, ok so I HAVE A BLACK CAT-PURR-CCINO FOR WHISKERS.
I can't believe I have to go to the Unfreezing Festival without you.
Who will do all our special friendship traditions with me?
dingaling!

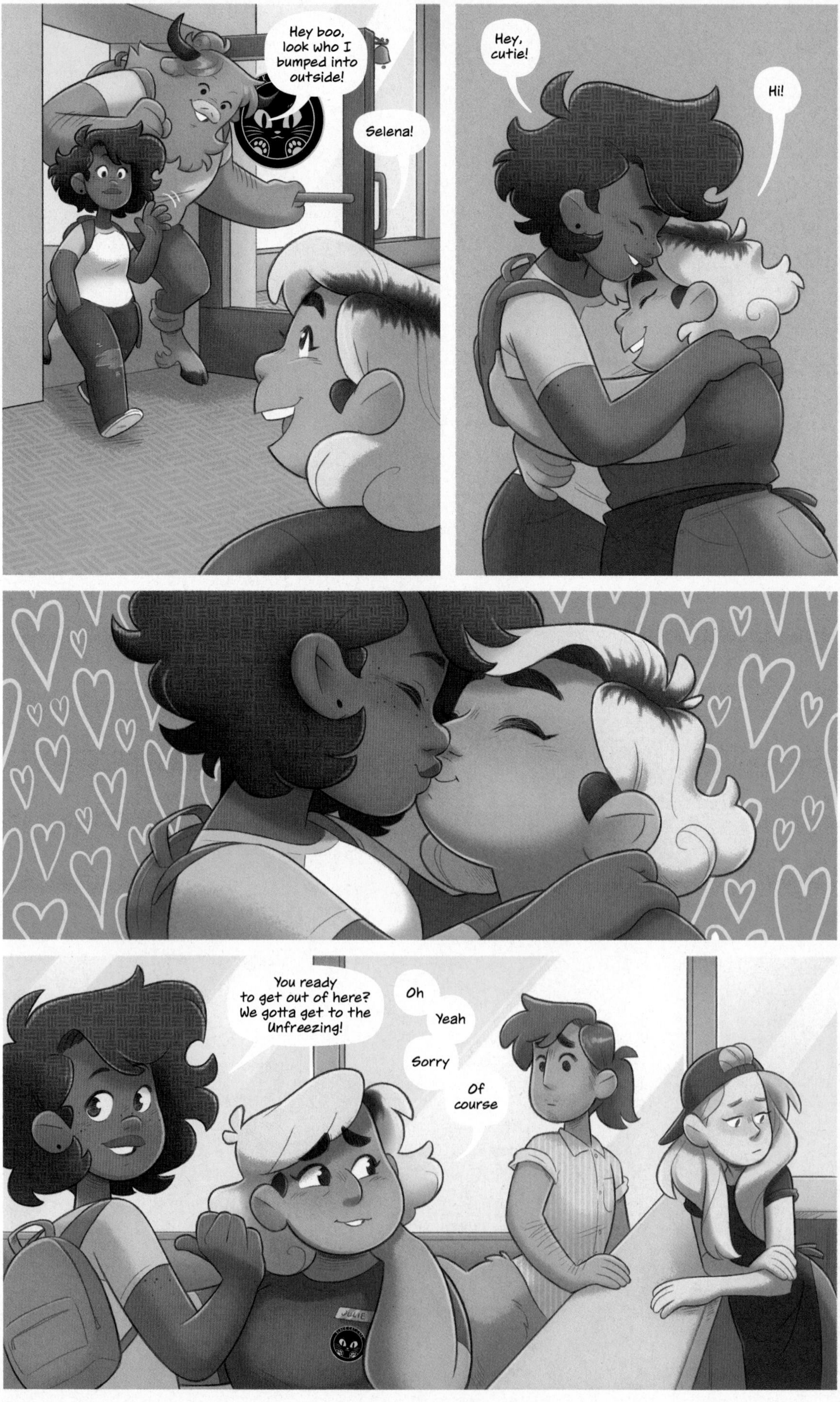
Hey boo, look who I bumped into outside!
Selena!
Hey, cutie!
Hi!
You ready to get out of here? We gotta get to the Unfreezing!
Oh
Yeah
Sorry
Of course

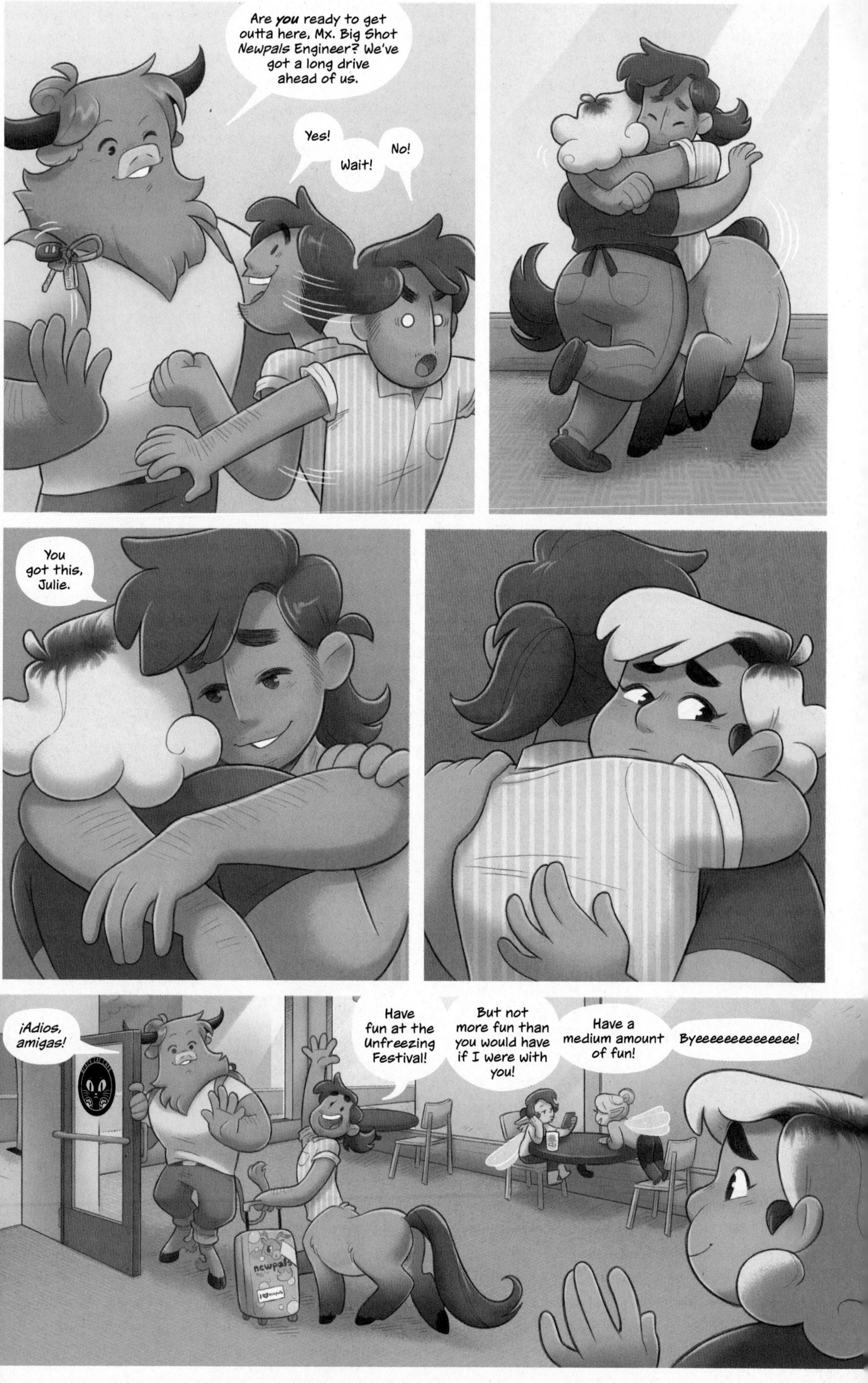
Are *you* ready to get outta here, Mx. Big Shot Newpals Engineer? We've got a long drive ahead of us.
Yes!
Wait!
No!
You got this, Julie.
¡Adios, amigas!
Have fun at the Unfreezing Festival!
But not more fun than you would have if I were with you!
Have a medium amount of fun!
Byeeeeeeeeeeeeee!

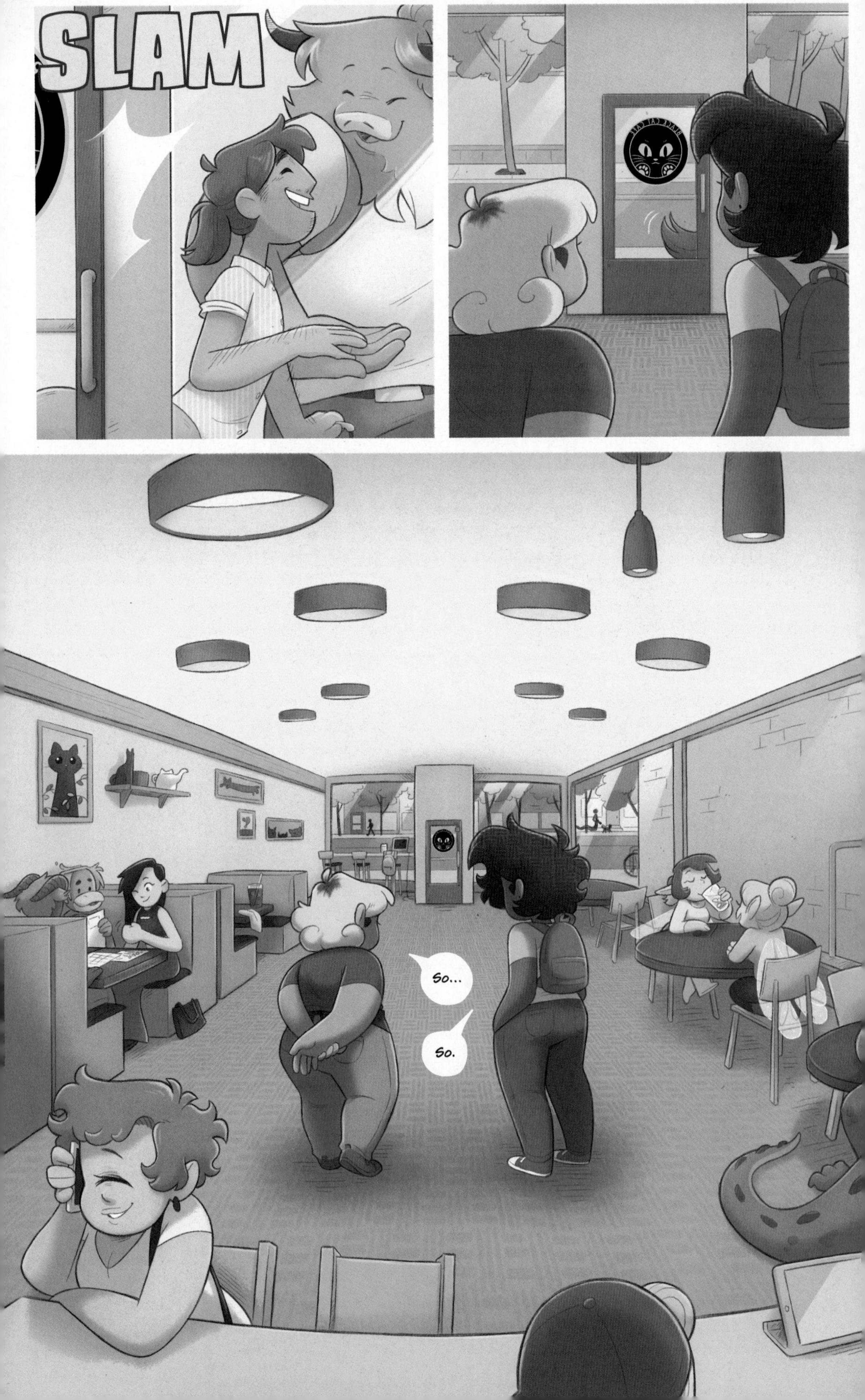
SLAM
So...
So.

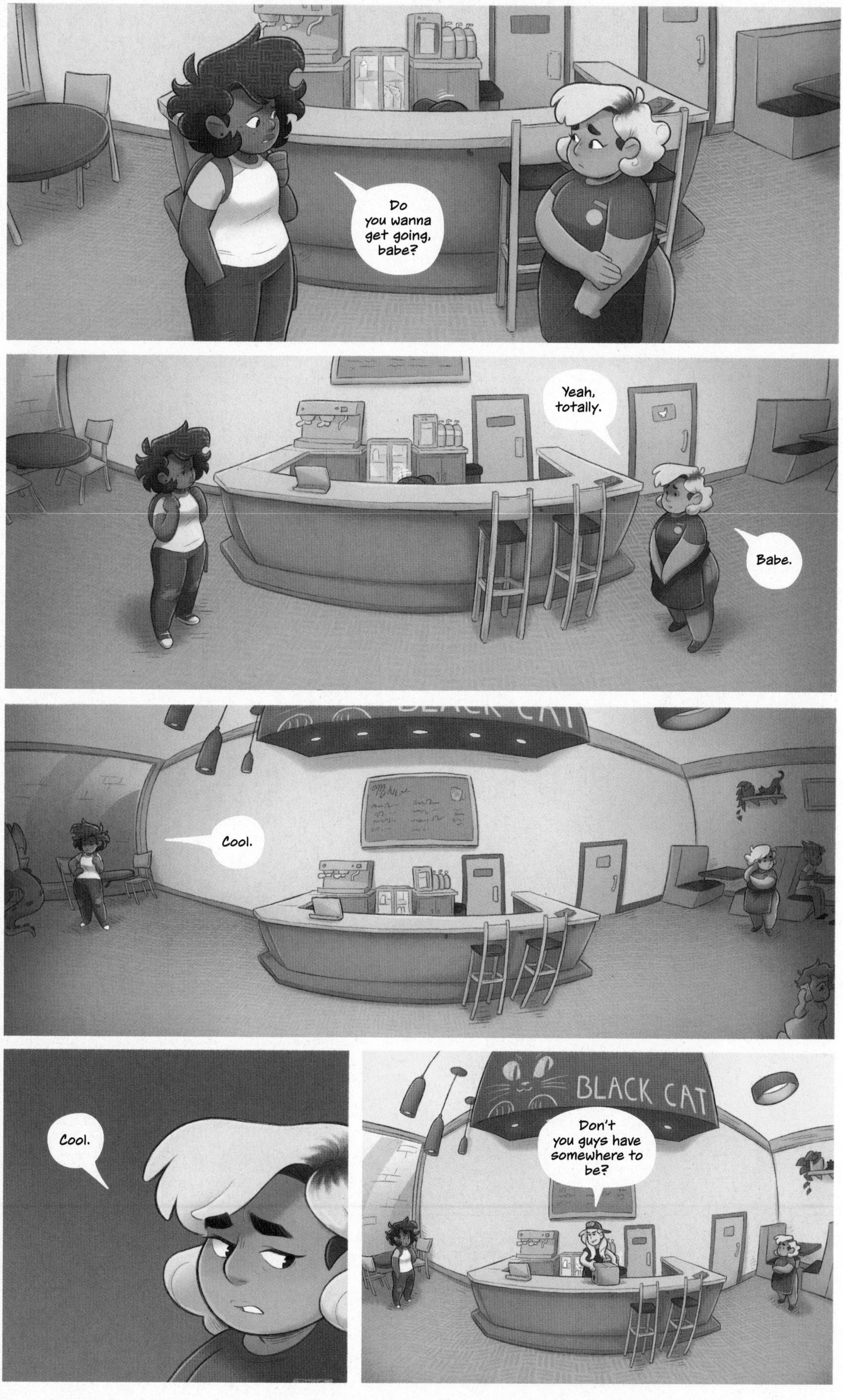
Do you wanna get going, babe?
Yeah, totally.
Babe.
Cool.
Cool.
BLACK CAT
Don't you guys have somewhere to be?

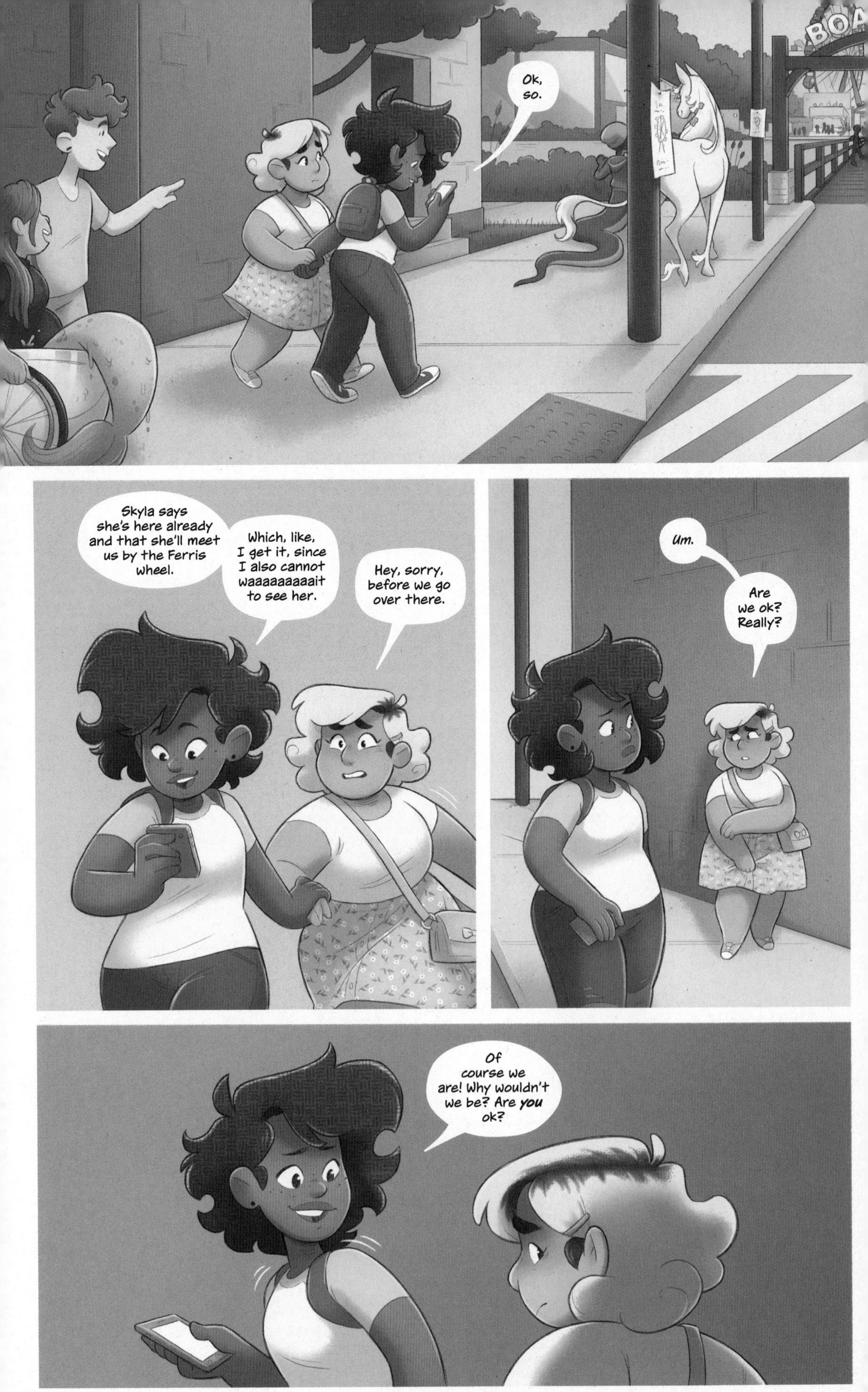
Ok, so.
Skyla says she's here already and that she'll meet us by the Ferris wheel.
Which, like, I get it, since I also cannot waaaaaaaaait to see her.
Hey, sorry, before we go over there.
Um.
Are we ok? Really?
Of course we are! Why wouldn't we be? Are *you* ok?

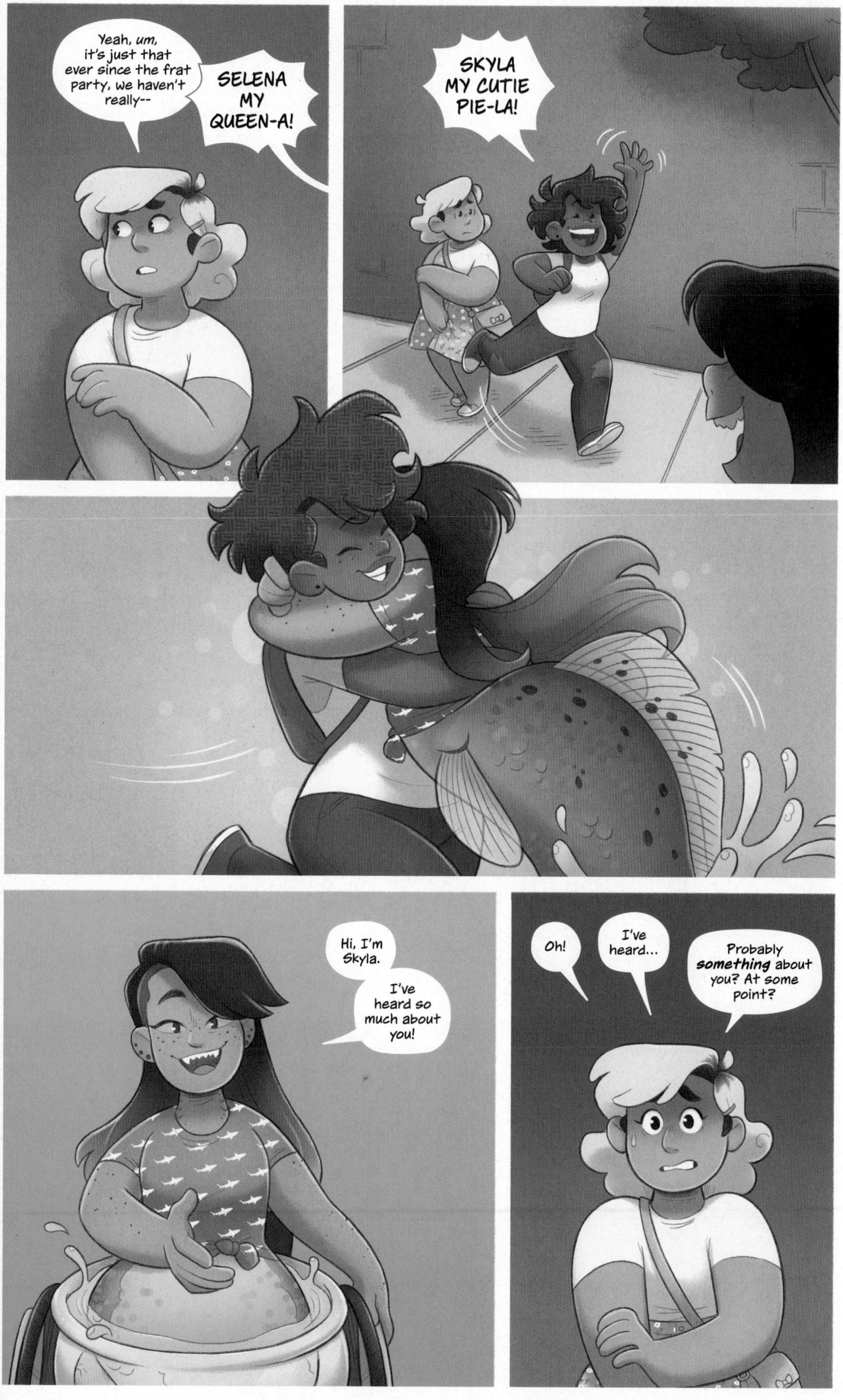

Yeah, *um*, it's just that ever since the frat party, we haven't really--
SELENA MY QUEEN-A!
SKYLA MY CUTIE PIE-LA!
Hi, I'm Skyla.
I've heard so much about you!
Oh!
I've heard...
Probably **something** about you? At some point?

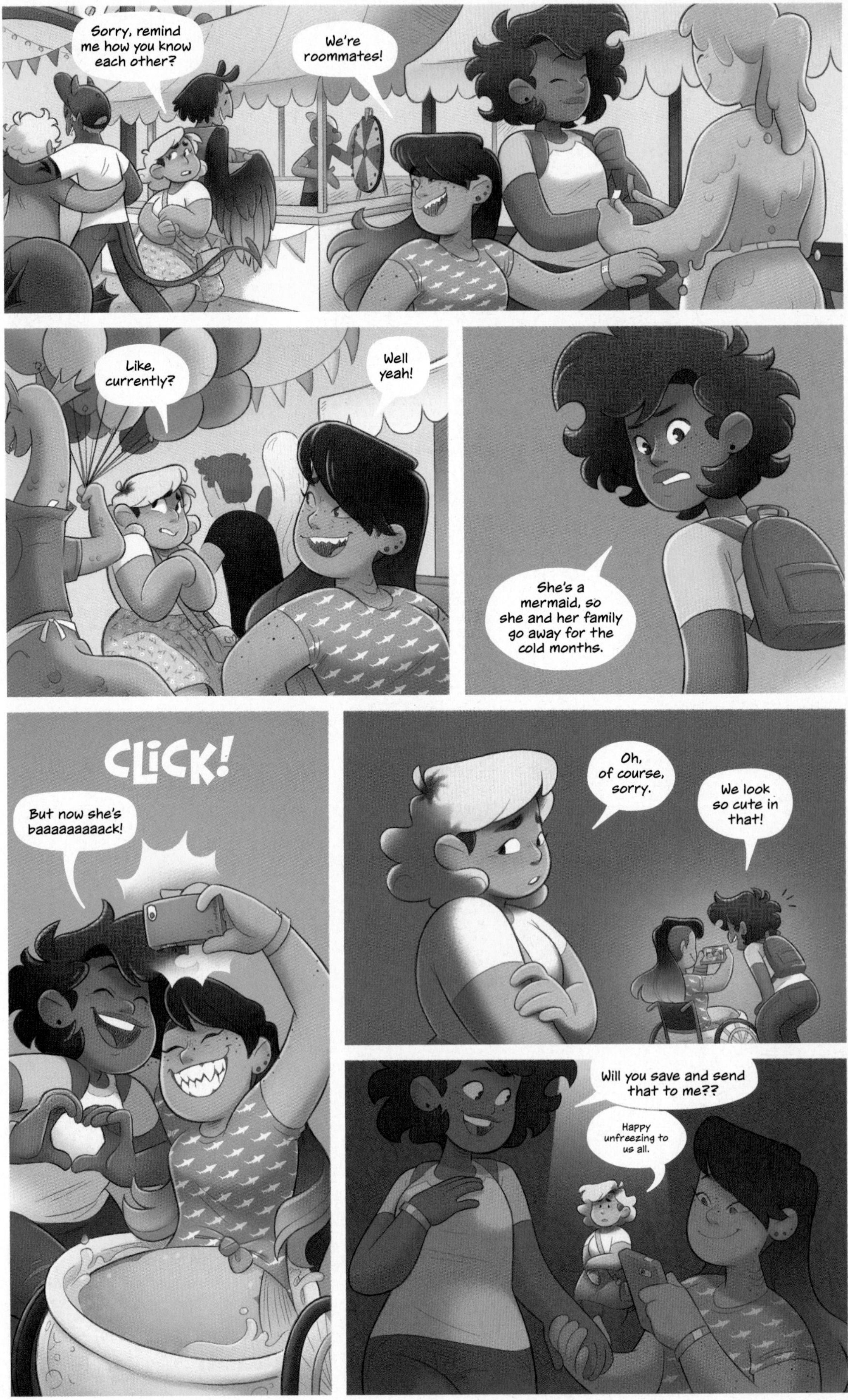
Sorry, remind me how you know each other?
We're roommates!
Like, currently?
Well yeah!
She's a mermaid, so she and her family go away for the cold months.
CLICK!
But now she's baaaaaaaaack!
Oh, of course, sorry.
We look so cute in that!
Will you save and send that to me??
Happy unfreezing to us all.

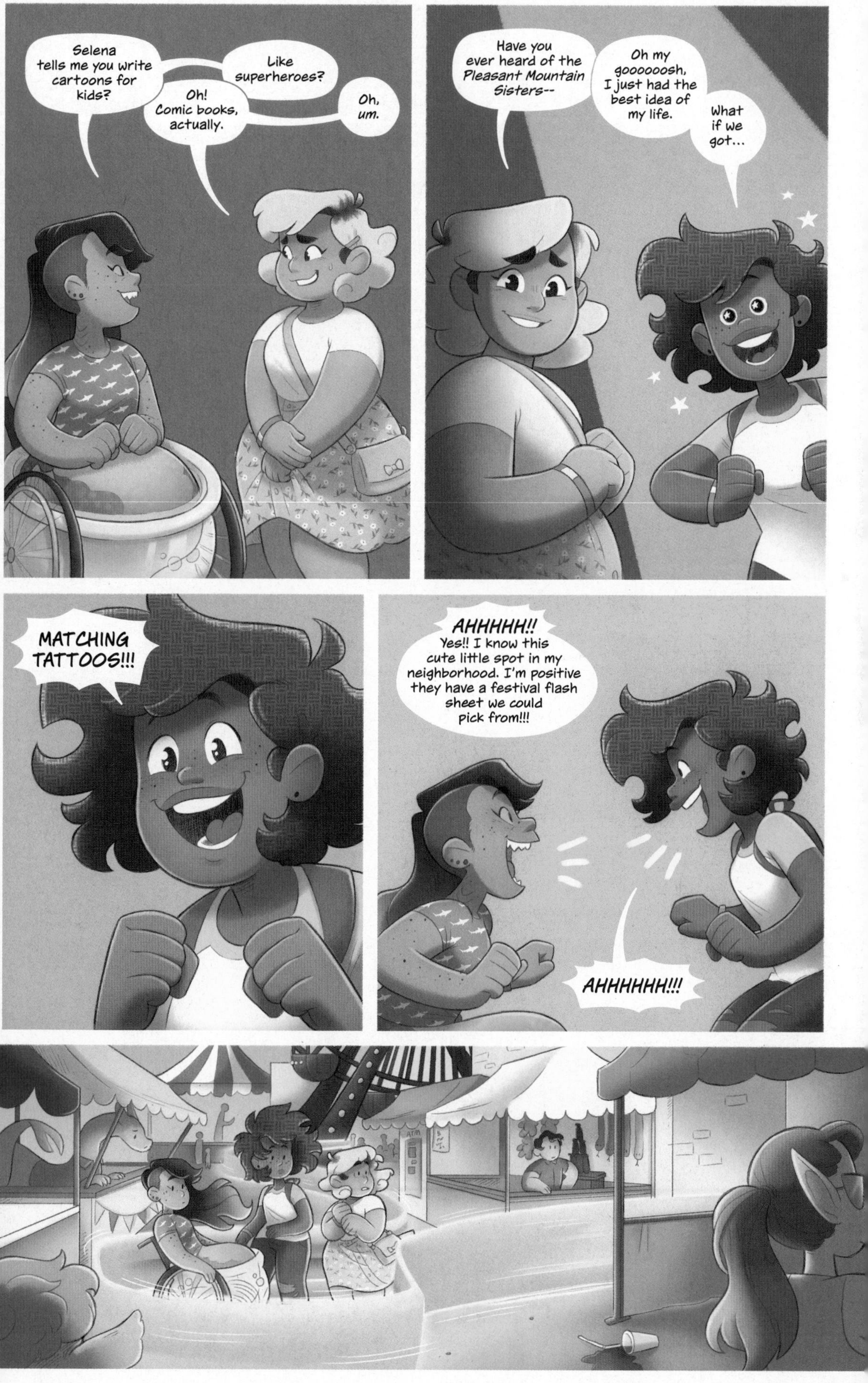
Selena tells me you write cartoons for kids?
Like superheroes?
Oh! Comic books, actually.
Oh, um.
Have you ever heard of the *Pleasant Mountain Sisters*--
Oh my goooooosh, I just had the best idea of my life.
What if we got...
MATCHING TATTOOS!!!
AHHHHH!!
Yes!! I know this cute little spot in my neighborhood. I'm positive they have a festival flash sheet we could pick from!!!
AHHHHHH!!!

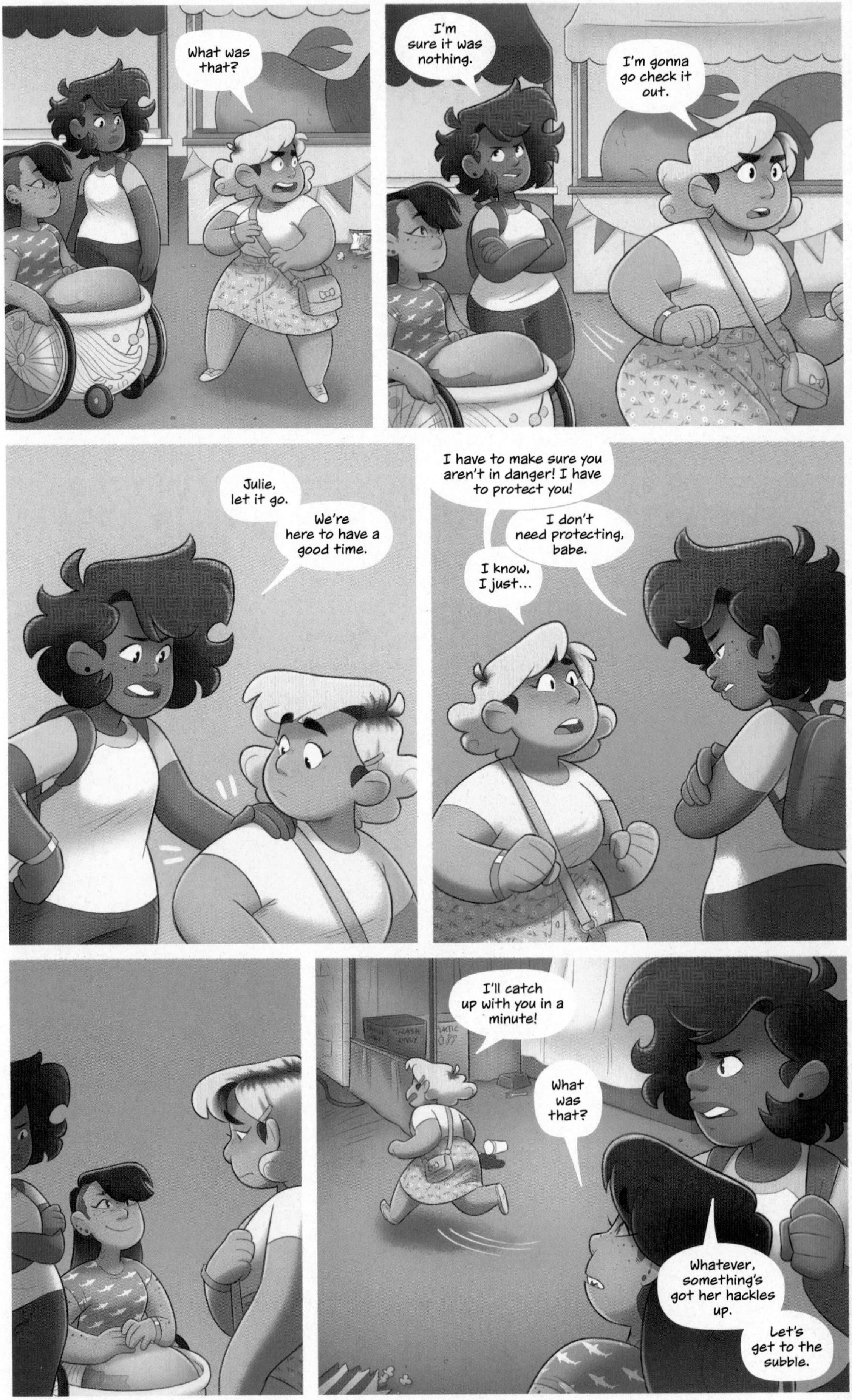
What was that?
I'm sure it was nothing.
I'm gonna go check it out.
Julie, let it go.
We're here to have a good time.
I have to make sure you aren't in danger! I have to protect you!
I don't need protecting, babe.
I know, I just...
I'll catch up with you in a minute!
TRASH ONLY
What was that?
Whatever, something's got her hackles up.
Let's get to the subble.

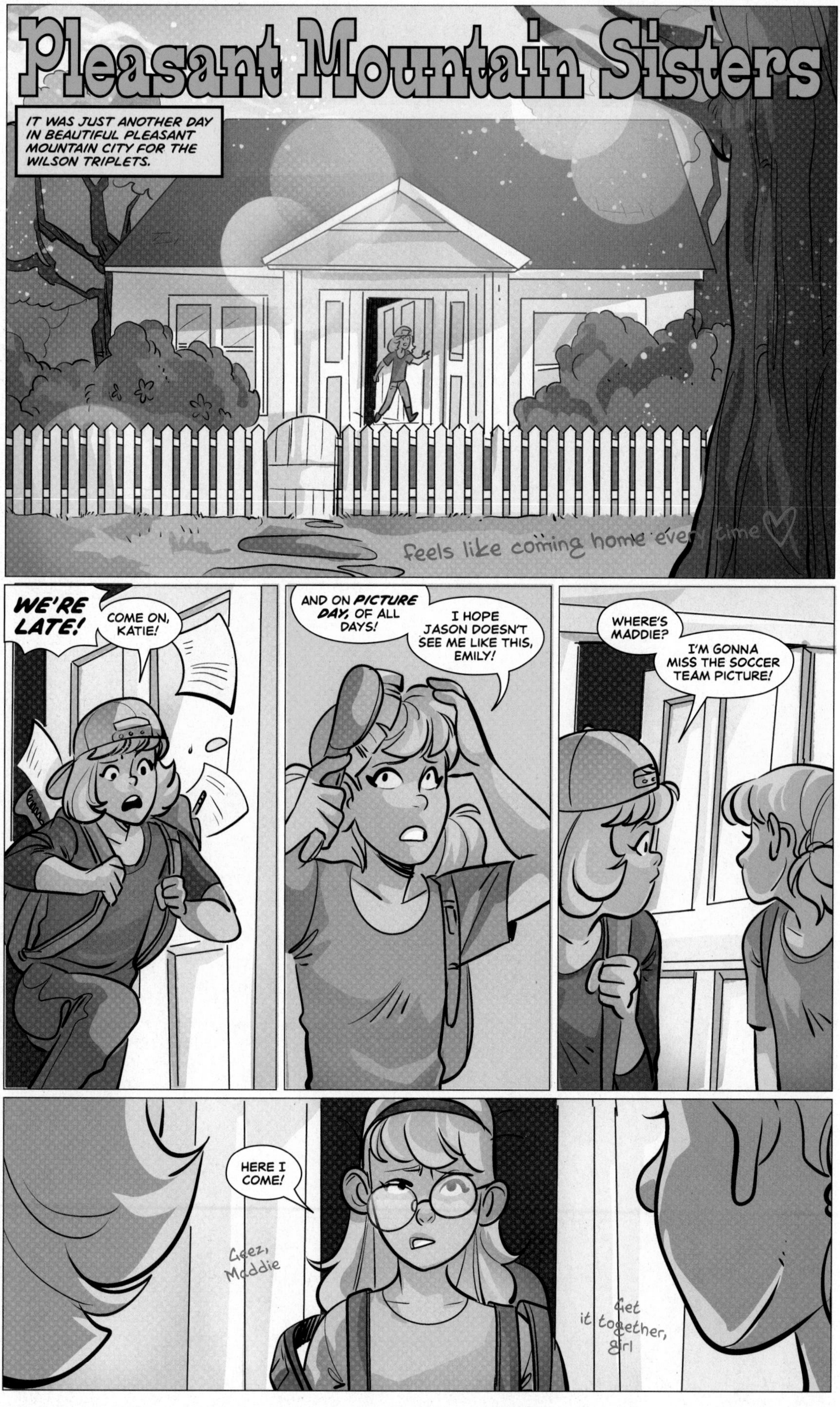
Pleasant Mountain Sisters
IT WAS JUST ANOTHER DAY IN BEAUTIFUL PLEASANT MOUNTAIN CITY FOR THE WILSON TRIPLETS.
feels like coming home every time
WE'RE LATE!
COME ON, KATIE!
AND ON PICTURE DAY, OF ALL DAYS!
I HOPE JASON DOESN'T SEE ME LIKE THIS, EMILY!
WHERE'S MADDIE?
I'M GONNA MISS THE SOCCER TEAM PICTURE!
HERE I COME!
Geez, Maddie
Get it together, girl

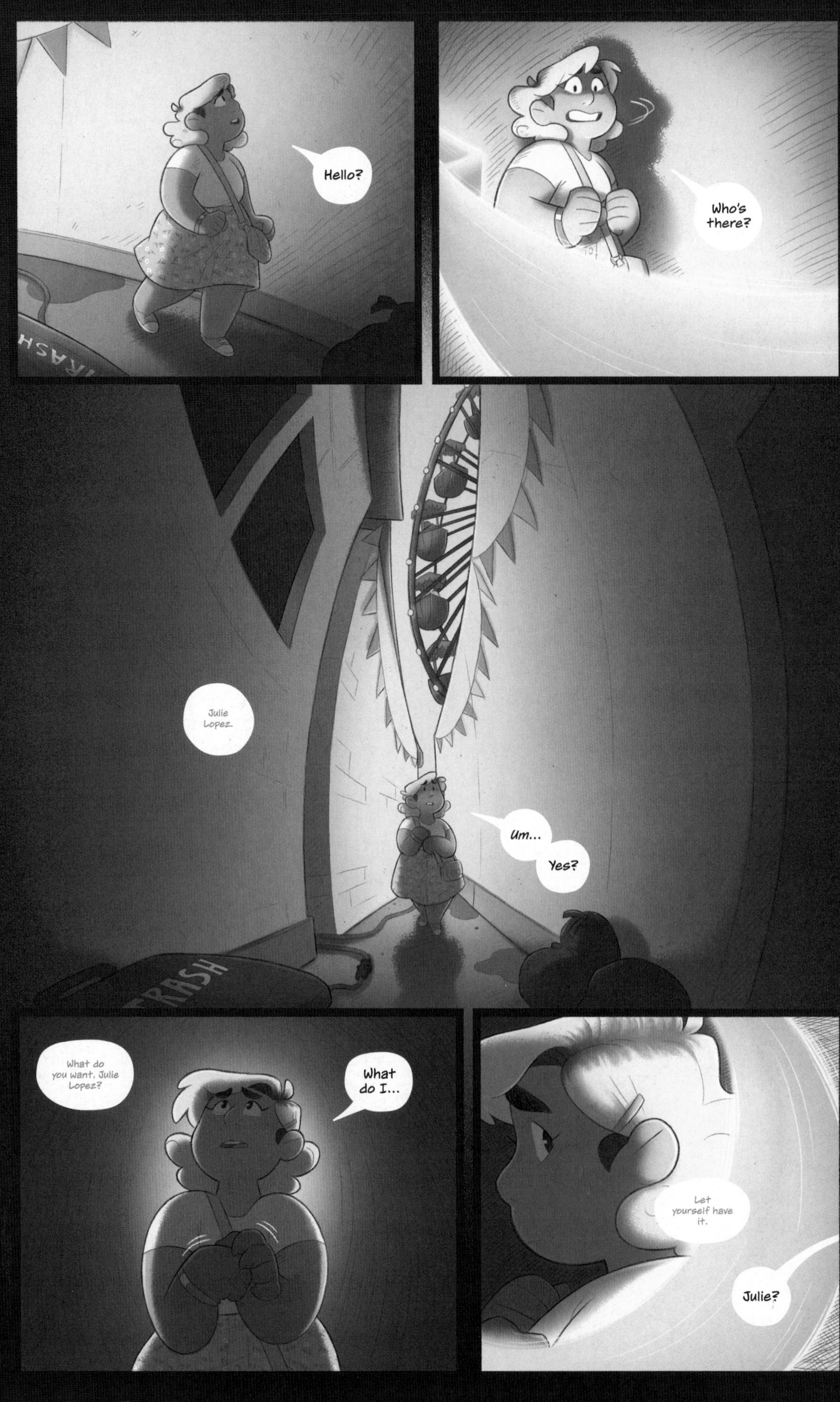

Hello?
Who's there?
TRASH
Julie Lopez.
Um...
Yes?
TRASH
What do you want, Julie Lopez?
What do I...
Let yourself have it.
Julie?

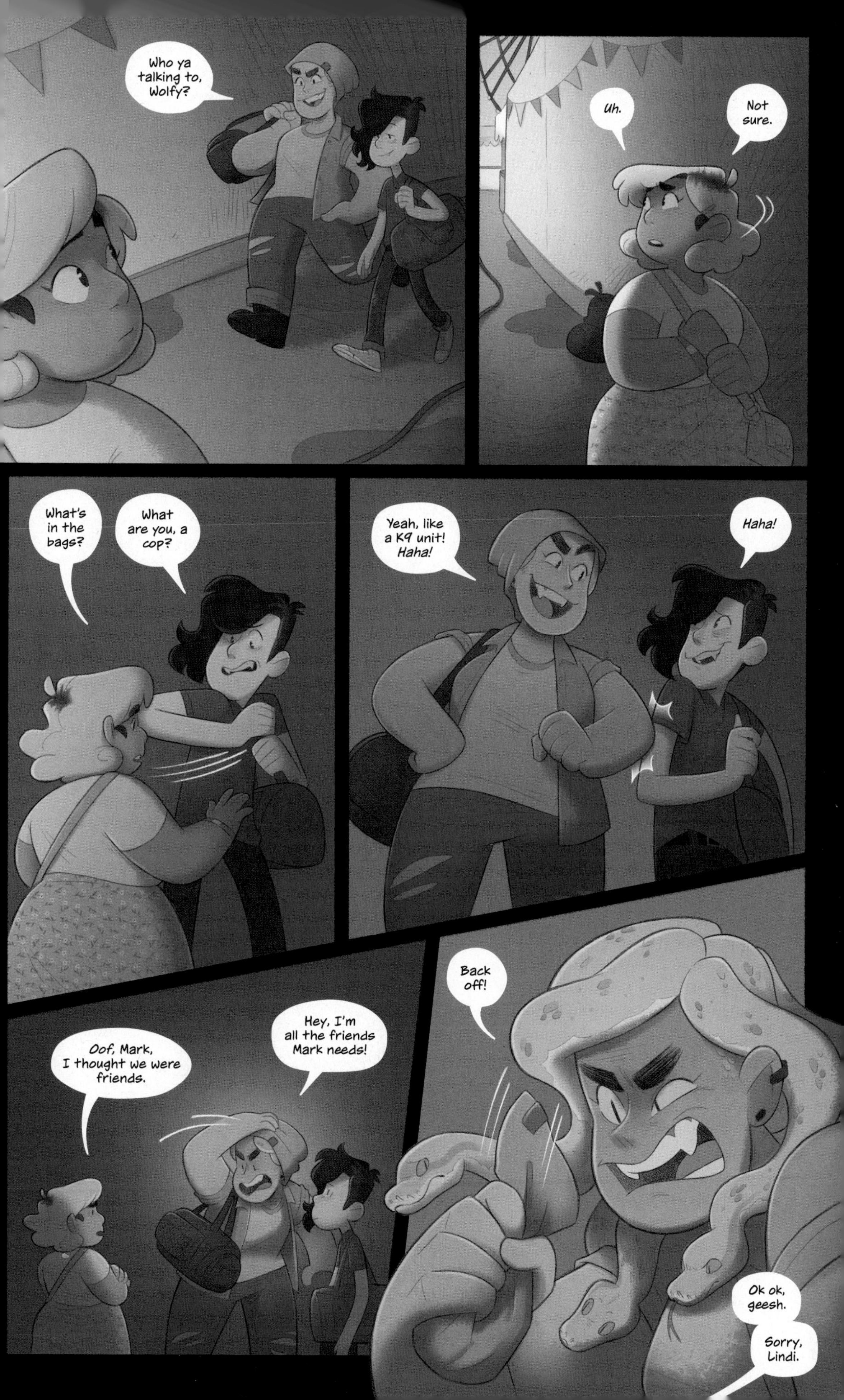
Who ya talking to, Wolfy?
Uh.
Not sure.
What's in the bags?
What are you, a cop?
Yeah, like a K9 unit! Haha!
Haha!
Oof, Mark, I thought we were friends.
Hey, I'm all the friends Mark needs!
Back off!
Ok ok, geesh.
Sorry, Lindi.

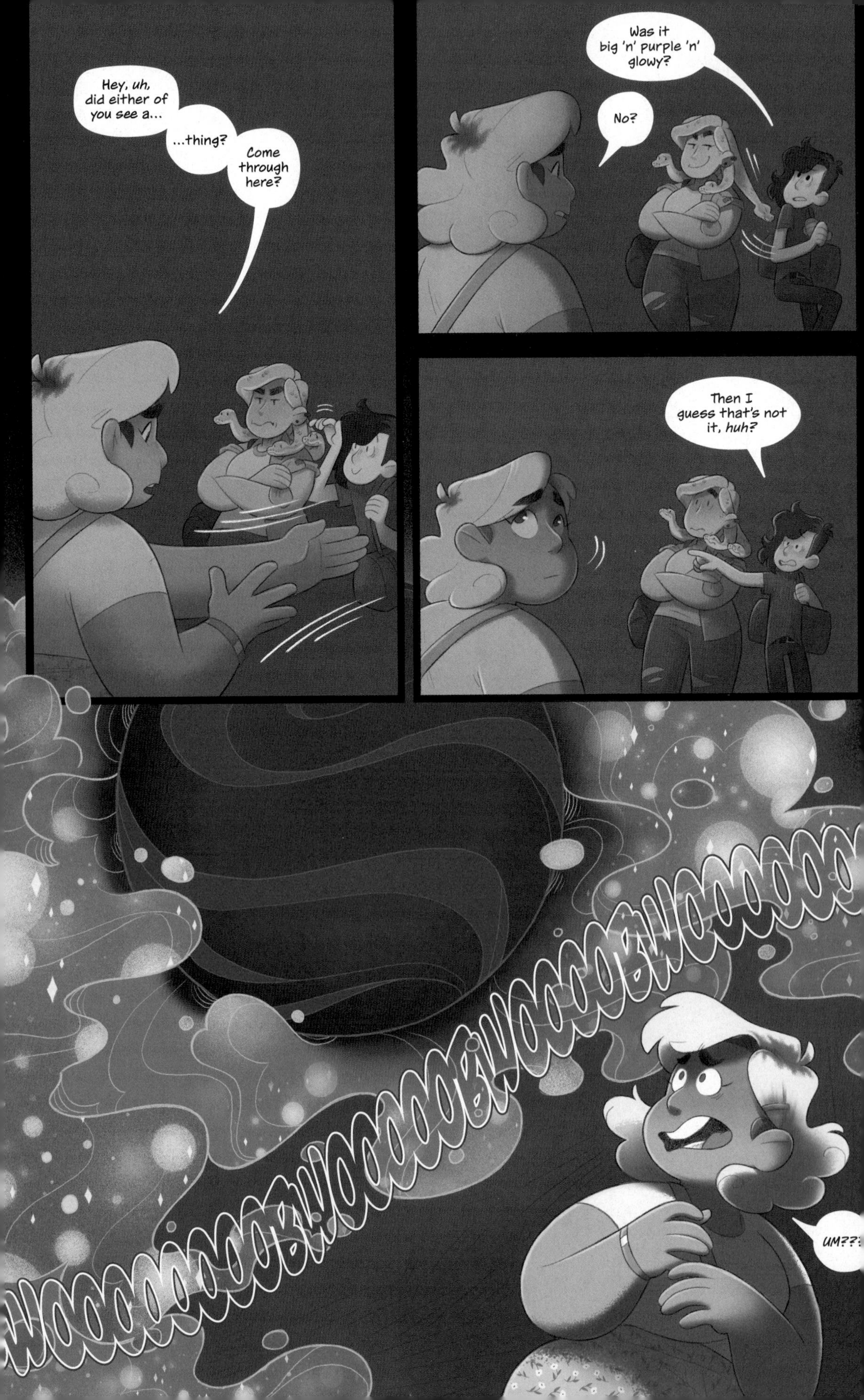
Hey, uh, did either of you see a...
...thing?
Come through here?
Was it big 'n' purple 'n' glowy?
No?
Then I guess that's not it, *huh*?
WOOOOOOOOOBWOOOOOOBWOOOOOOBWOOOOOOO
UM???

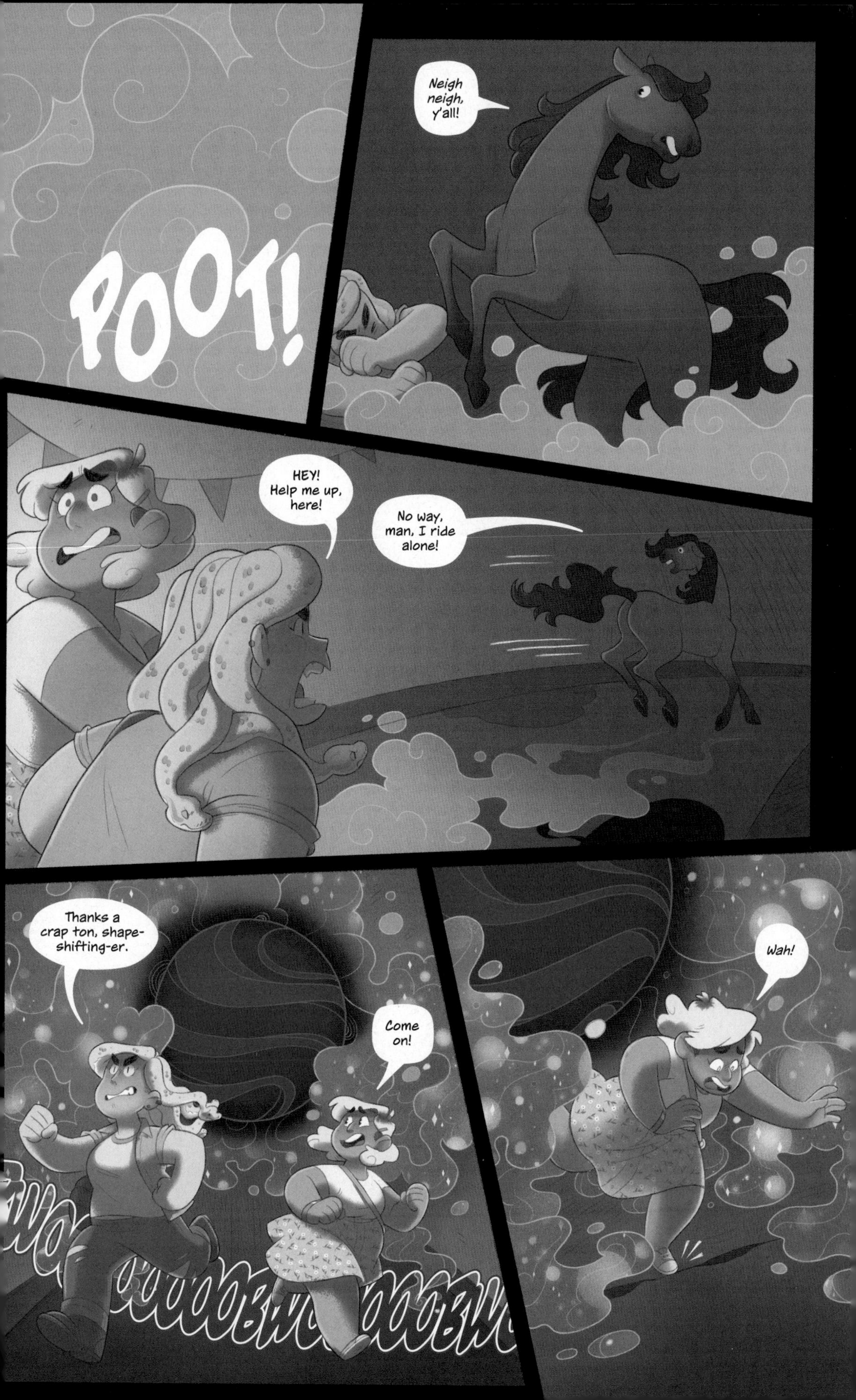
POOT!
Neigh neigh, Y'all!
HEY! Help me up, here!
No way, man, I ride alone!
Thanks a crap ton, shape-shifting-er.
Come on!
BWOOOOBWOOOOBWO
Wah!

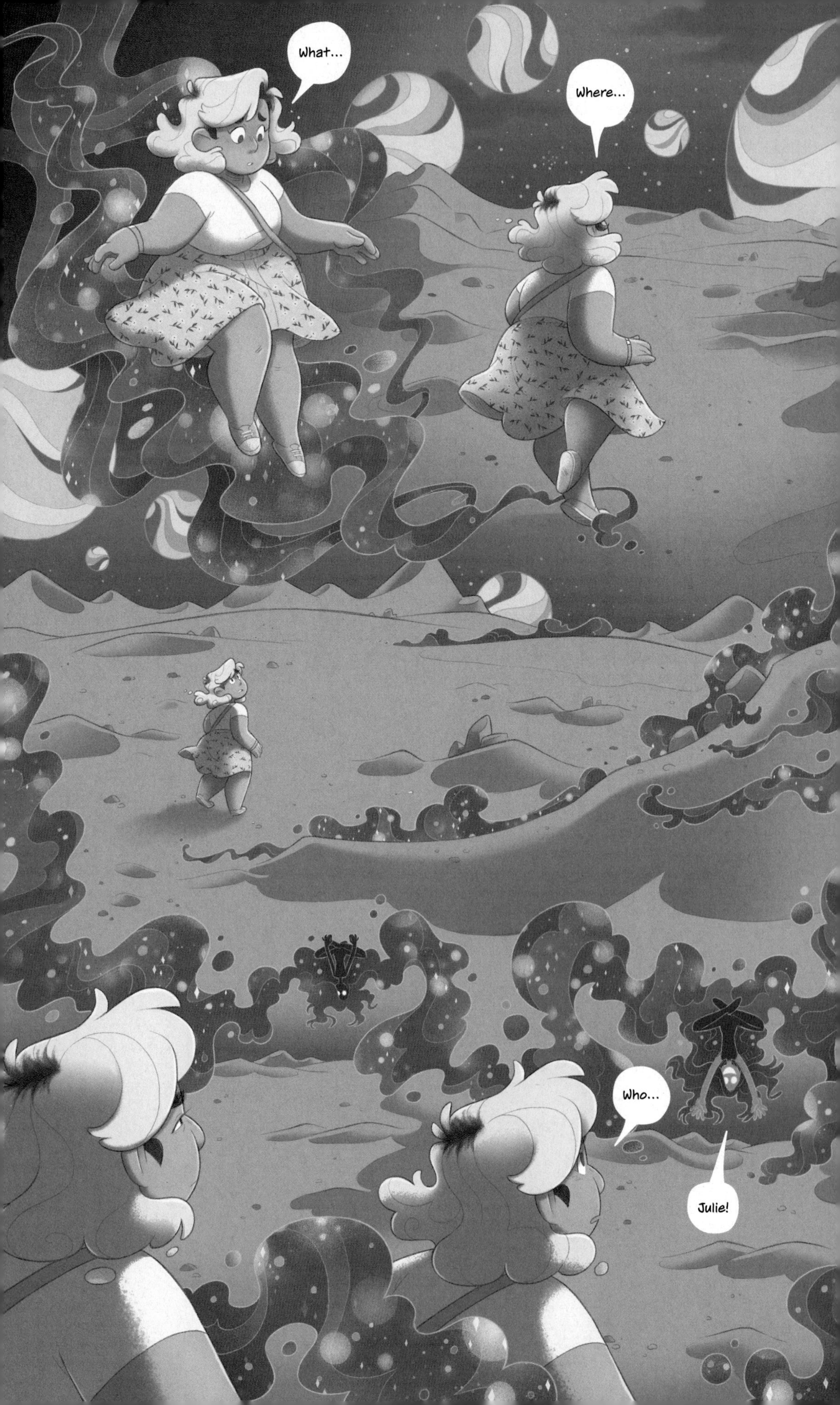
What...
Where...
Who...
Julie!

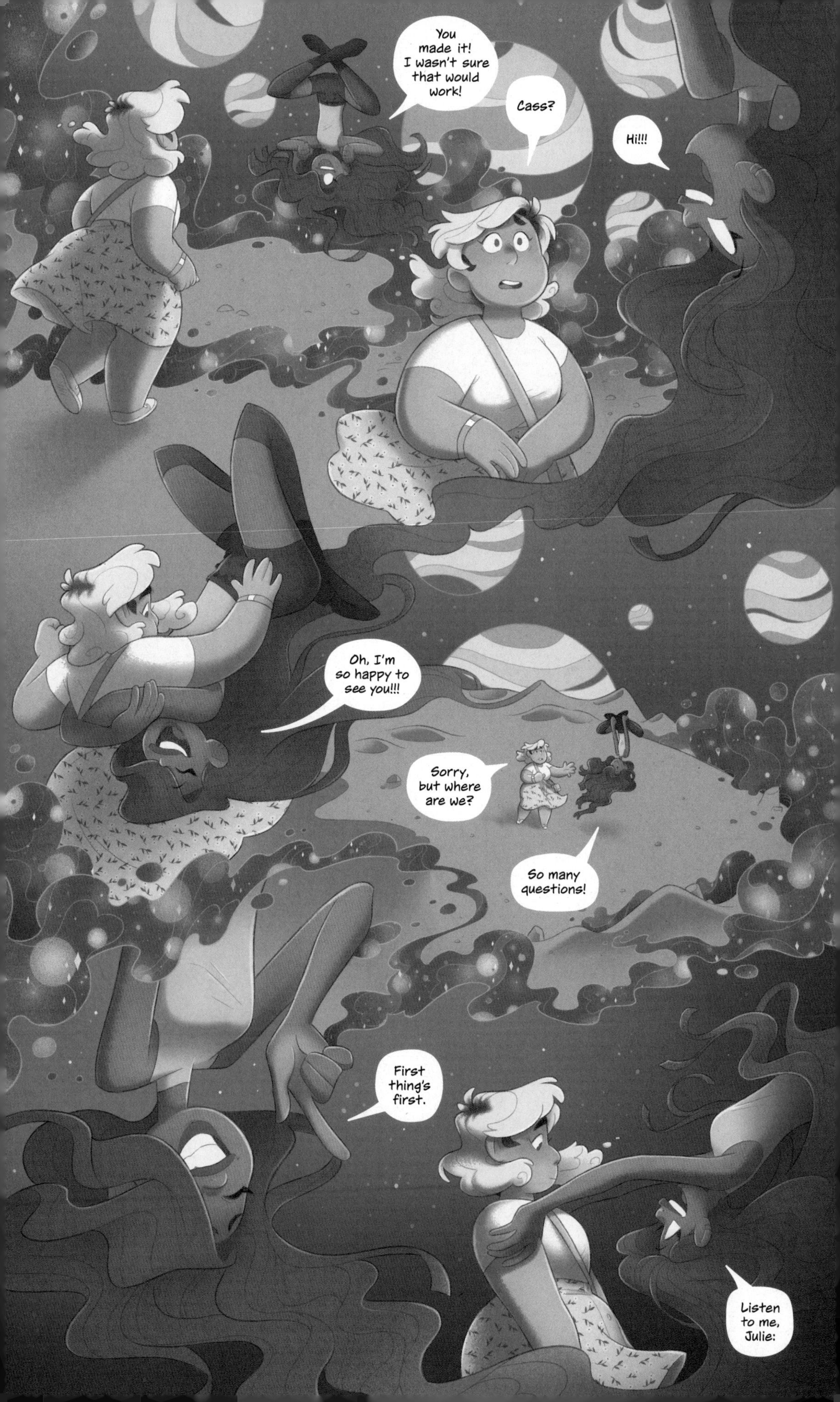
You made it! I wasn't sure that would work!
Cass?
Hi!!!
Oh, I'm so happy to see you!!!
Sorry, but where are we?
So many questions!
First thing's first.
Listen to me, Julie:

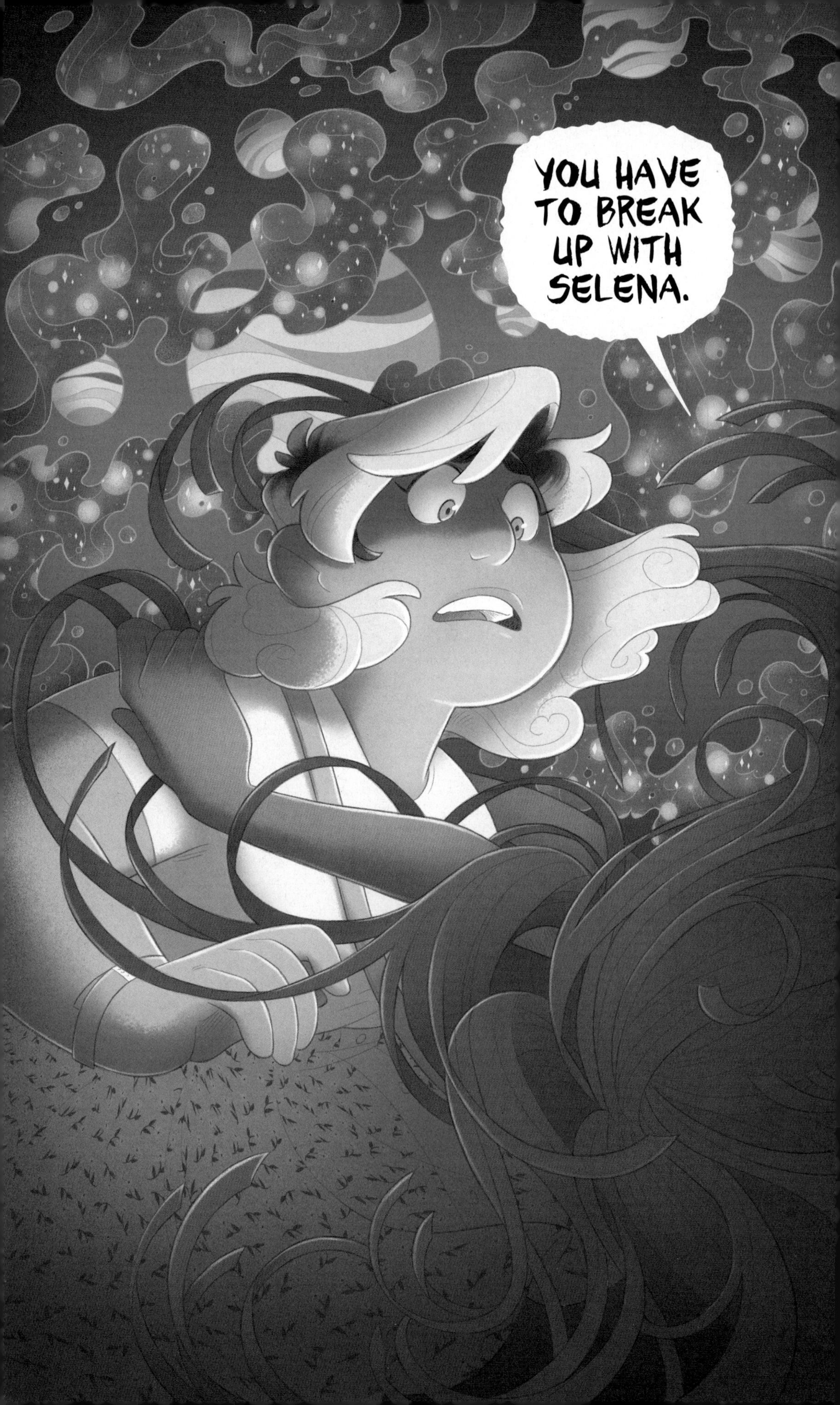
YOU HAVE TO BREAK UP WITH SELENA.

newPals

Super Fun Pages!

Chet and Manuel have arrived at Newpals headquarters! Help them solve this crossword puzzle!

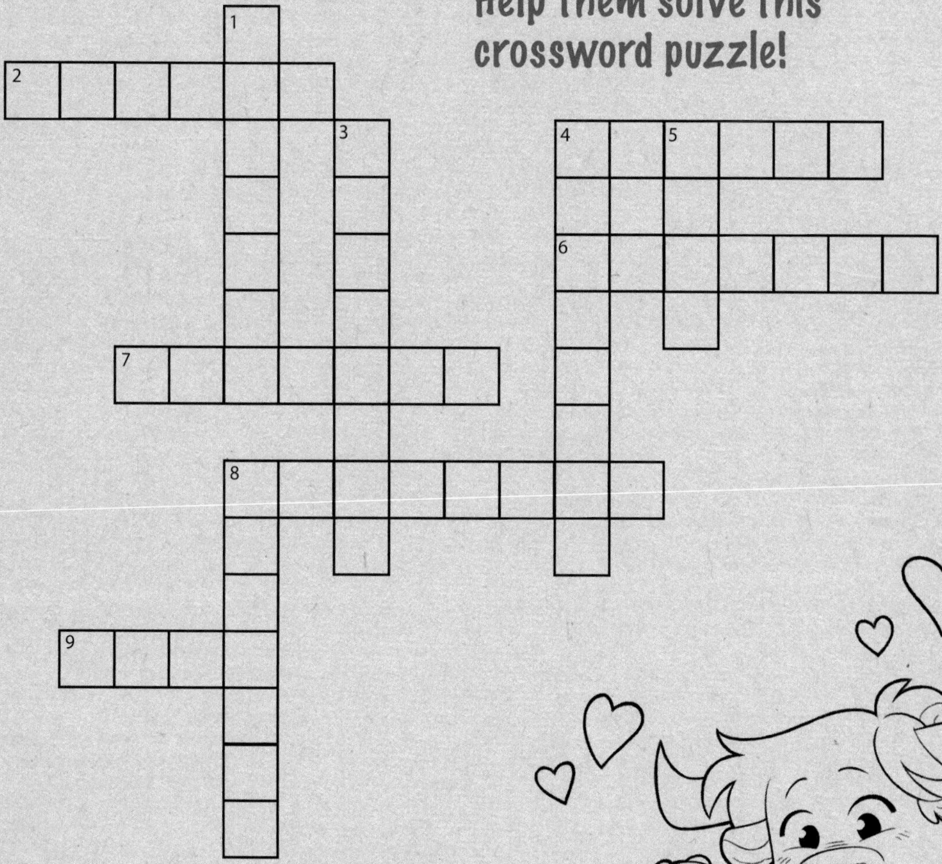

Across

2. Used to change a Newpal's color
4. Like a western Witch
6. I Was A _____ Werewolf
7. Chet's job
8. Half bull
9. Cappuccino milk

Down

1. Half horse
3. Mountain Sisters adjective
4. Advice for Chet and Manuel
5. 1988 Best Actress
8. Half fish

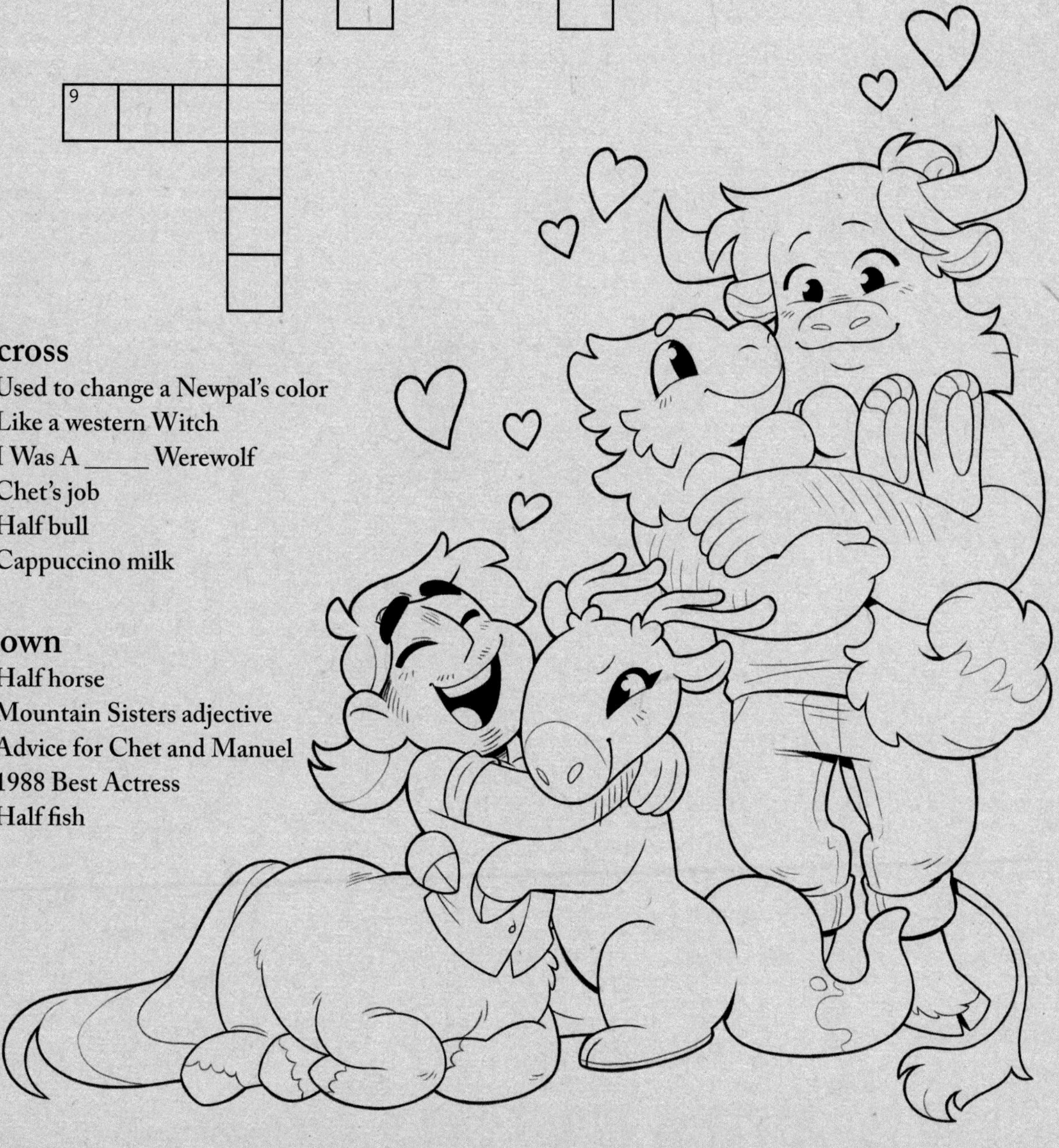

CHAPTER TWO

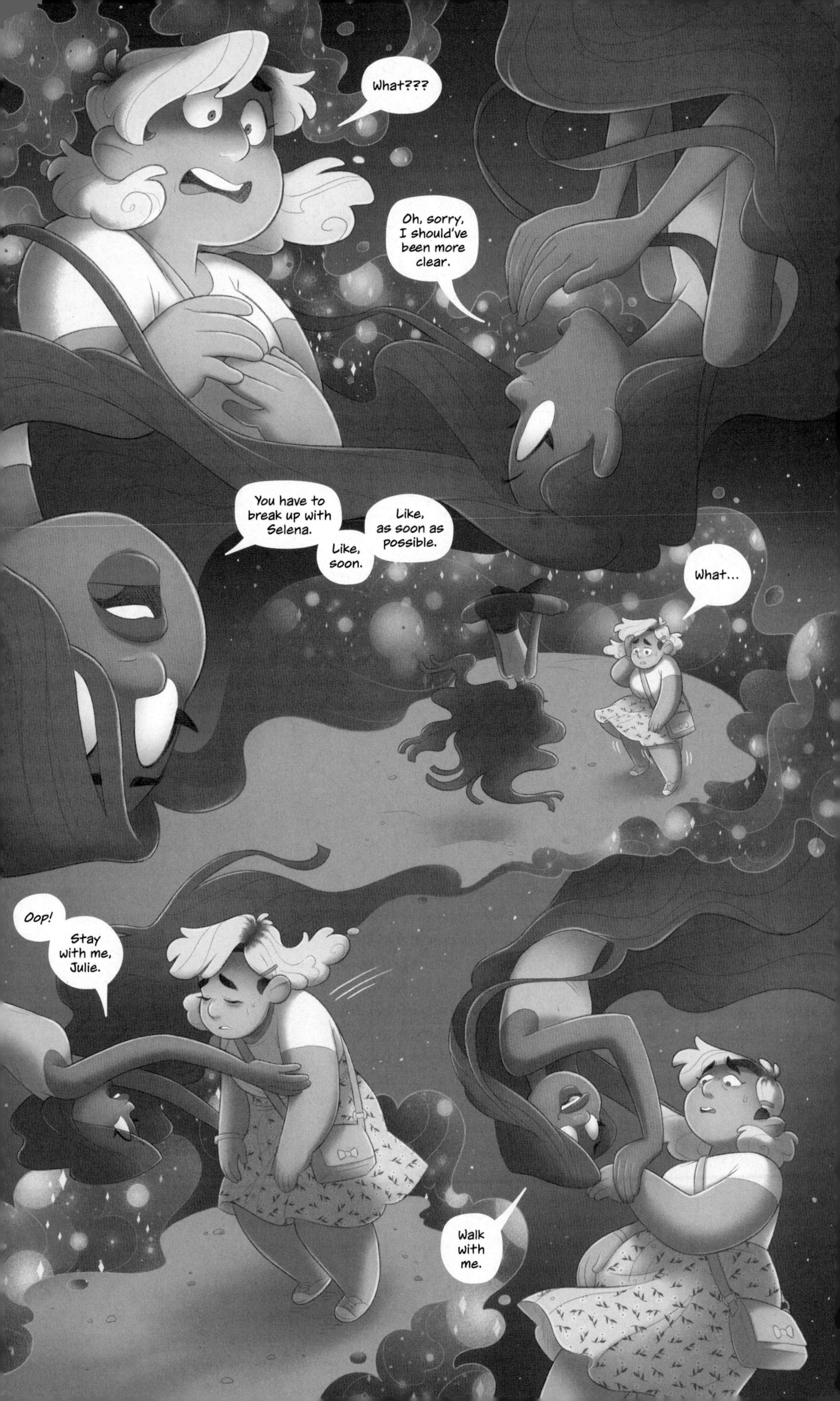
What???
Oh, sorry, I should've been more clear.
You have to break up with Selena.
Like, soon.
Like, as soon as possible.
What...
Oop!
Stay with me, Julie.
Walk with me.

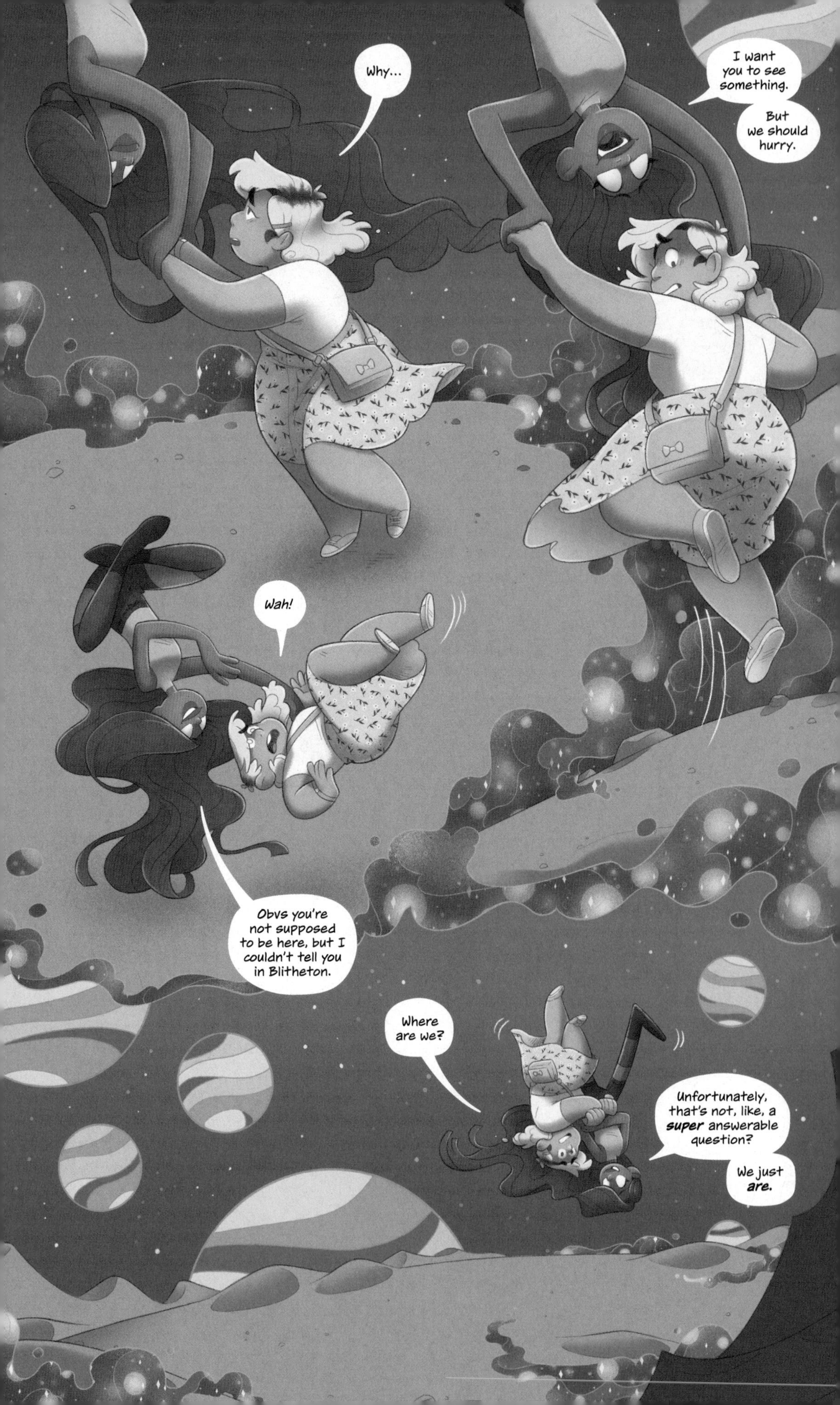
Why...
I want you to see something.
But we should hurry.
Wah!
Obvs you're not supposed to be here, but I couldn't tell you in Blitheton.
Where are we?
Unfortunately, that's not, like, a *super* answerable question?
We just *are.*

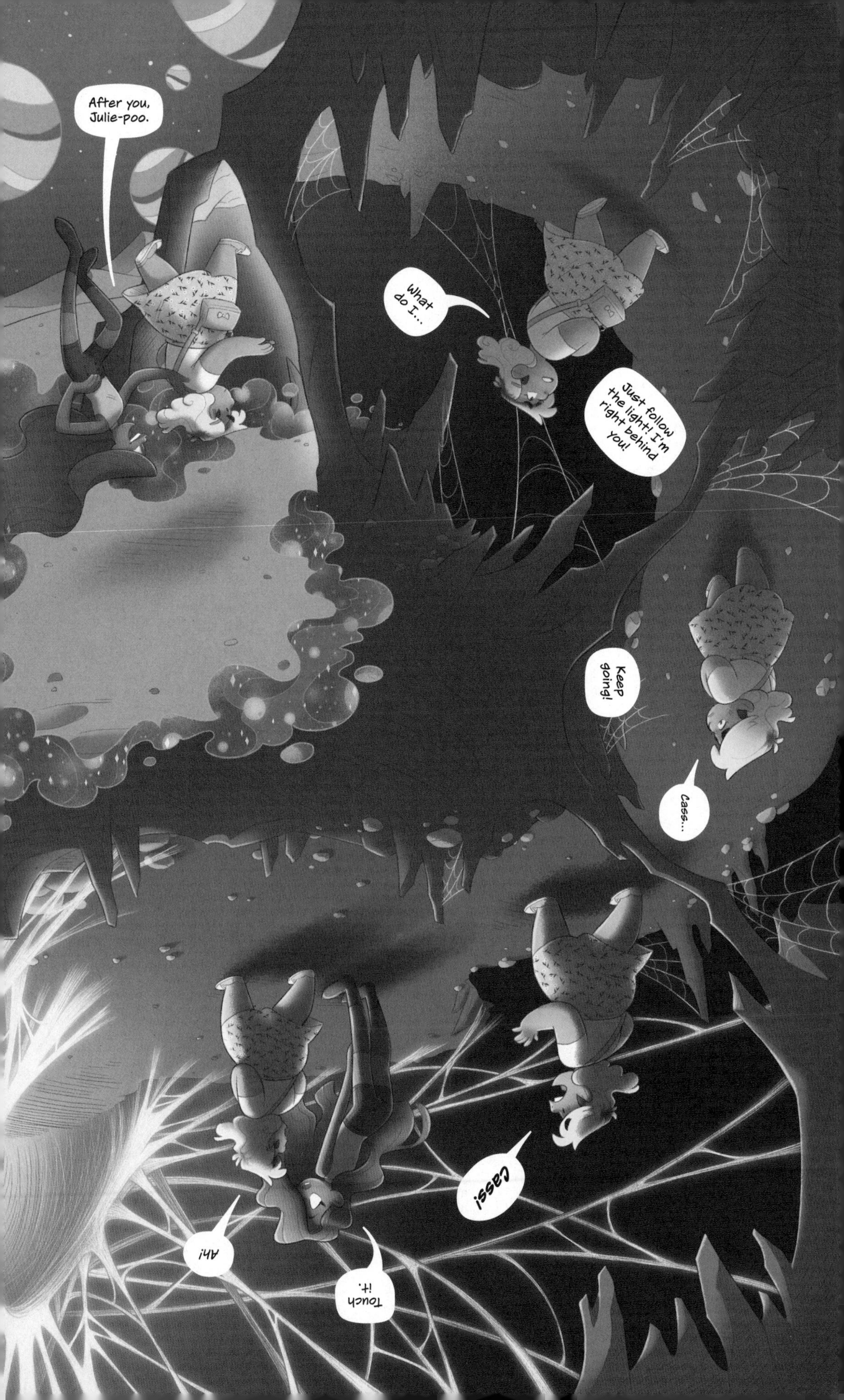
After you, Julie-poo.
What do I...
Just follow the light! I'm right behind you!
Keep going!
Cass...
Cass!
Ah!
Touch it.

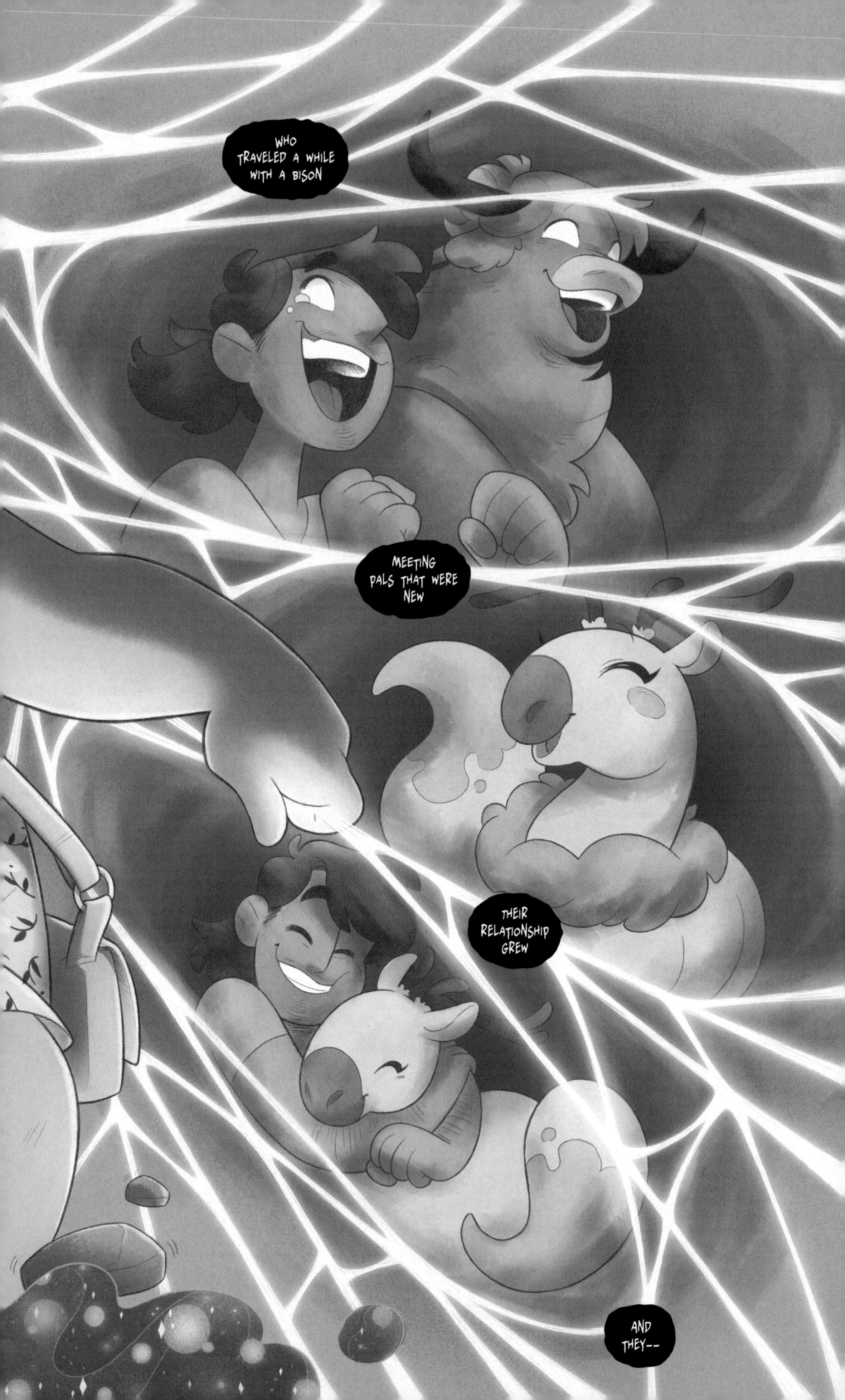
WHO TRAVELED A WHILE WITH A BISON
MEETING PALS THAT WERE NEW
THEIR RELATIONSHIP GREW
AND THEY--

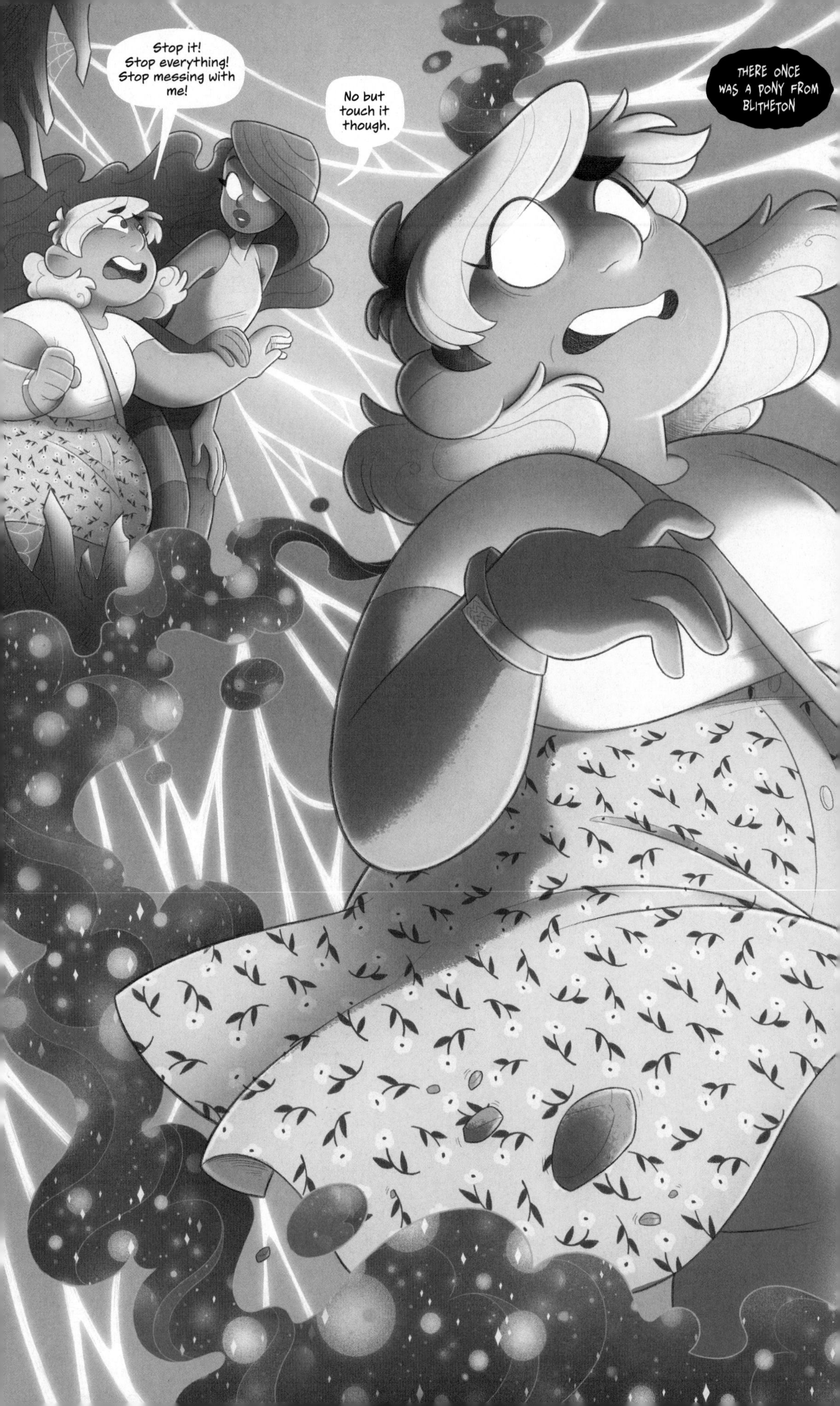
Stop it!
Stop everything!
Stop messing with
me!
No but
touch it
though.
THERE ONCE
WAS A PONY FROM
BLITHETON

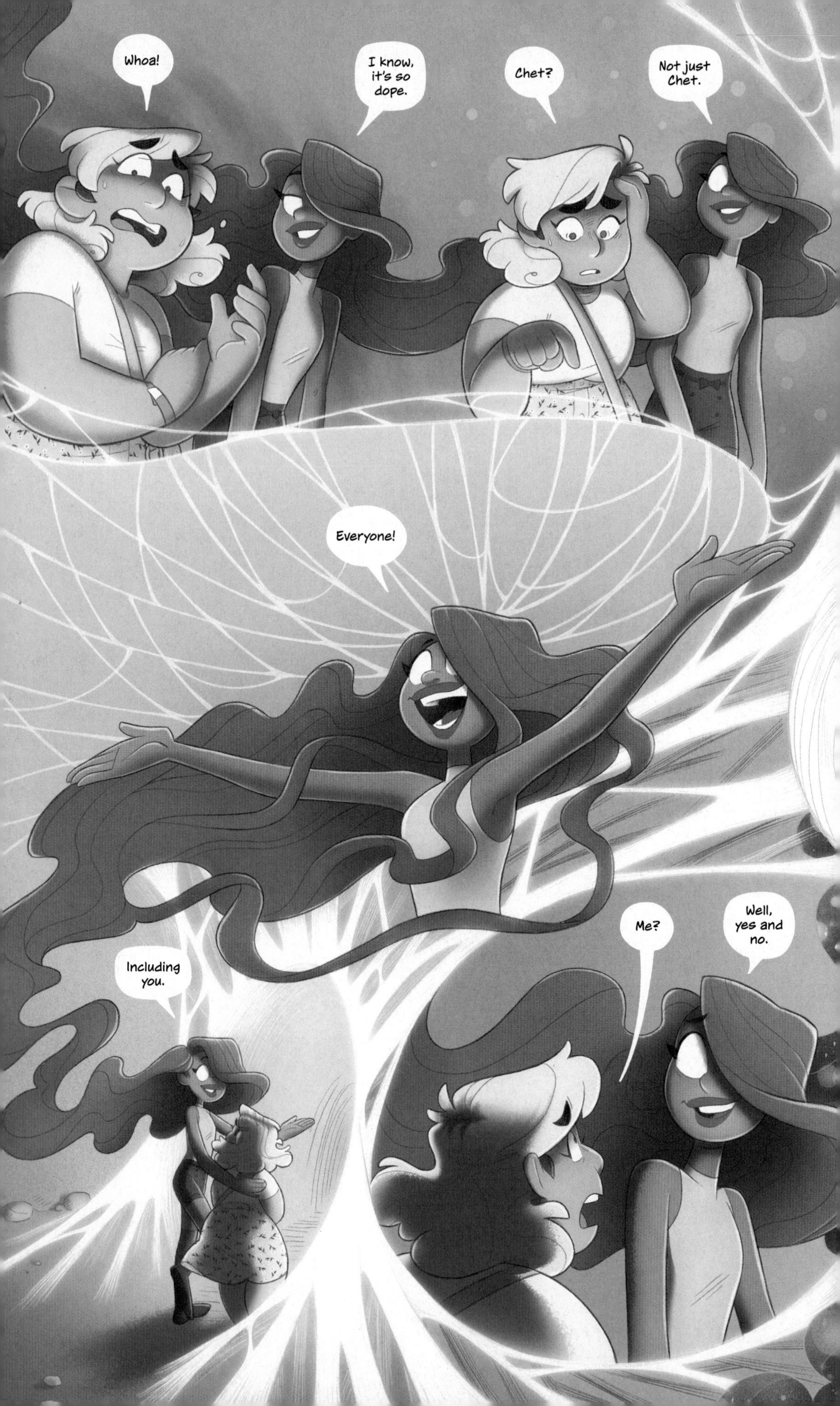
Whoa!
I know, it's so dope.
Chet?
Not just Chet.
Everyone!
Including you.
Me?
Well, yes and no.

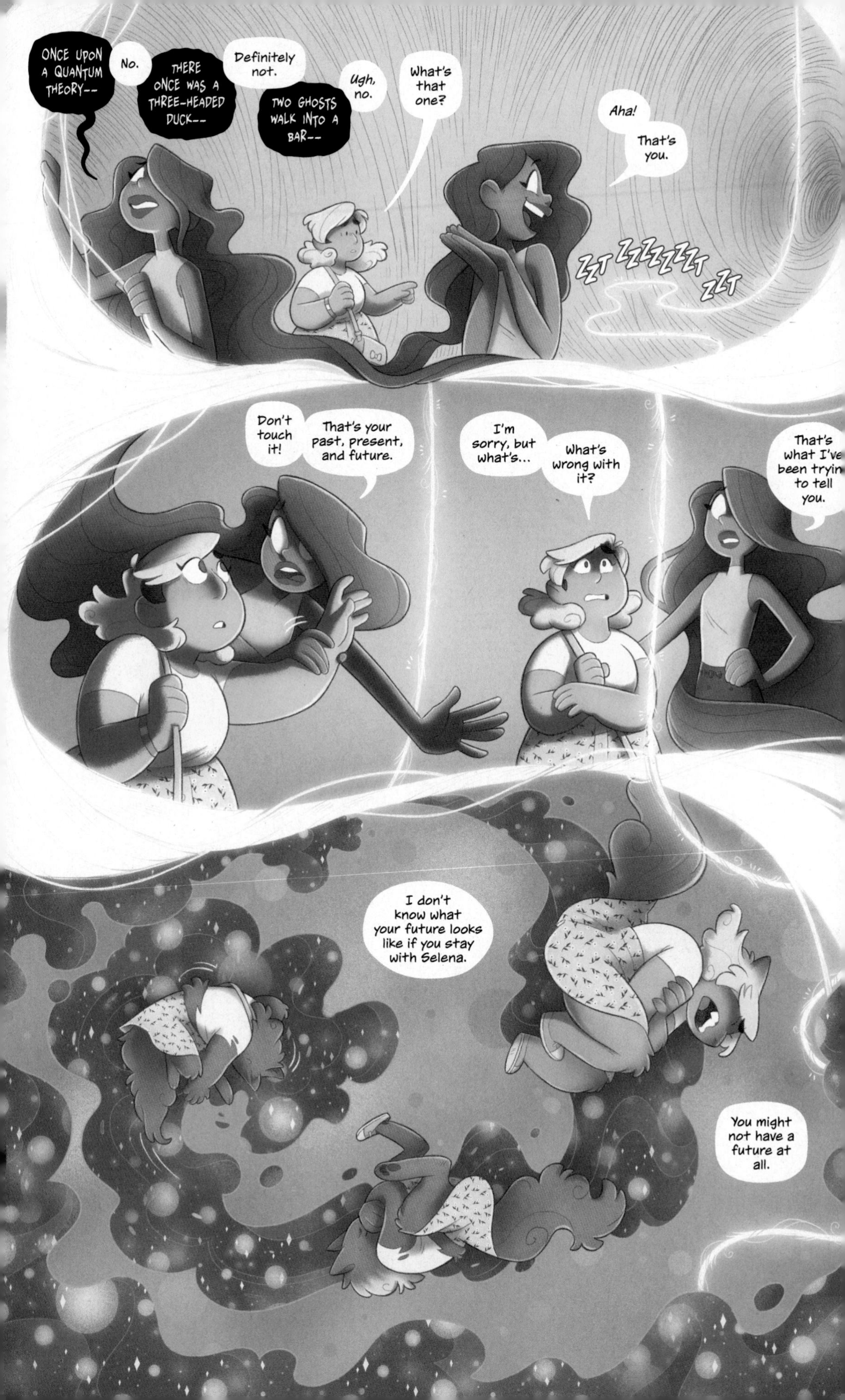
ONCE UPON A QUANTUM THEORY--
No.
THERE ONCE WAS A THREE-HEADED DUCK--
Definitely not.
TWO GHOSTS WALK INTO A BAR--
Ugh, no.
What's that one?
Aha!
That's you.
ZZT ZZZZZZZT ZZT
Don't touch it!
That's your past, present, and future.
I'm sorry, but what's...
What's wrong with it?
That's what I've been tryin' to tell you.
I don't know what your future looks like if you stay with Selena.
You might not have a future at all.

GASP!

Where's Cass?

Whoa there, tiger, slow down.

When did I wolf-out??

The nurse said it was your body's self-defense.

Totally natural.

HALF OFF SCUE WHEN YOU RIDE WIT

SUBBLE

What happened?

I was hoping you could tell us.

We were getting ready to get on the subble when *Lindi* comes tearing after us yelling about needing *"emergency surfaces."*

And then we found you passed out in the alley.

And here we are.

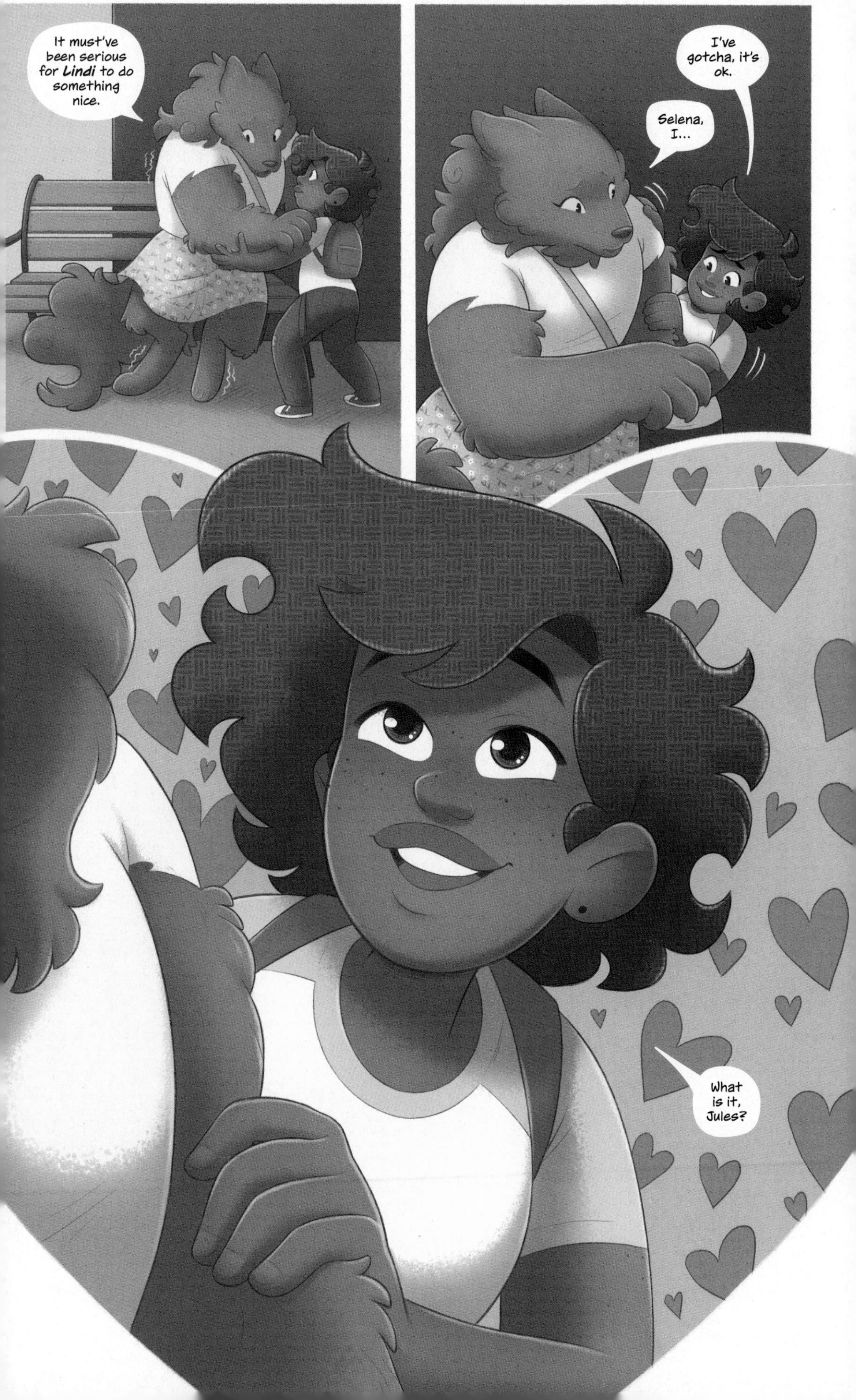
It must've been serious for *Lindi* to do something nice.
Selena, I...
I've gotcha, it's ok.
What is it, Jules?

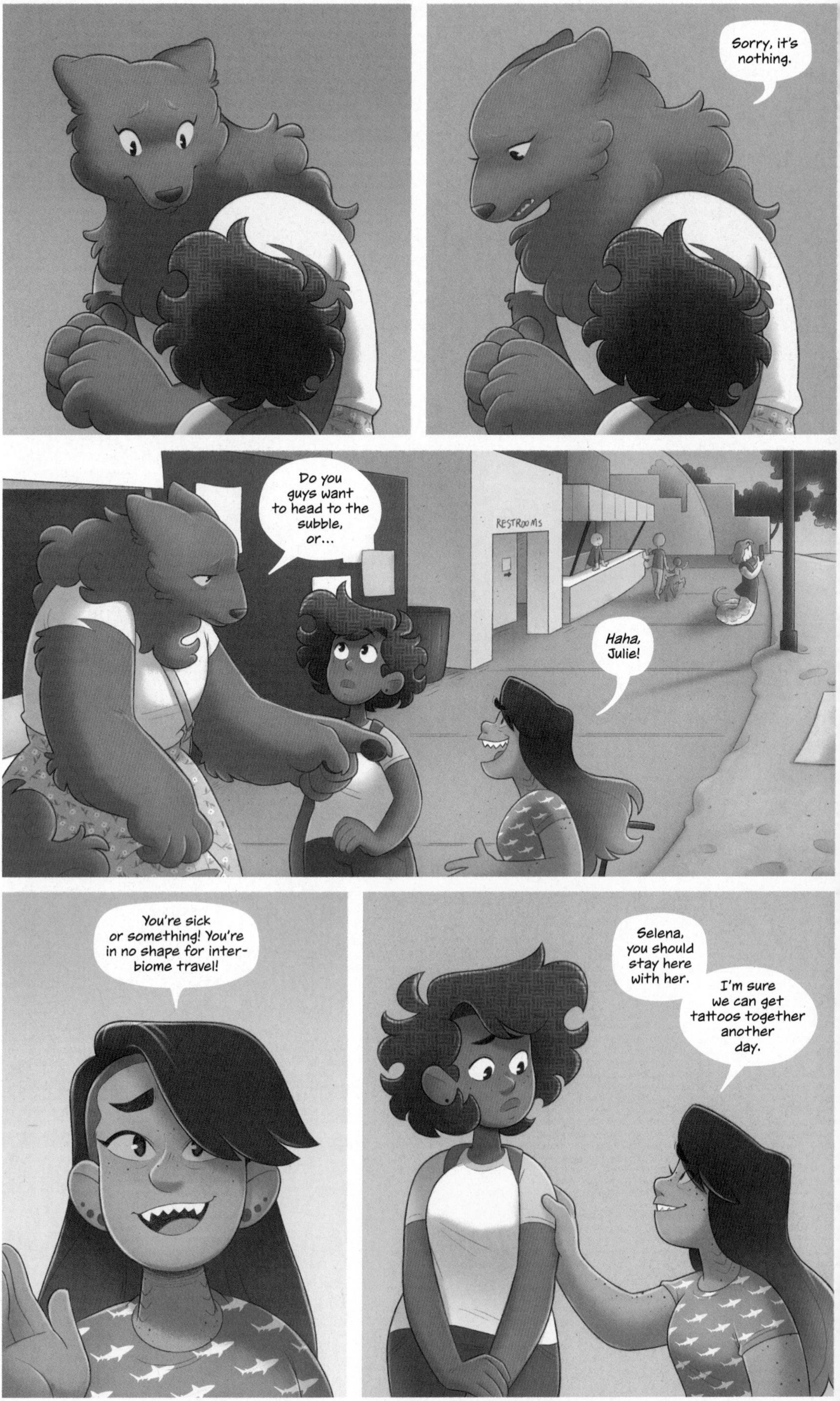

Sorry, it's nothing.
Do you guys want to head to the subble, or...
RESTROOMS
Haha, Julie!
You're sick or something! You're in no shape for inter-biome travel!
Selena, you should stay here with her.
I'm sure we can get tattoos together another day.

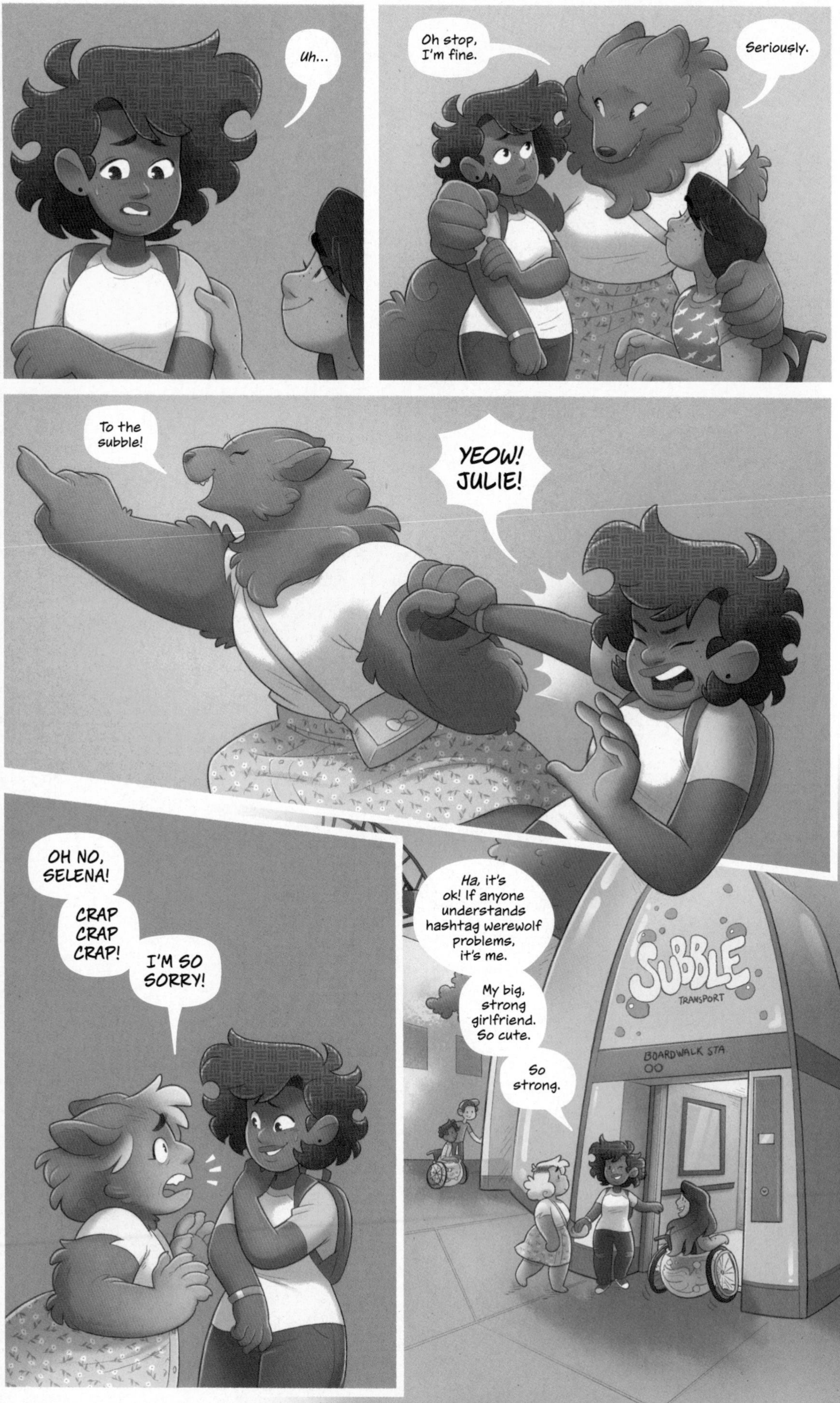
Uh...
Oh stop, I'm fine.
Seriously.
To the subble!
YEOW! JULIE!
OH NO, SELENA!
CRAP CRAP CRAP!
I'M SO SORRY!
Ha, it's ok! If anyone understands hashtag werewolf problems, it's me.
My big, strong girlfriend. So cute.
So strong.
SUBBLE
TRANSPORT
BOARDWALK STA

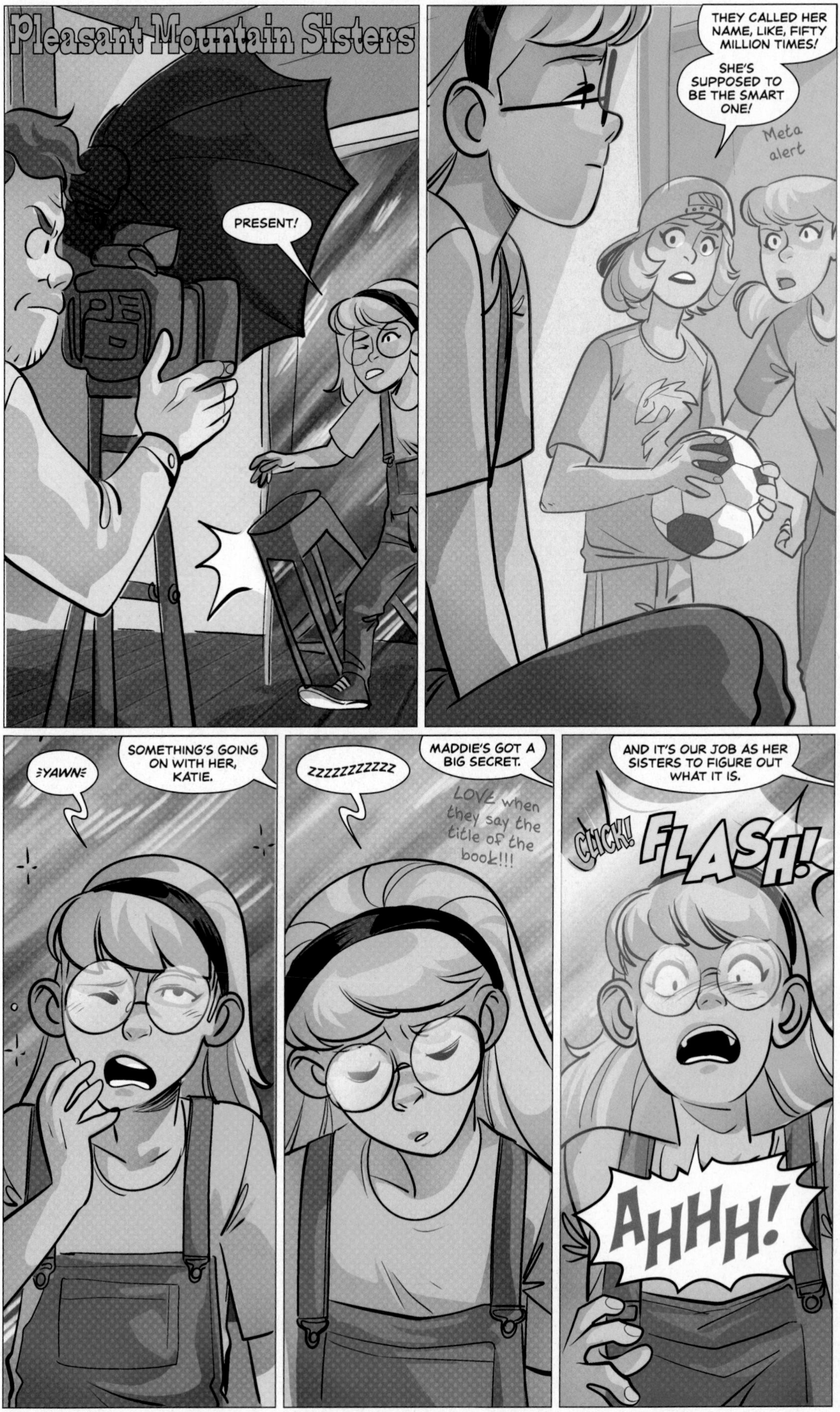

Pleasant Mountain Sisters
PRESENT!
THEY CALLED HER NAME, LIKE, FIFTY MILLION TIMES!
SHE'S SUPPOSED TO BE THE SMART ONE!
Meta alert
YAWN
SOMETHING'S GOING ON WITH HER, KATIE.
ZZZZZZZZZZZ
MADDIE'S GOT A BIG SECRET.
LOVE when they say the title of the book!!!
AND IT'S OUR JOB AS HER SISTERS TO FIGURE OUT WHAT IT IS.
CLICK!
FLASH!
AHHH!

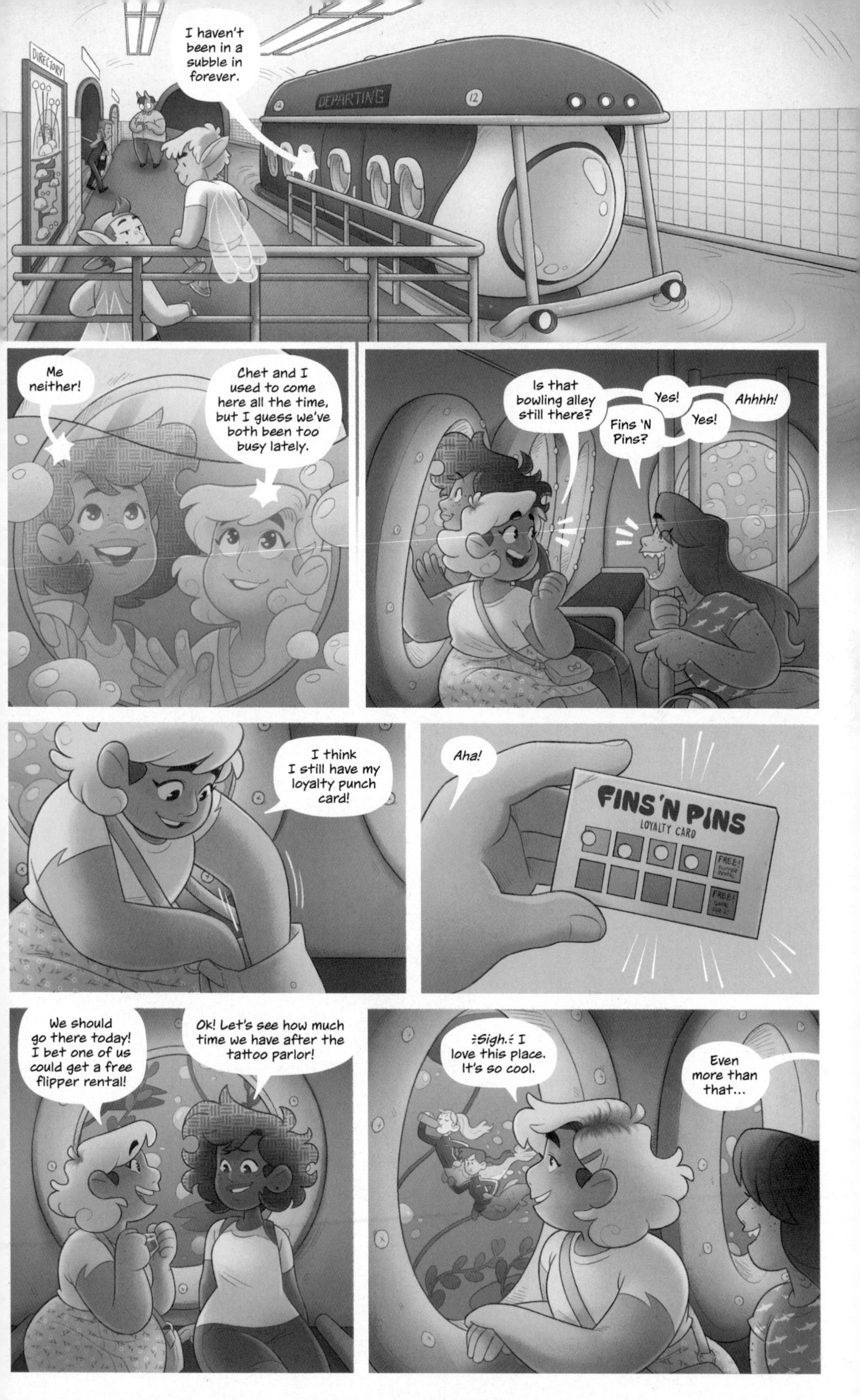
I haven't been in a subble in forever.
DIRECTORY
DEPARTING
12
Me neither!
Chet and I used to come here all the time, but I guess we've both been too busy lately.
Is that bowling alley still there?
Fins 'N Pins?
Yes!
Yes!
Ahhhh!
I think I still have my loyalty punch card!
Aha!
FINS 'N PINS
LOYALTY CARD
FREE!
FREE!
We should go there today! I bet one of us could get a free flipper rental!
Ok! Let's see how much time we have after the tattoo parlor!
≈Sigh.≈ I love this place. It's so cool.
Even more than that…

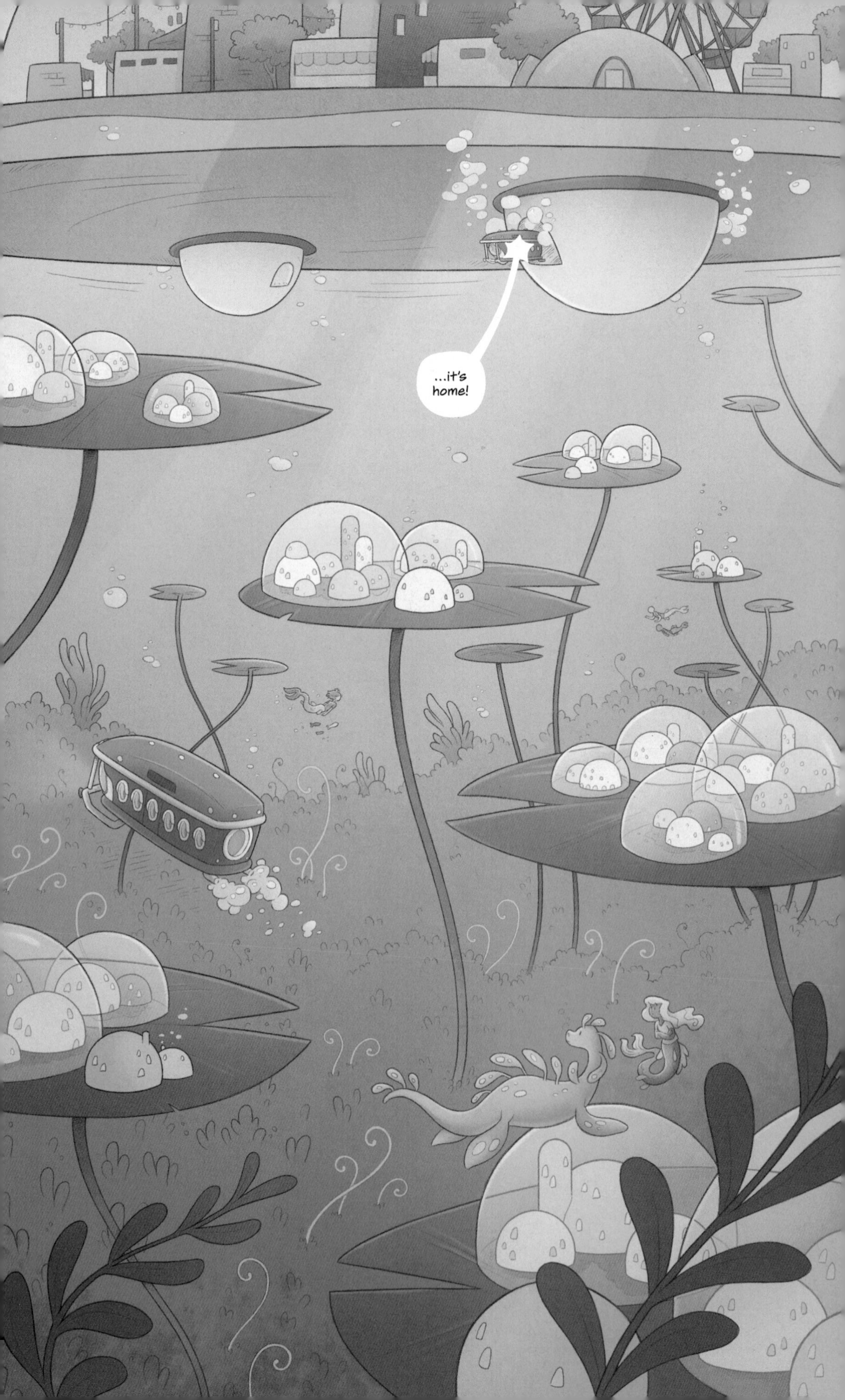
...it's home!

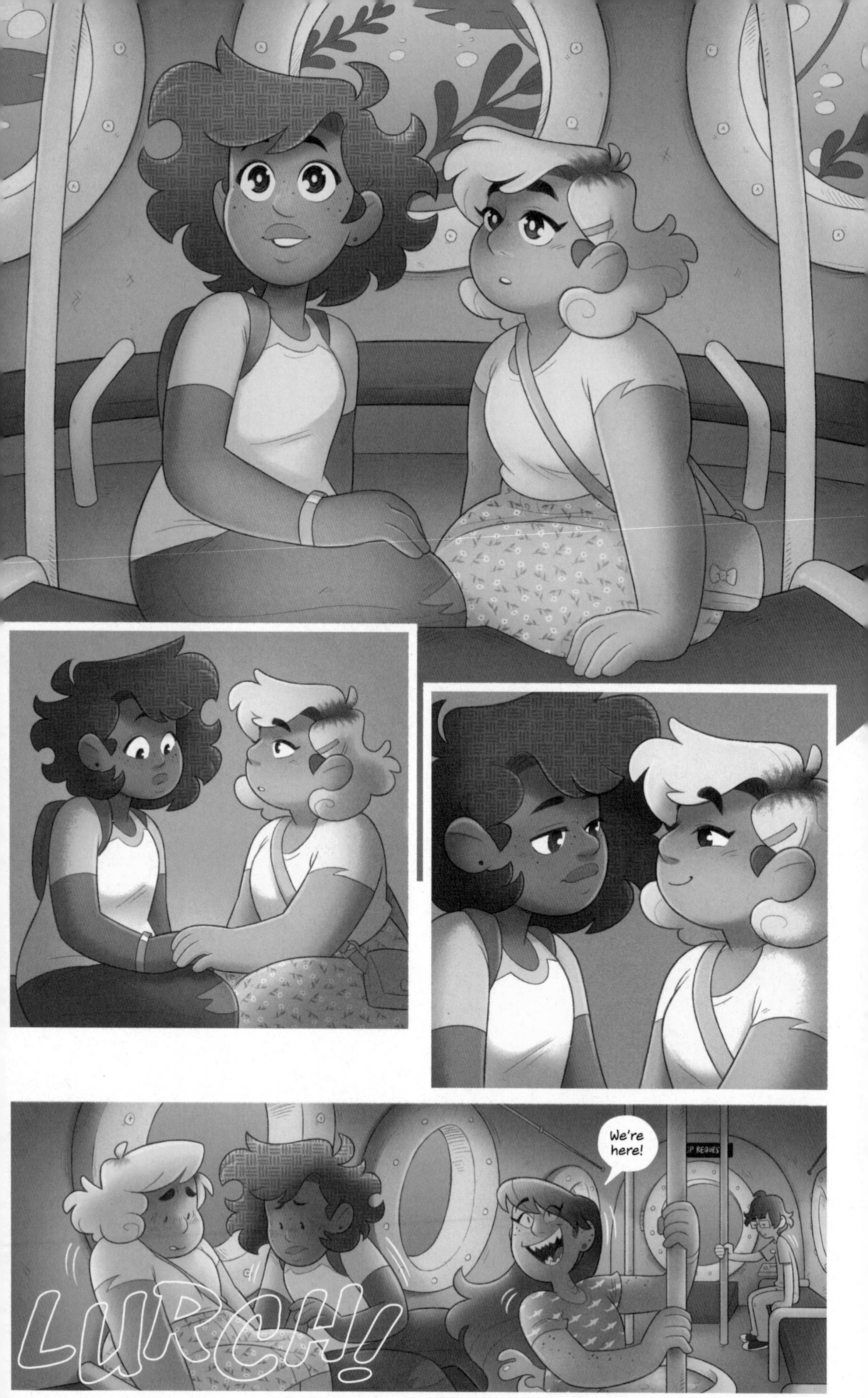
We're here!
LURCH!

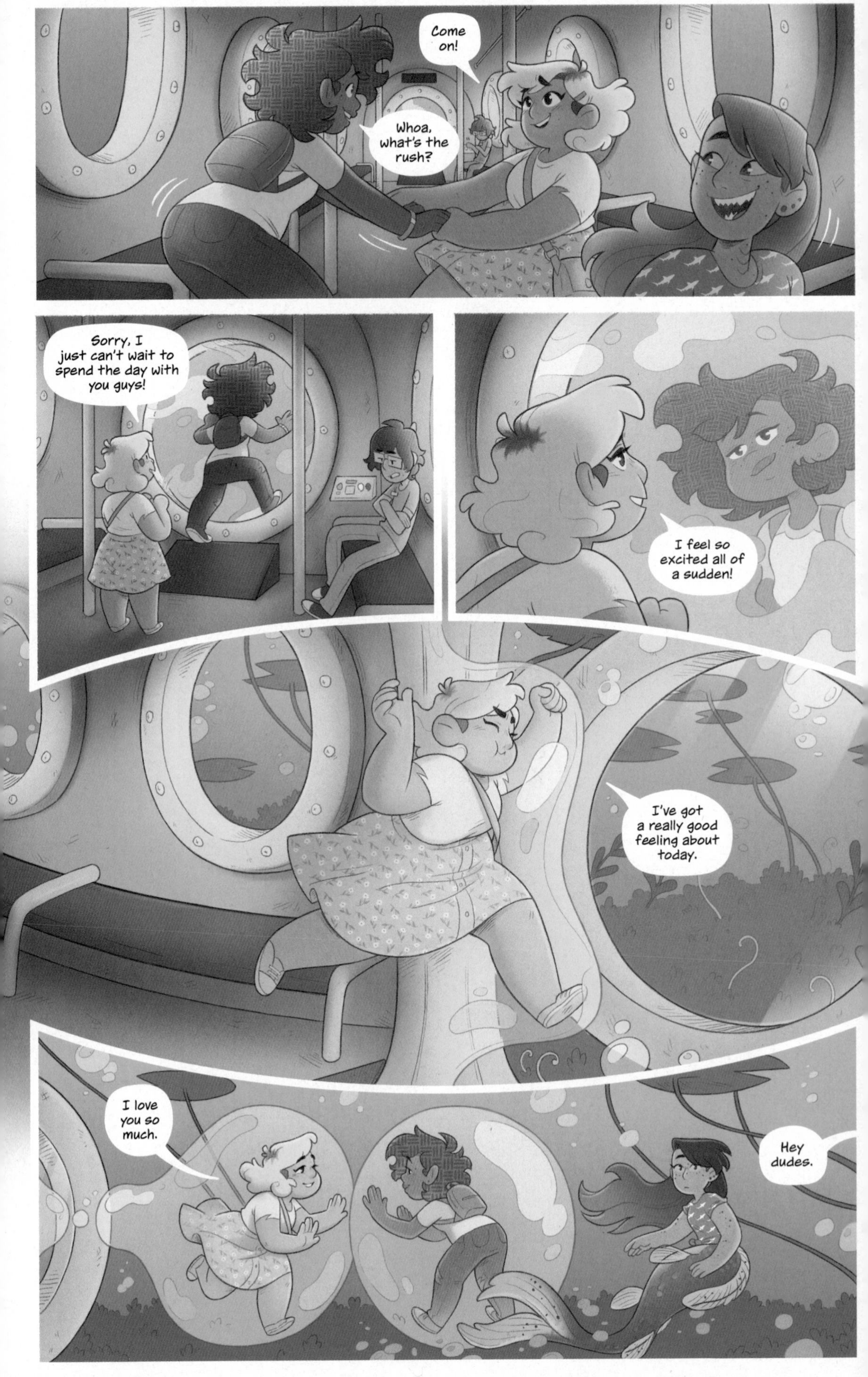
Come on!
Whoa, what's the rush?
Sorry, I just can't wait to spend the day with you guys!
I feel so excited all of a sudden!
I've got a really good feeling about today.
I love you so much.
Hey dudes.

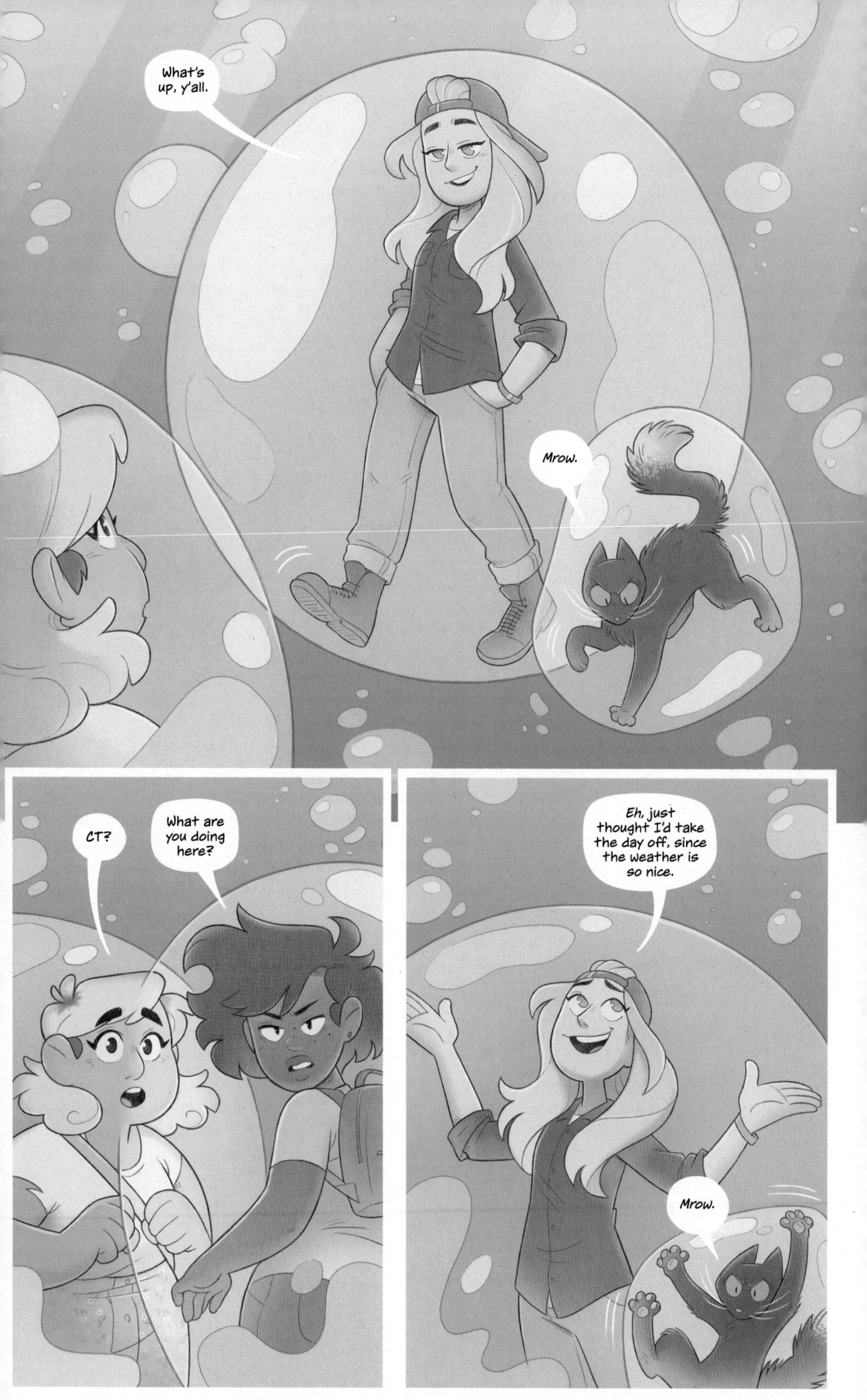
What's up, y'all.
Mrow.
CT?
What are you doing here?
Eh, just thought I'd take the day off, since the weather is so nice.
Mrow.

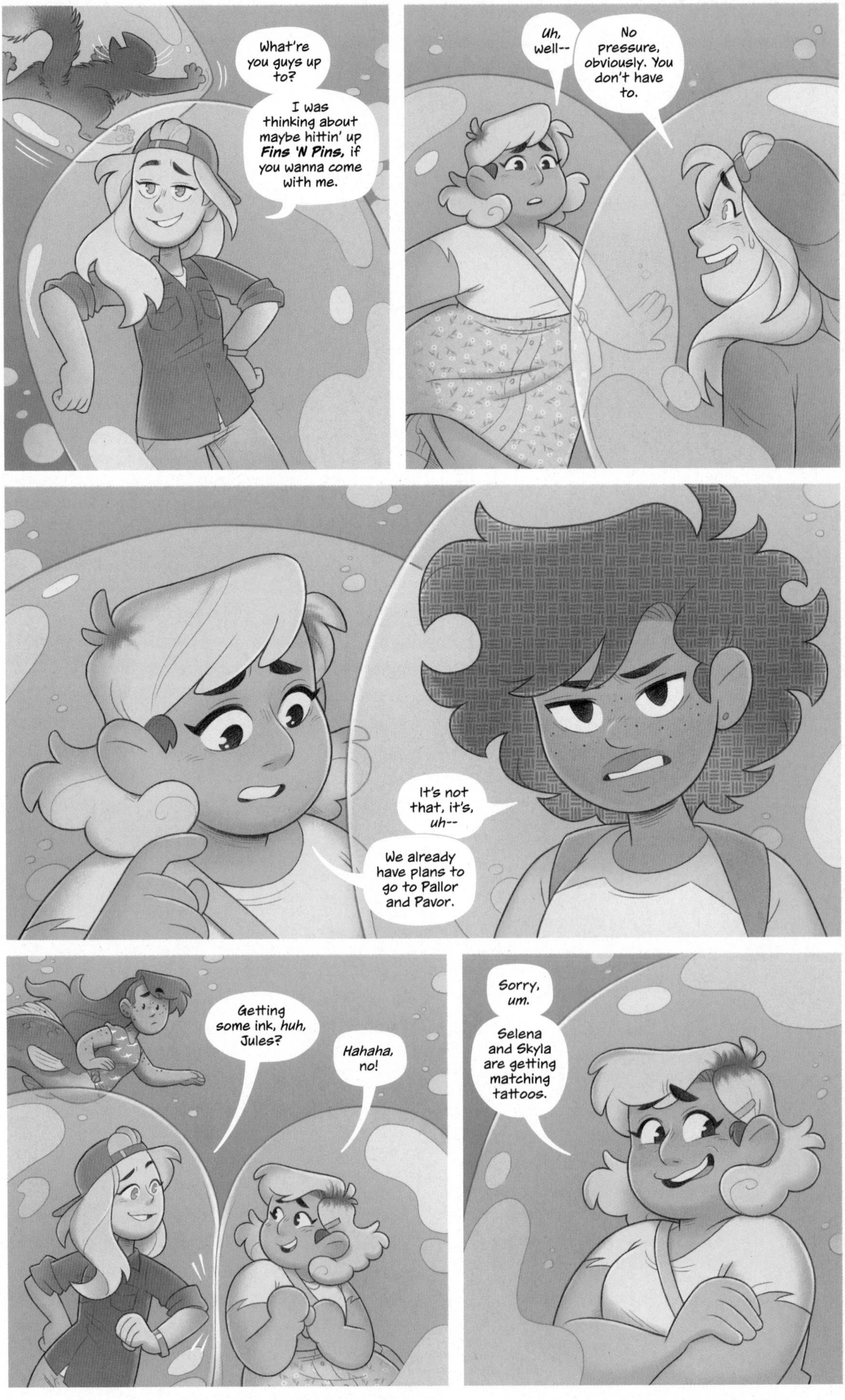
What're you guys up to?
I was thinking about maybe hittin' up **Fins 'N Pins,** if you wanna come with me.
Uh, well--
No pressure, obviously. You don't have to.
It's not that, it's, *uh*--
We already have plans to go to Pallor and Pavor.
Getting some ink, *huh,* Jules?
Hahaha, no!
Sorry, *um.*
Selena and Skyla are getting matching tattoos.

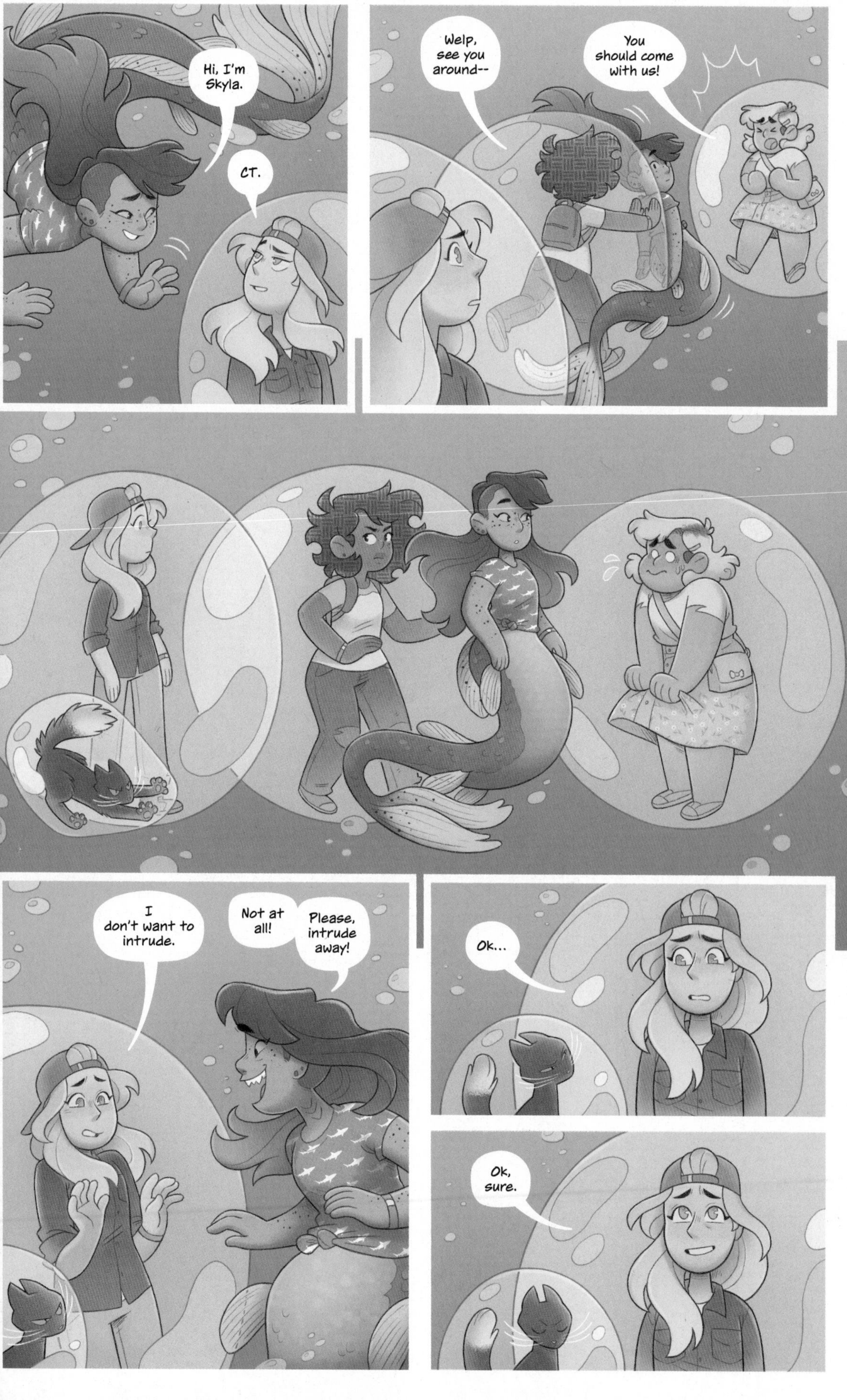
Hi, I'm Skyla.
CT.
Welp, see you around--
You should come with us!
I don't want to intrude.
Not at all!
Please, intrude away!
Ok...
Ok, sure.

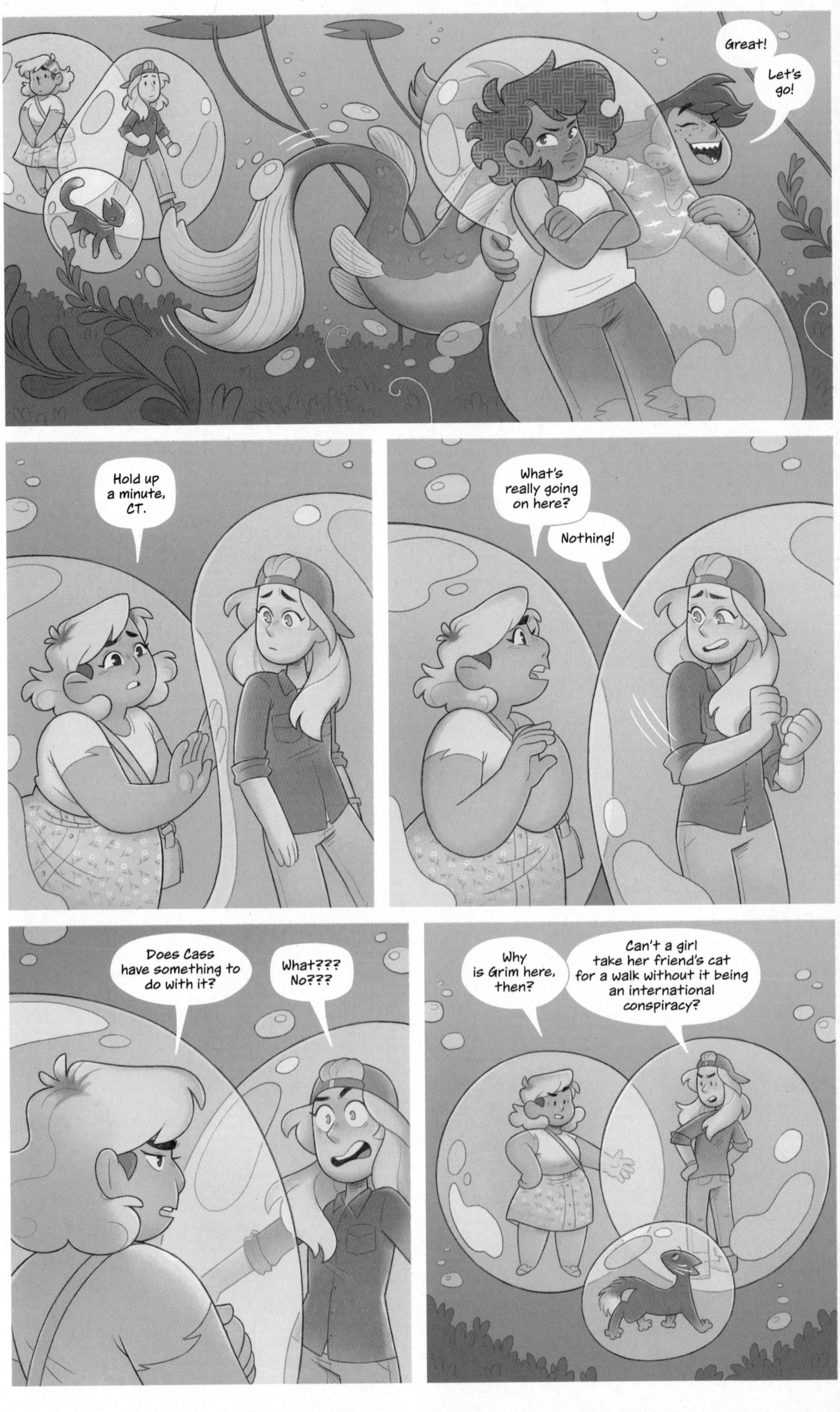
Great!
Let's go!
Hold up a minute, CT.
What's really going on here?
Nothing!
Does Cass have something to do with it?
What??? No???
Why is Grim here, then?
Can't a girl take her friend's cat for a walk without it being an international conspiracy?

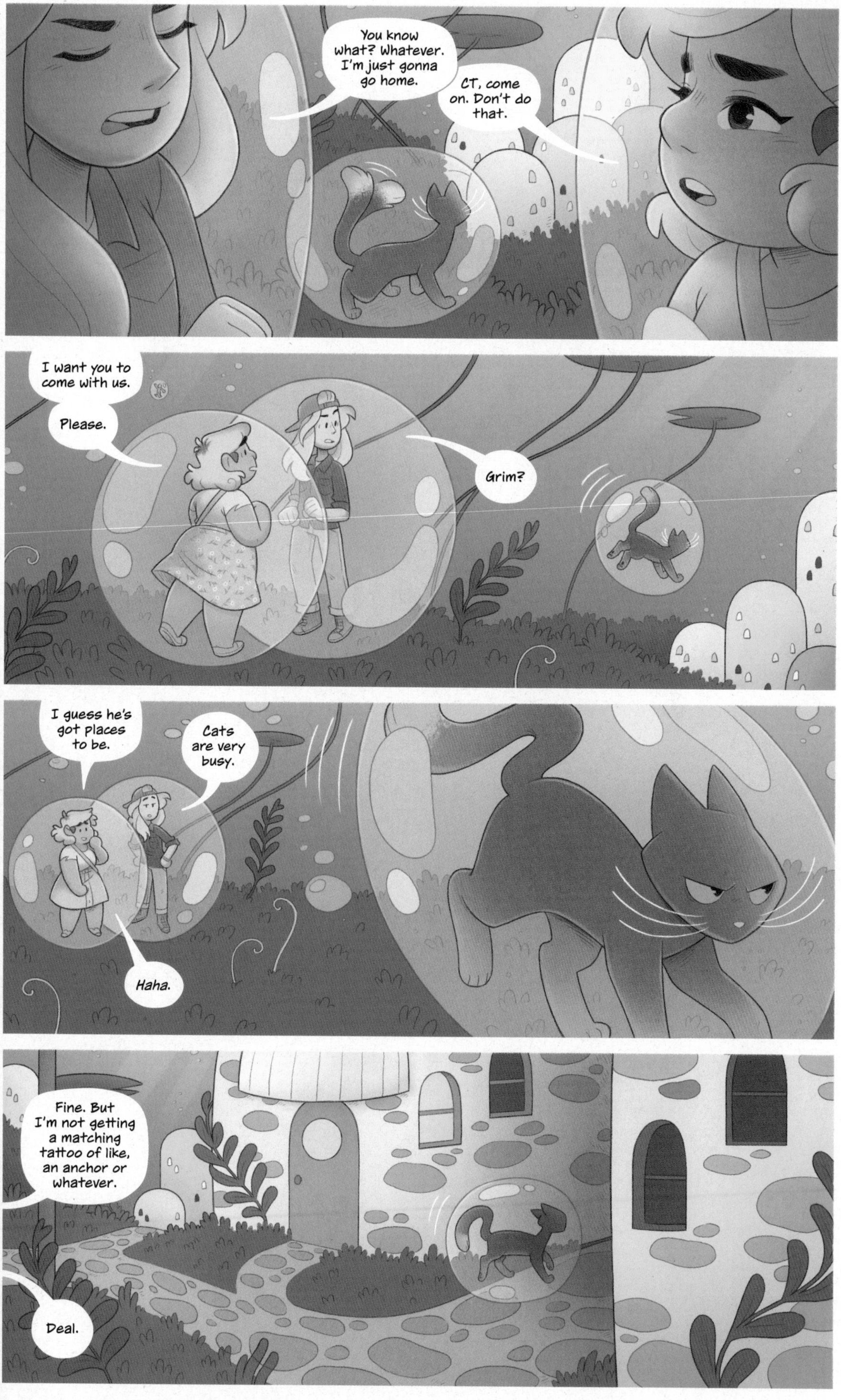
You know what? Whatever. I'm just gonna go home.
CT, come on. Don't do that.
I want you to come with us.
Please.
Grim?
I guess he's got places to be.
Cats are very busy.
Haha.
Fine. But I'm not getting a matching tattoo of like, an anchor or whatever.
Deal.

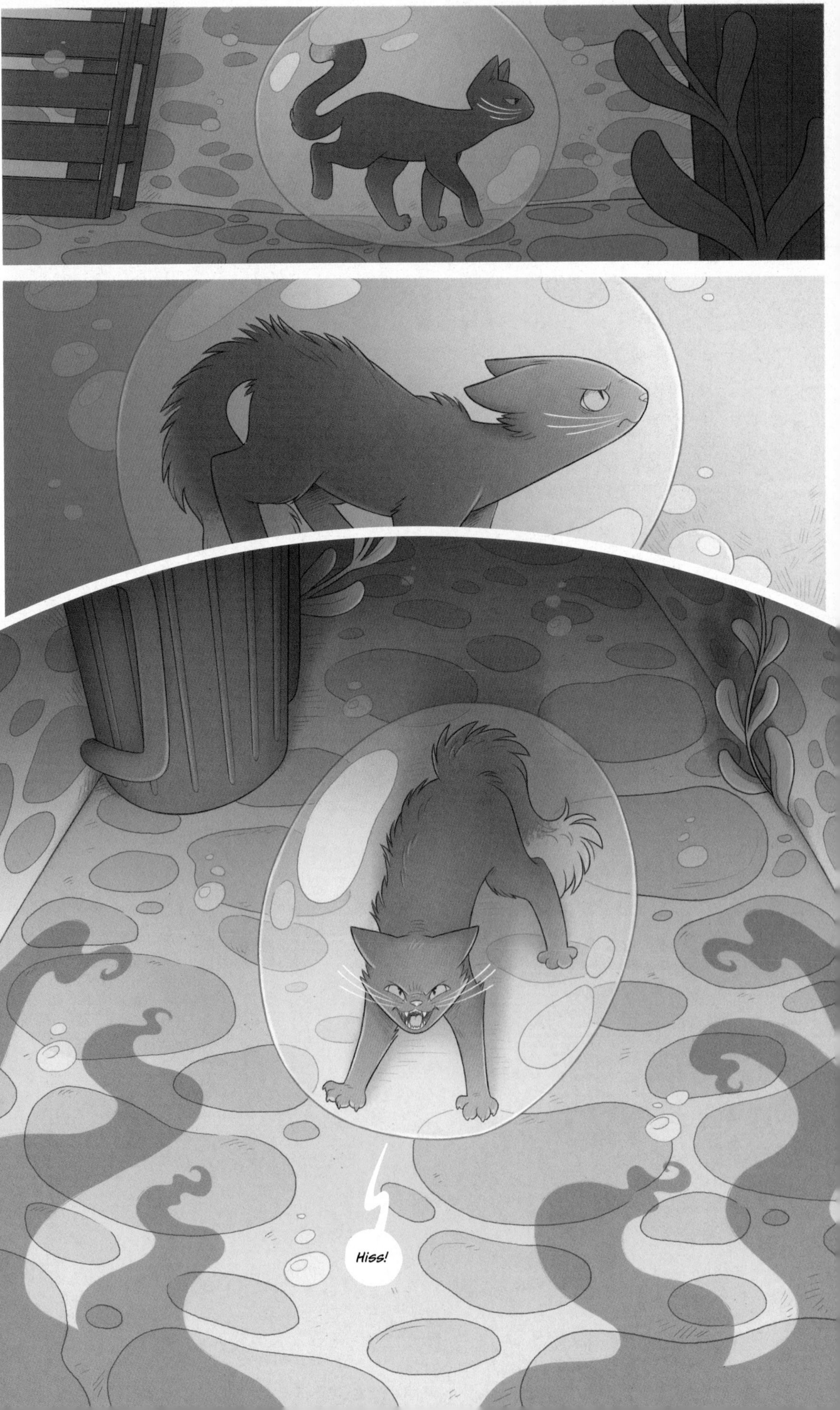
Hiss!

newPals

Super Fun Pages!

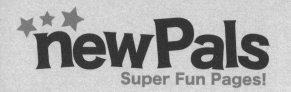

Help Chet and Manuel solve this fun and normal word search!

R	O	U	X	H	N	G	O	S	K	B	T	A	F	S
L	U	S	L	T	I	X	L	D	L	Q	A	A	D	U
C	K	N	S	S	L	A	X	I	S	R	C	A	F	S
I	H	G	O	E	P	G	T	U	V	E	K	C	D	P
G	Q	R	J	W	R	H	E	S	D	M	C	A	A	I
A	P	N	E	A	E	P	B	L	Y	I	A	D	N	C
M	X	N	V	T	R	U	S	J	P	T	L	P	G	I
A	H	C	O	M	L	I	D	E	R	E	B	U	E	O
V	J	N	V	I	R	T	U	A	L	U	N	A	R	U
C	O	N	N	I	V	I	N	G	R	J	L	K	T	S

NEWPALS	DECAF	BLACKCAT
GELPEN	ESPRESSO	BLITHETON
VIRTUAL	MOCHA	MAGIC

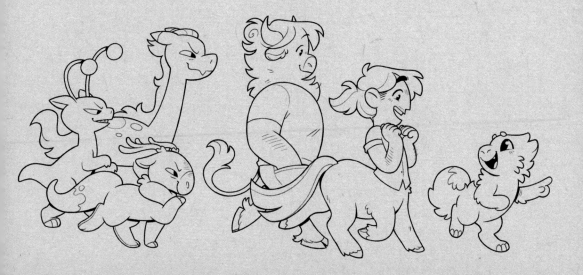

CHAPTER THREE

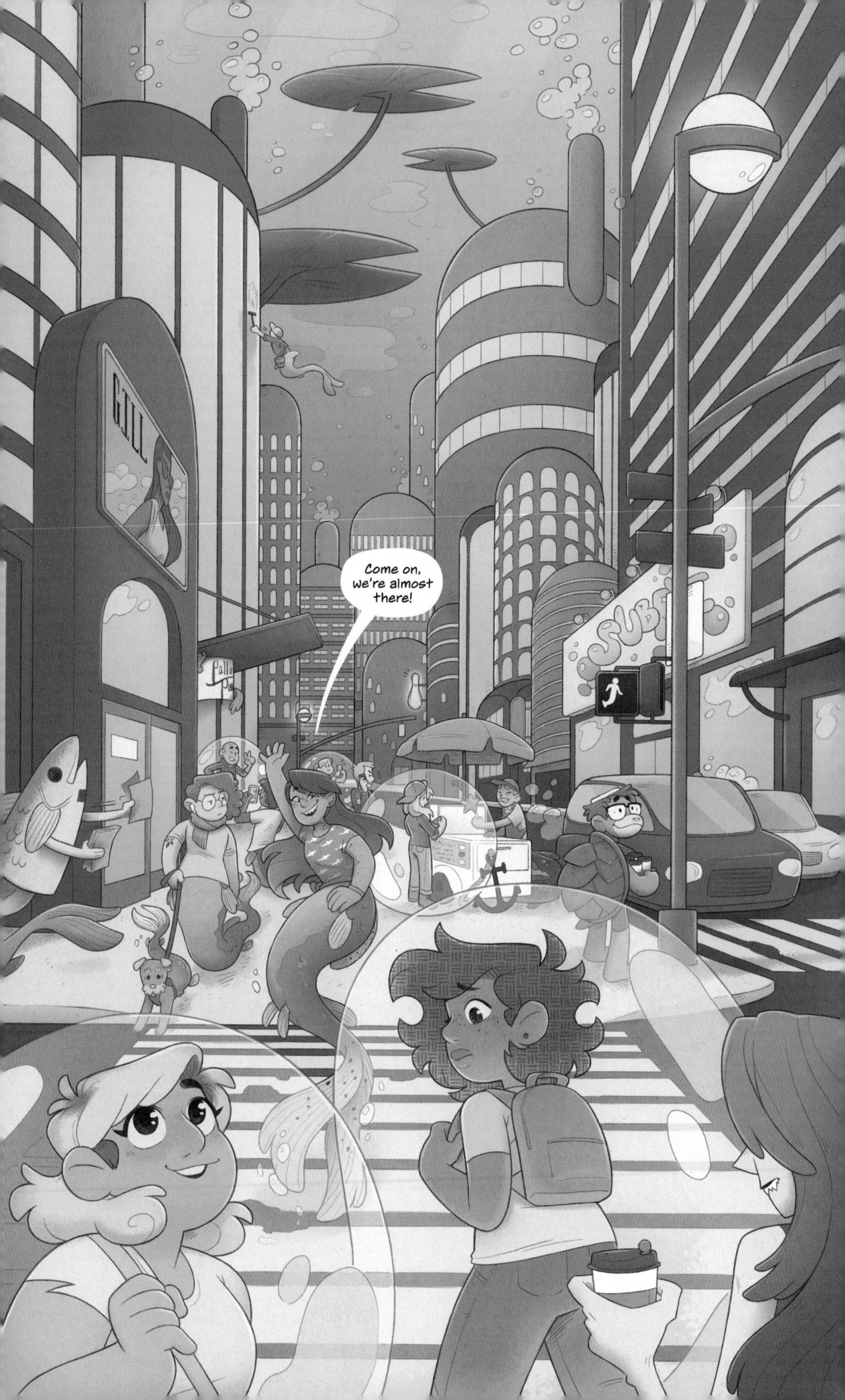
GILL
Come on, we're almost there!

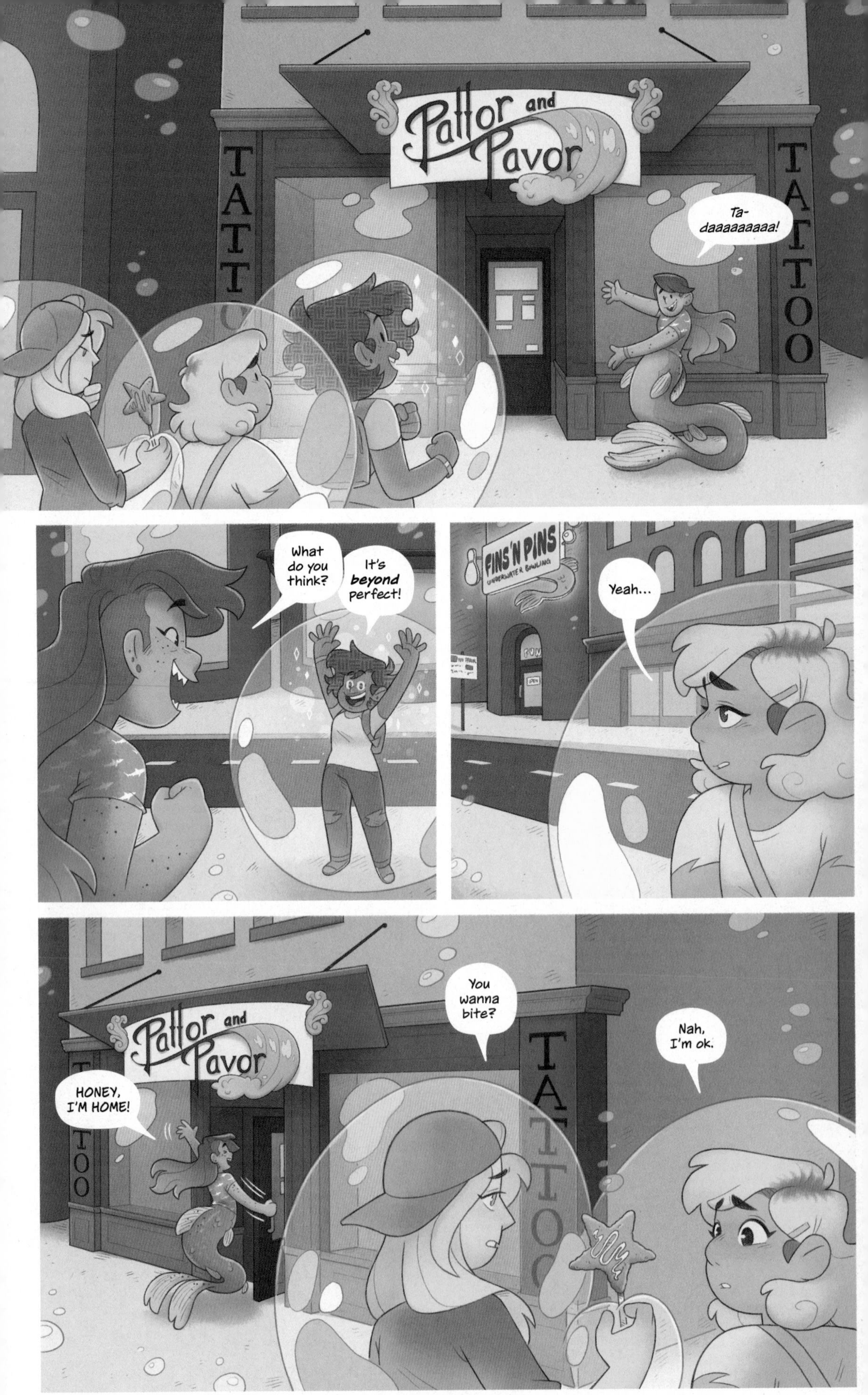
Pallor and Pavor
TATTOO
TATTOO
Ta-daaaaaaaaa!
What do you think?
It's **beyond** perfect!
FINS 'N PINS
UNDERWATER BOWLING
Yeah...
Pallor and Pavor
TATTOO
TATTOO
HONEY, I'M HOME!
You wanna bite?
Nah, I'm ok.

"What's wrong, Jules?

"No one is making you get a tattoo."

"Sorry, it's nothing.

"I'm being a baby."

"Having an emotion doesn't make you a baby.

"You shouldn't have to apologize for having a feeling."

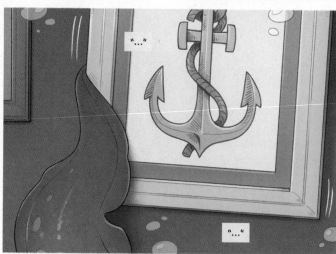

"..."

"..."

I guess you're right.

Y'all here for festival tats?

Yes!

Perfect!

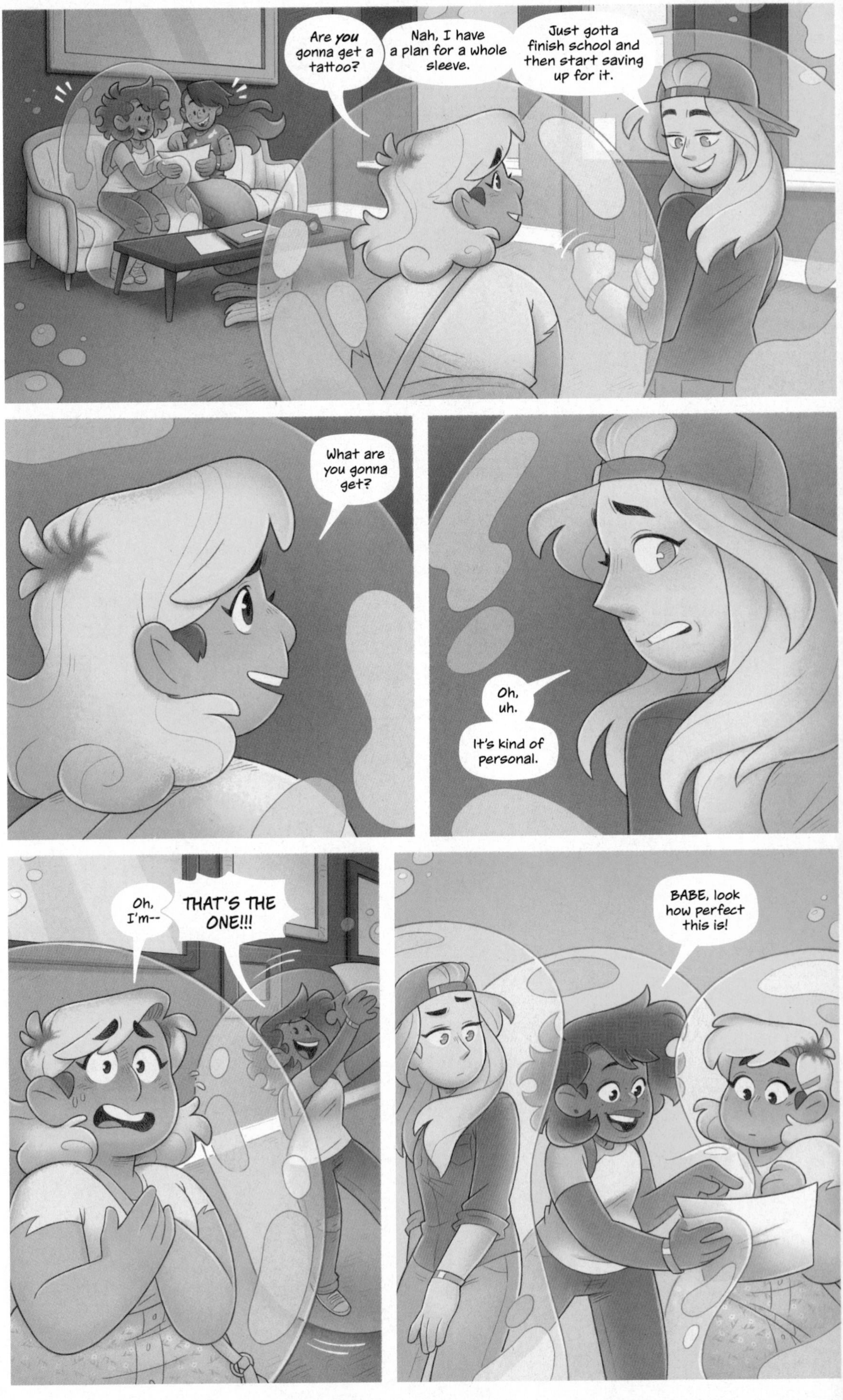
Are you gonna get a tattoo?
Nah, I have a plan for a whole sleeve.
Just gotta finish school and then start saving up for it.
What are you gonna get?
Oh, uh.
It's kind of personal.
Oh, I'm--
THAT'S THE ONE!!!
BABE, look how perfect this is!

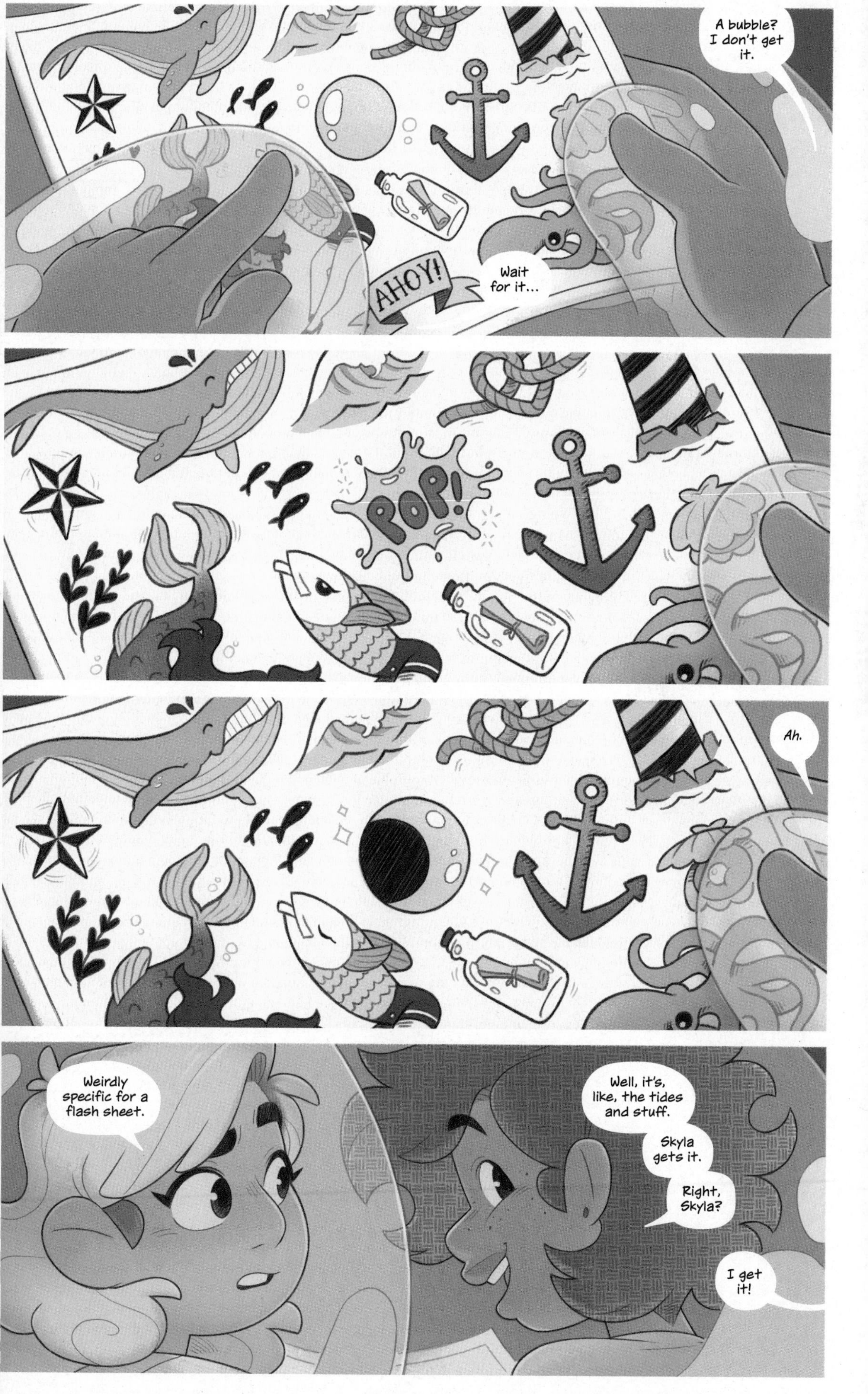

A bubble? I don't get it.
AHOY!
Wait for it...
POP!
Ah.
Weirdly specific for a flash sheet.
Well, it's, like, the tides and stuff.
Skyla gets it.
Right, Skyla?
I get it!

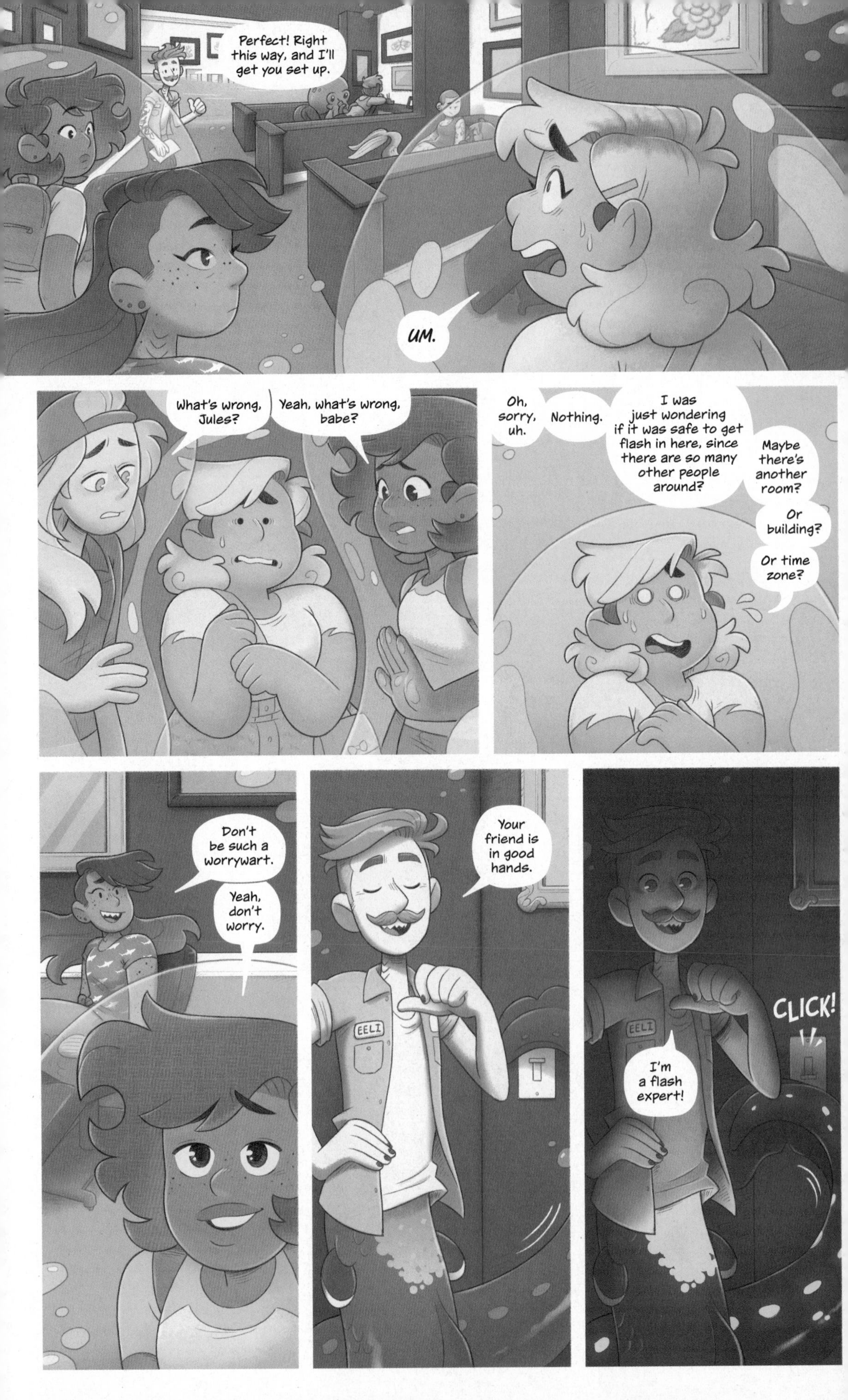
Perfect! Right this way, and I'll get you set up.
UM.
What's wrong, Jules?
Yeah, what's wrong, babe?
Oh, sorry, uh.
Nothing.
I was just wondering if it was safe to get flash in here, since there are so many other people around?
Maybe there's another room?
Or building?
Or time zone?
Don't be such a worrywart.
Yeah, don't worry.
Your friend is in good hands.
EELI
EELI
I'm a flash expert!
CLICK!

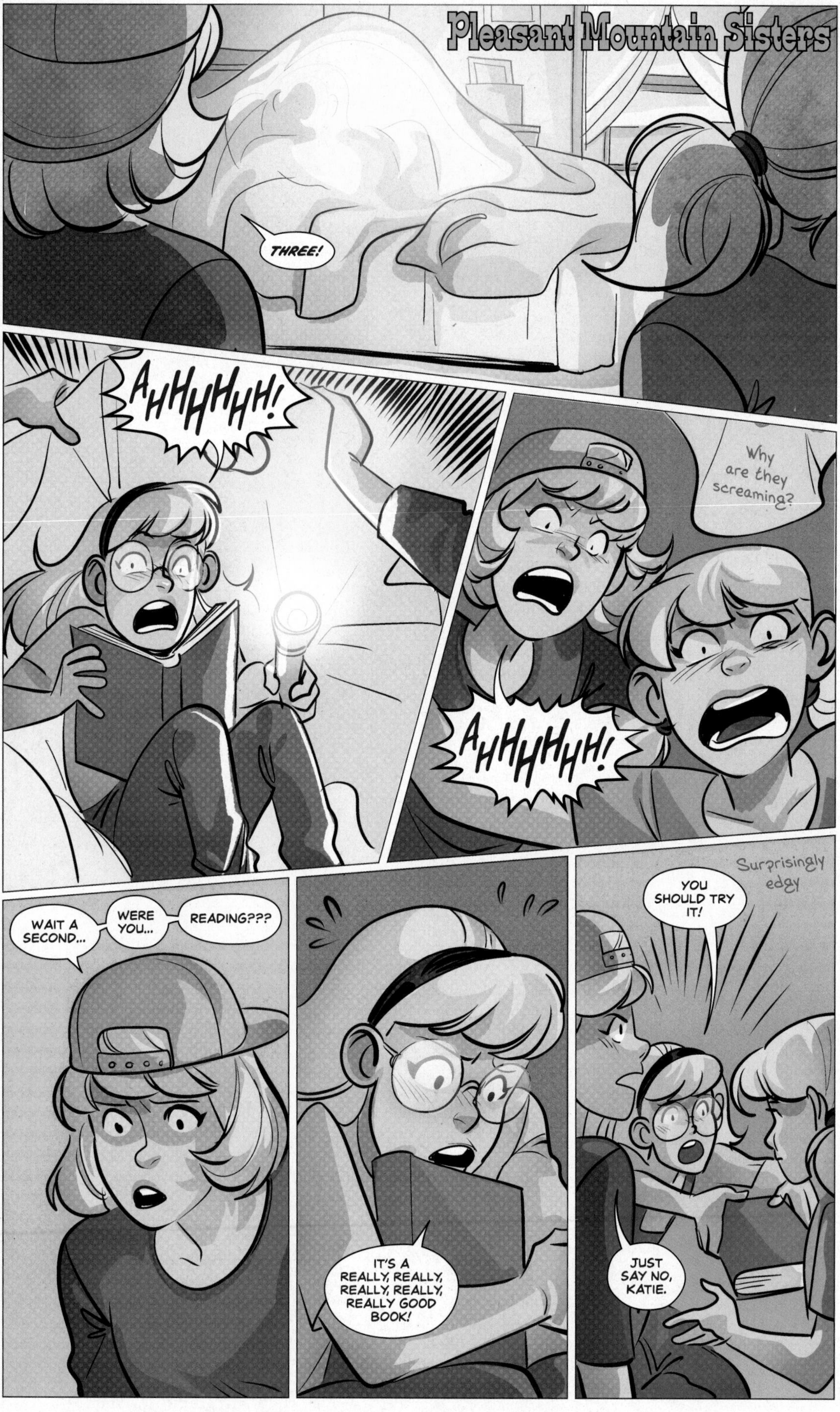
Pleasant Mountain Sisters
THREE!
AHHHHHH!
Why are they screaming?
AHHHHHH!
WAIT A SECOND...
WERE YOU...
READING???
IT'S A REALLY, REALLY, REALLY, REALLY, REALLY GOOD BOOK!
Surprisingly edgy
YOU SHOULD TRY IT!
JUST SAY NO, KATIE.

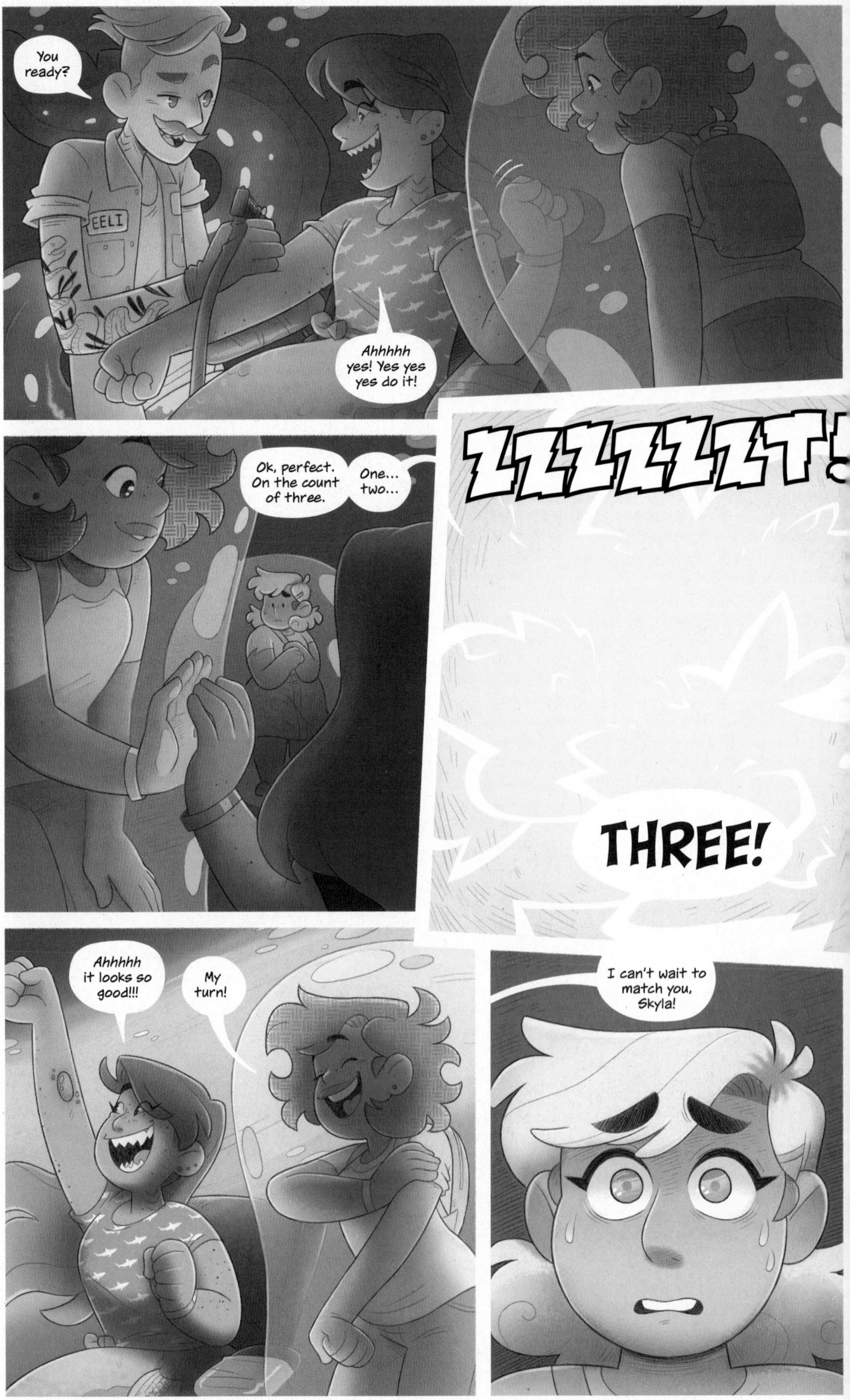

You ready?
Ahhhhh yes! Yes yes yes do it!
Ok, perfect. On the count of three.
One... two...
ZZZZZZZT!
THREE!
Ahhhhh it looks so good!!!
My turn!
I can't wait to match you, Skyla!

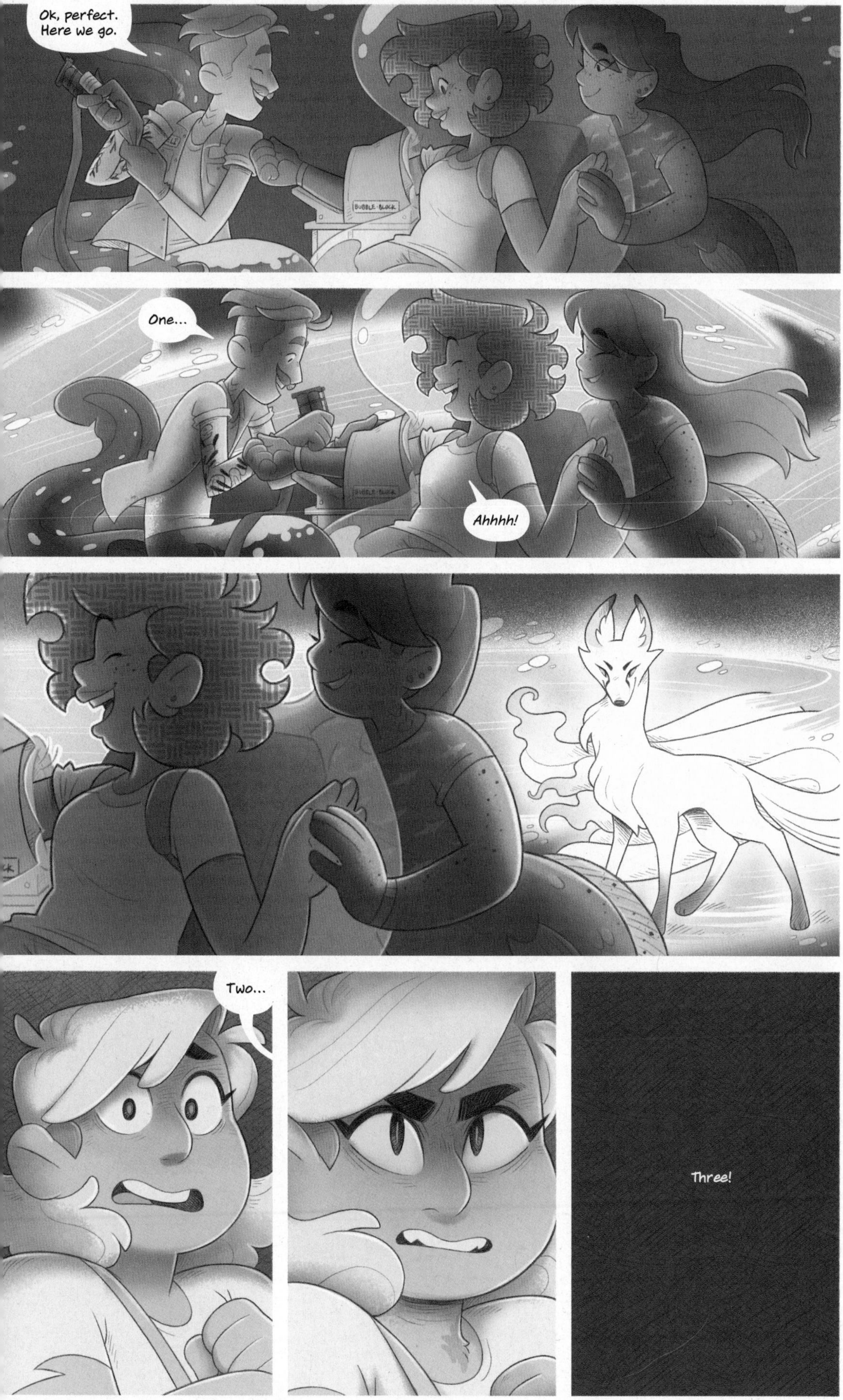
Ok, perfect.
Here we go.
BUBBLE-BLOCK
One...
Ahhhh!
Two...
Three!

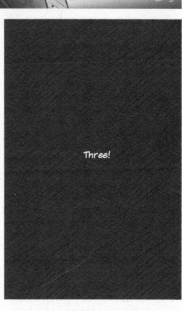

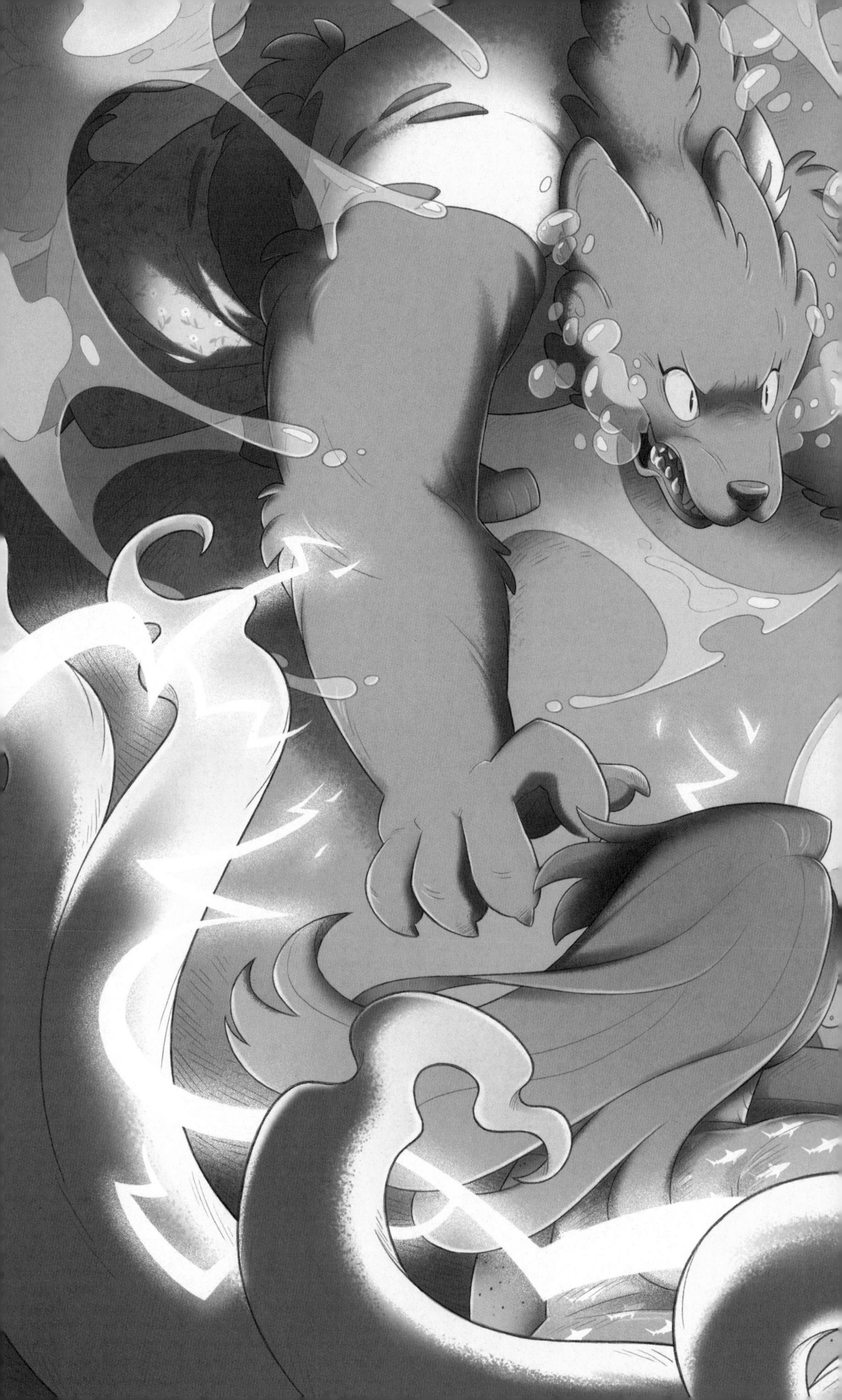

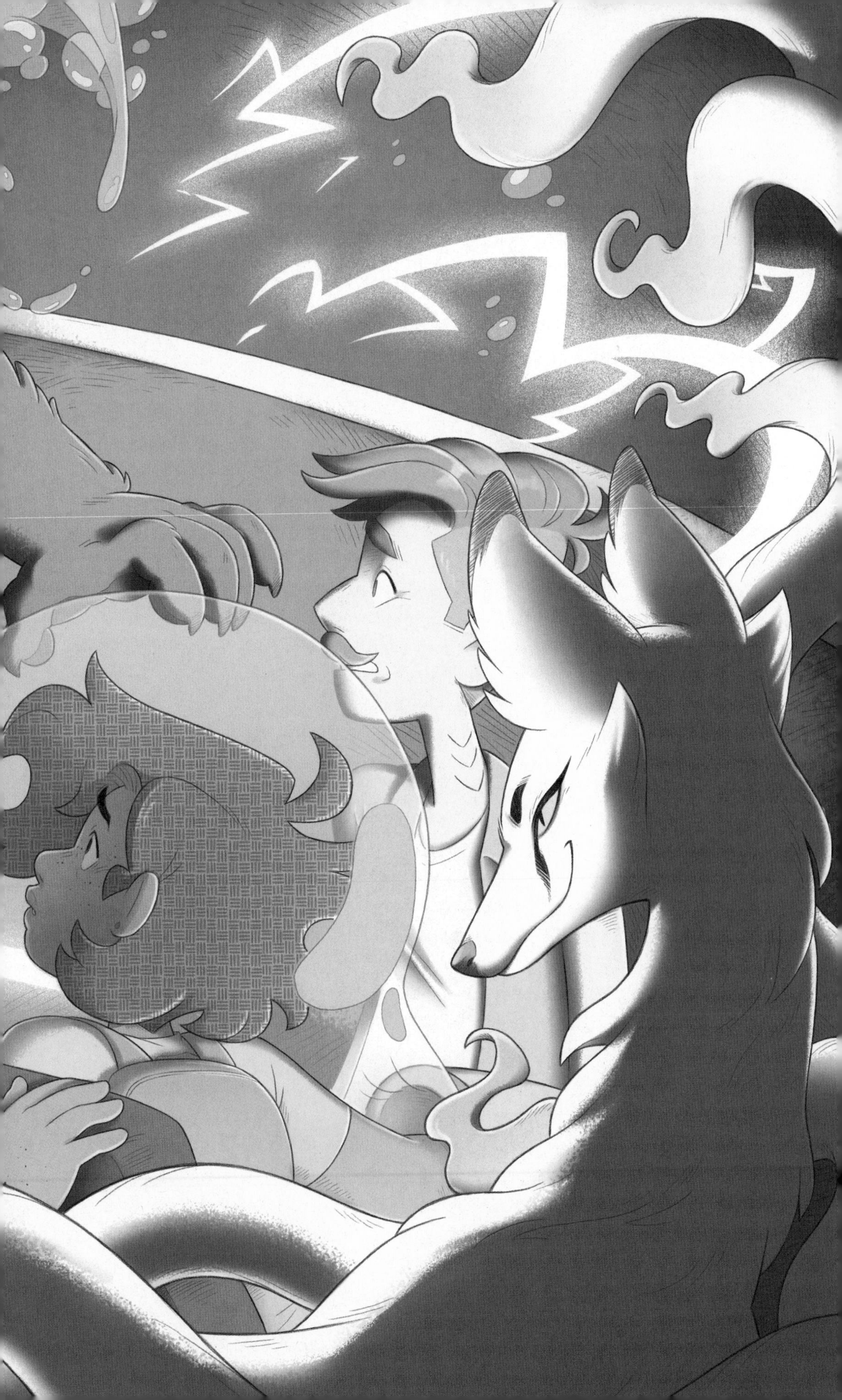

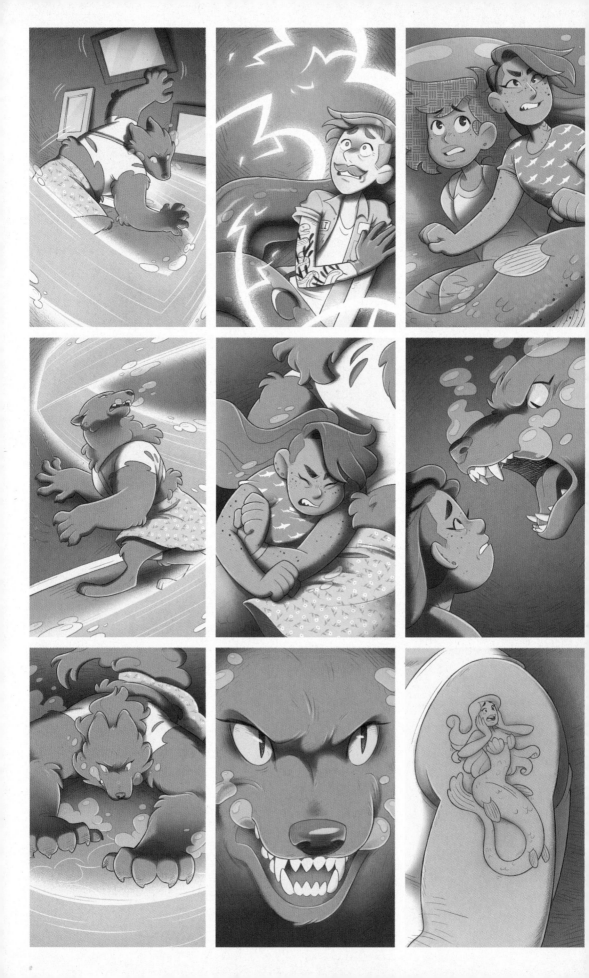

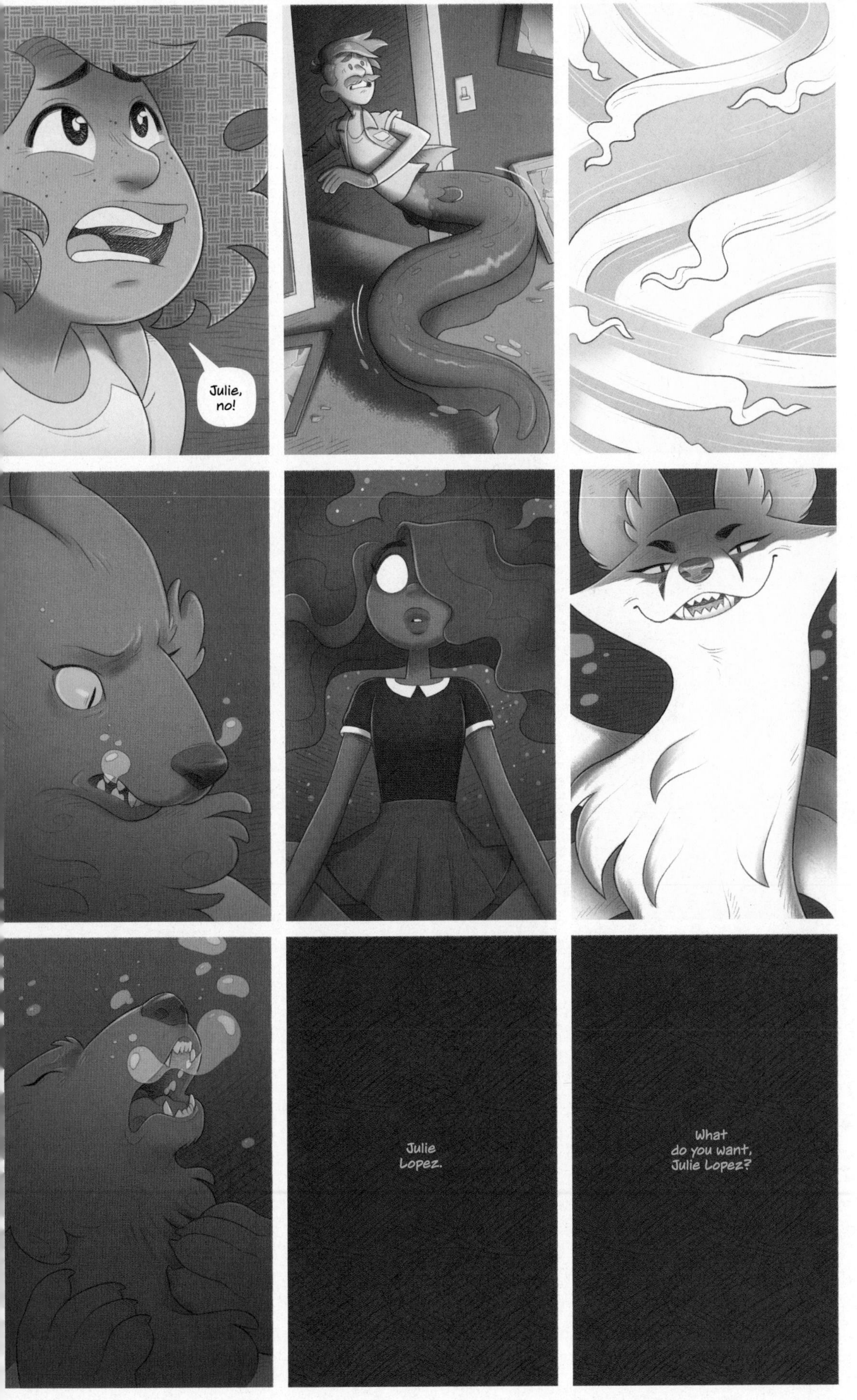
Julie, no!
Julie Lopez.
What do you want, Julie Lopez?

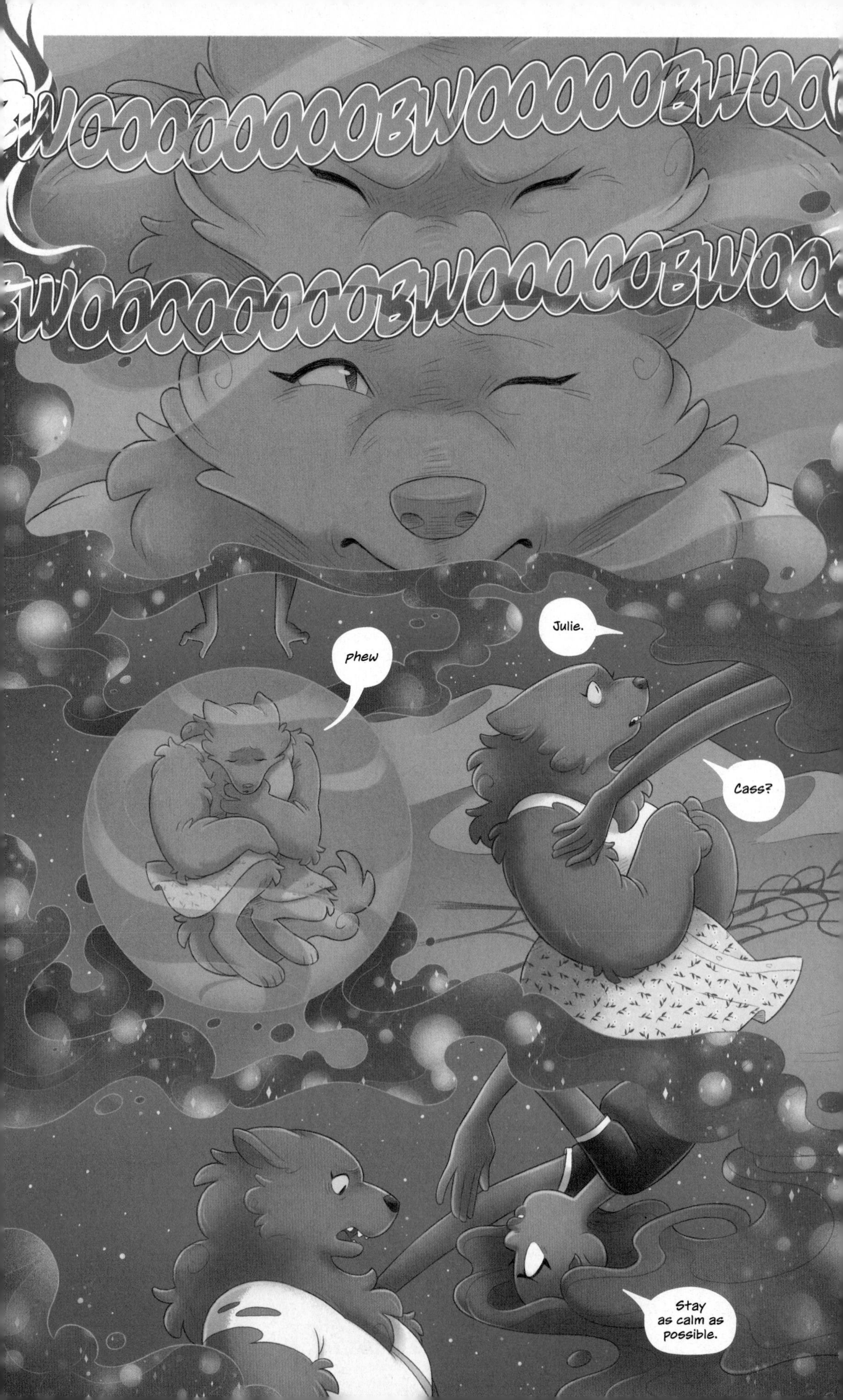
BWOOOOOOOOOBWOOOOOOBWOO
BWOOOOOOOOOBWOOOOOOBWOO
Phew
Julie.
Cass?
Stay as calm as possible.

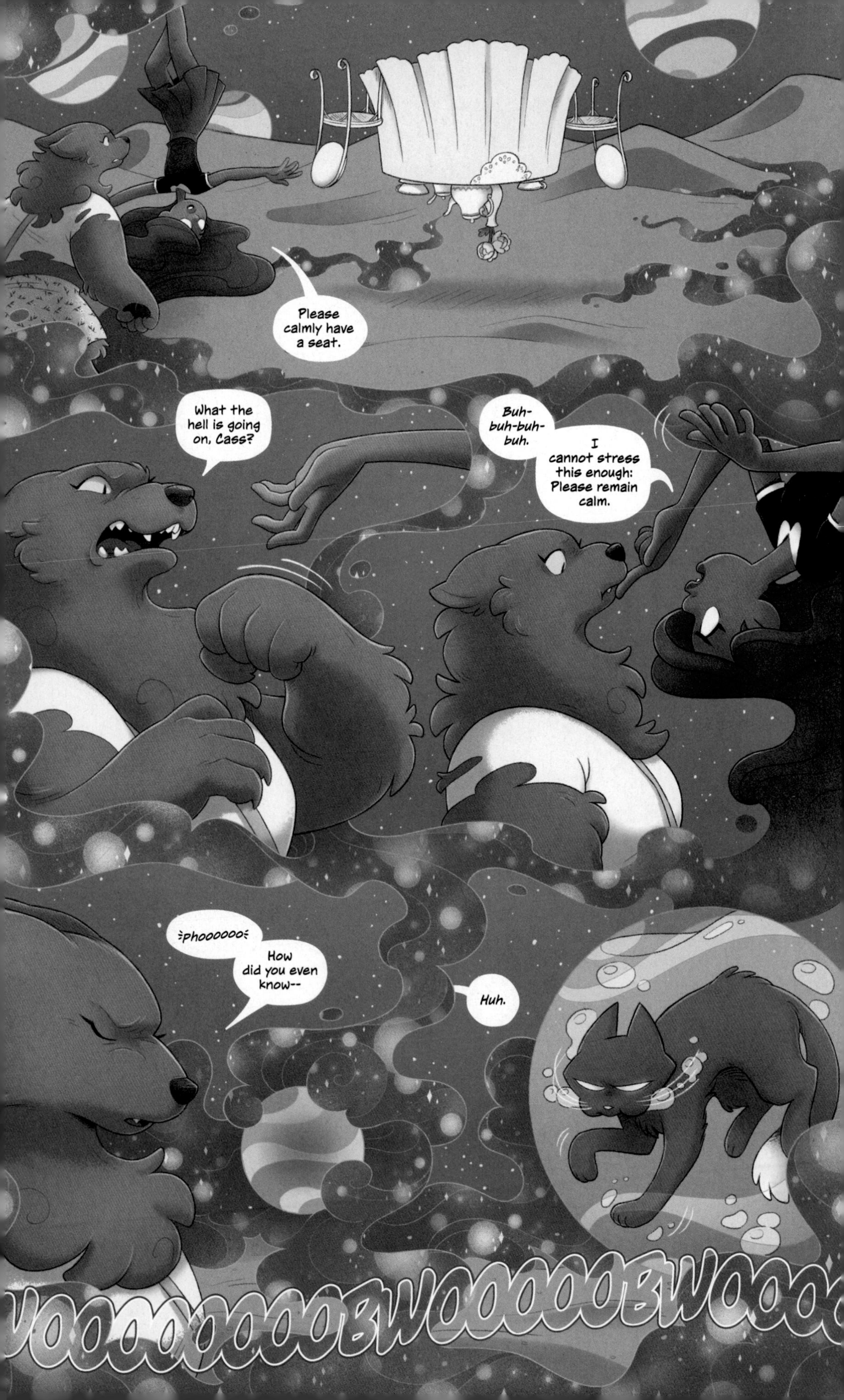
Please calmly have a seat.
What the hell is going on, Cass?
Buh-buh-buh-buh.
I cannot stress this enough: Please remain calm.
phoooooo
How did you even know--
Huh.
VOOOOOOOOOBWOOOOOOBWOOO

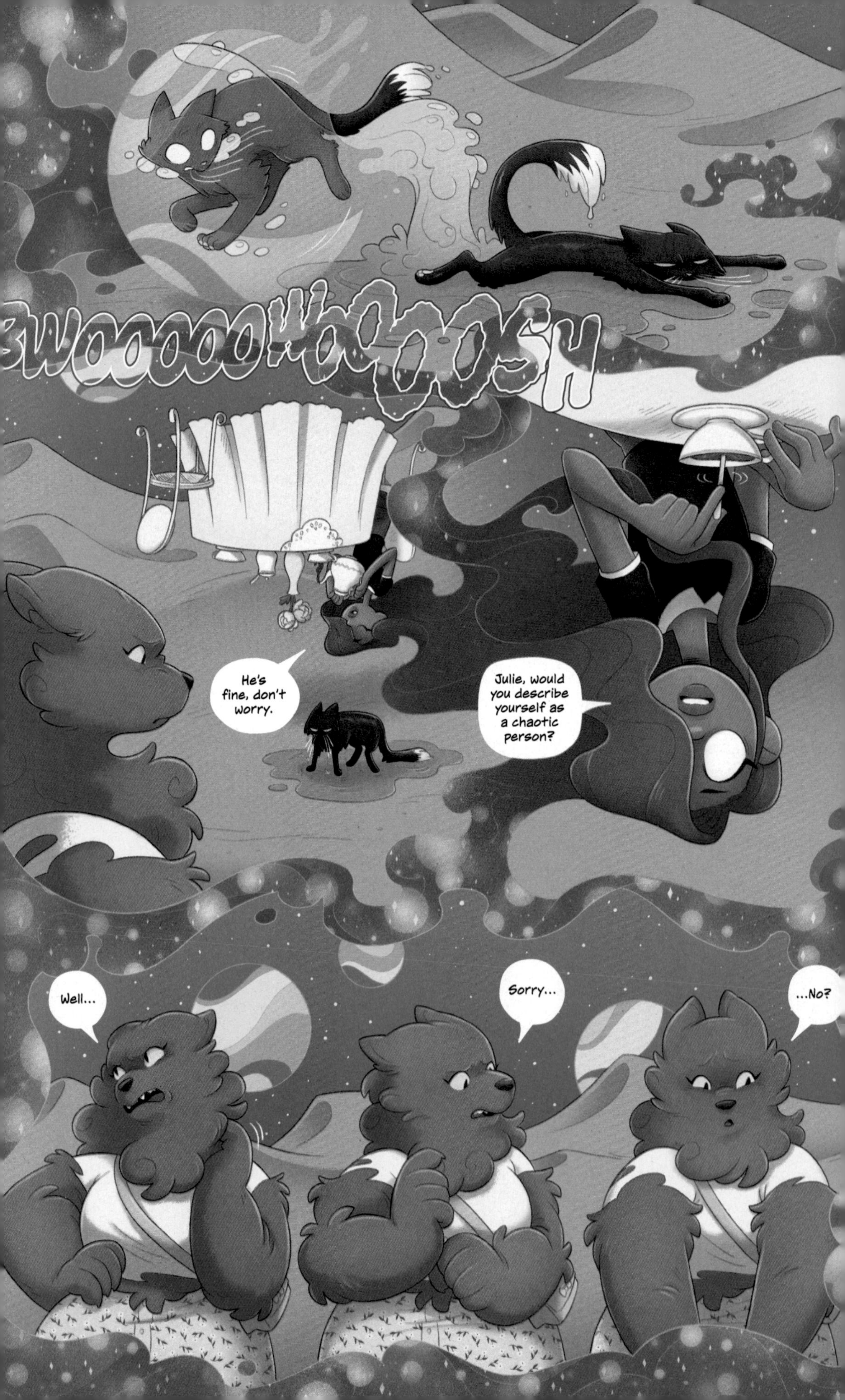
SWOOOOOWOOOOSH
He's fine, don't worry.
Julie, would you describe yourself as a chaotic person?
Well...
Sorry...
...No?

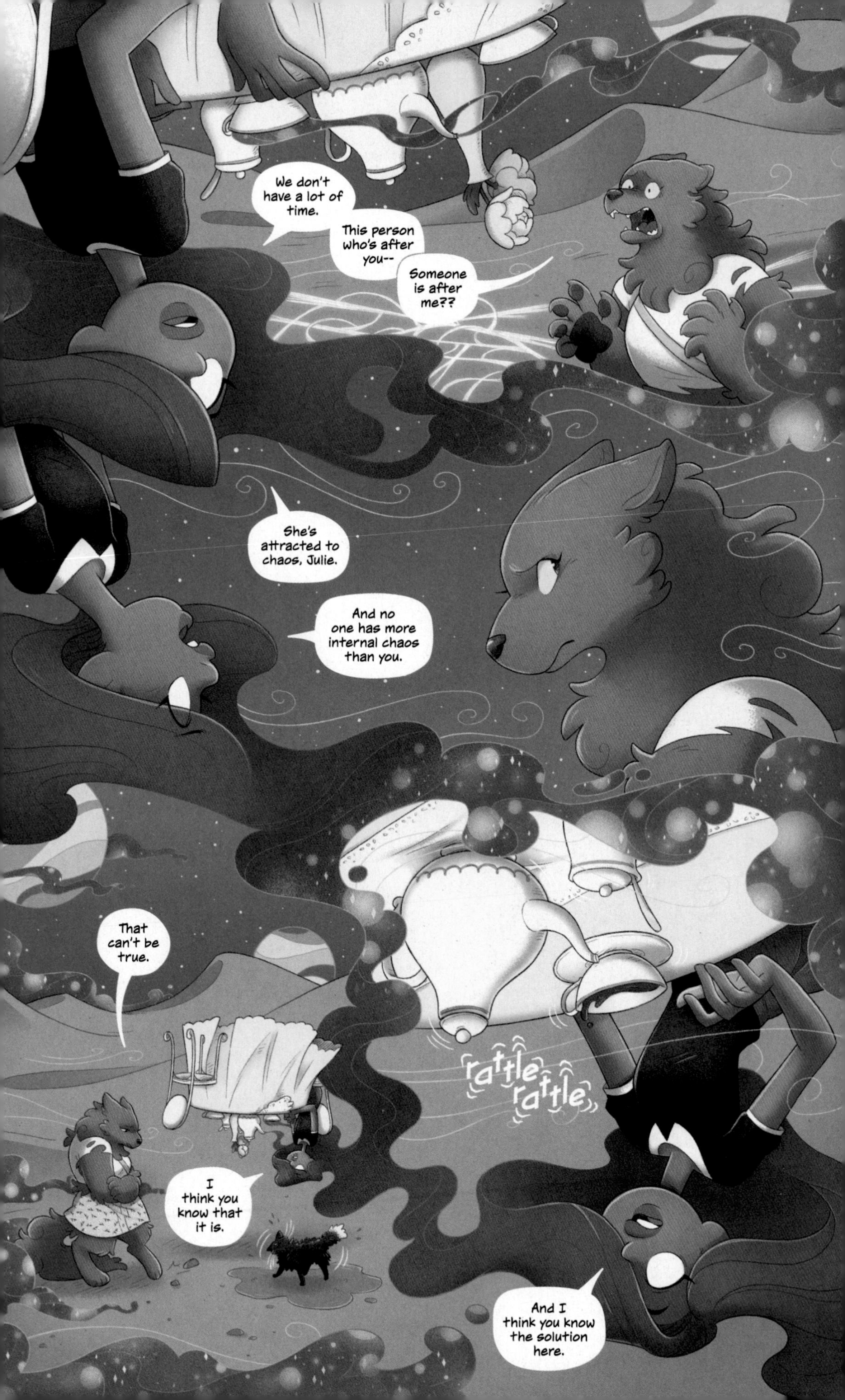
We don't have a lot of time.
This person who's after you--
Someone is after me??
She's attracted to chaos, Julie.
And no one has more internal chaos than you.
That can't be true.
rattle rattle
I think you know that it is.
And I think you know the solution here.

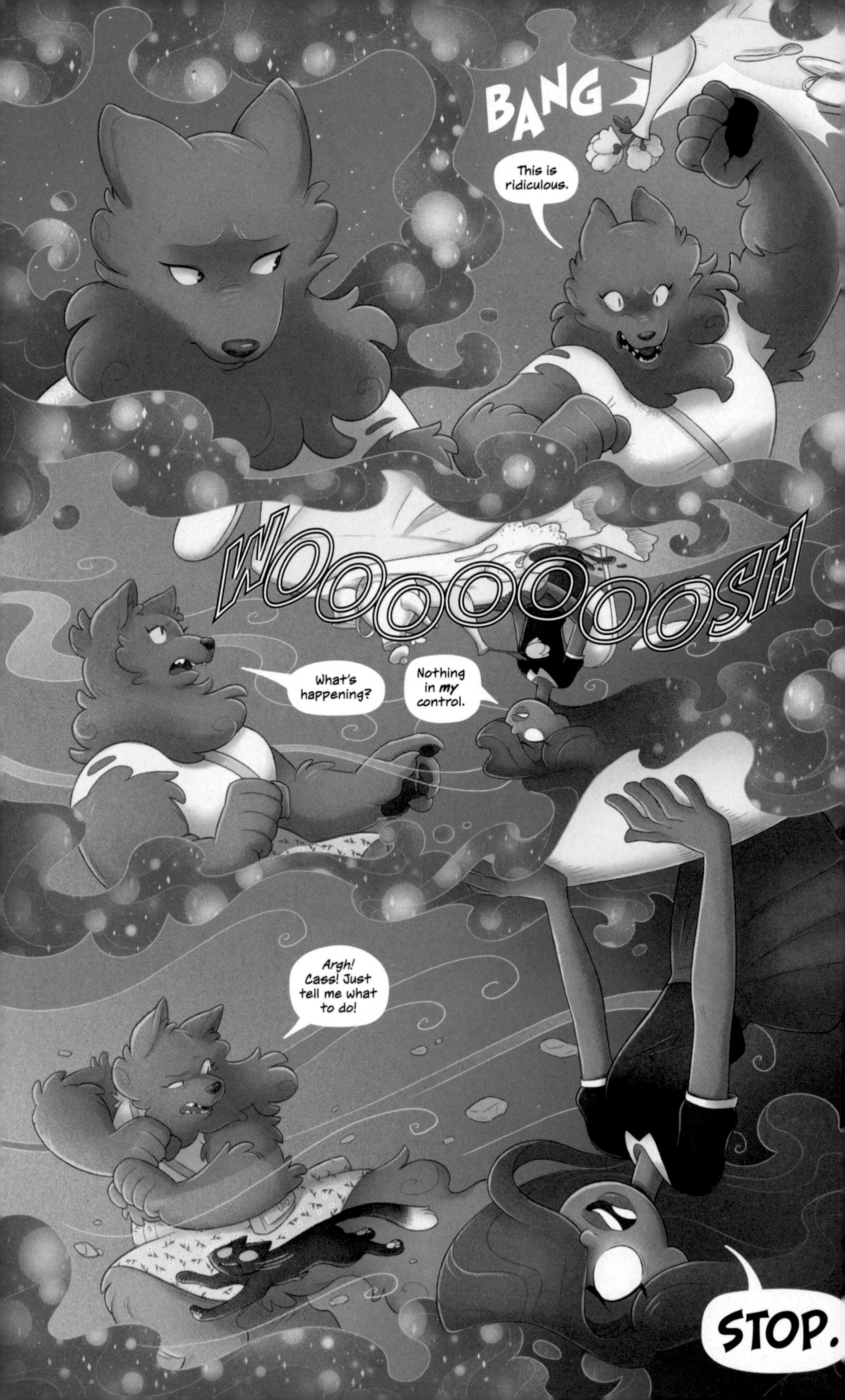
BANG
This is ridiculous.
WOOOOOOOOOSH
What's happening?
Nothing in *my* control.
Argh! Cass! Just tell me what to do!
STOP.

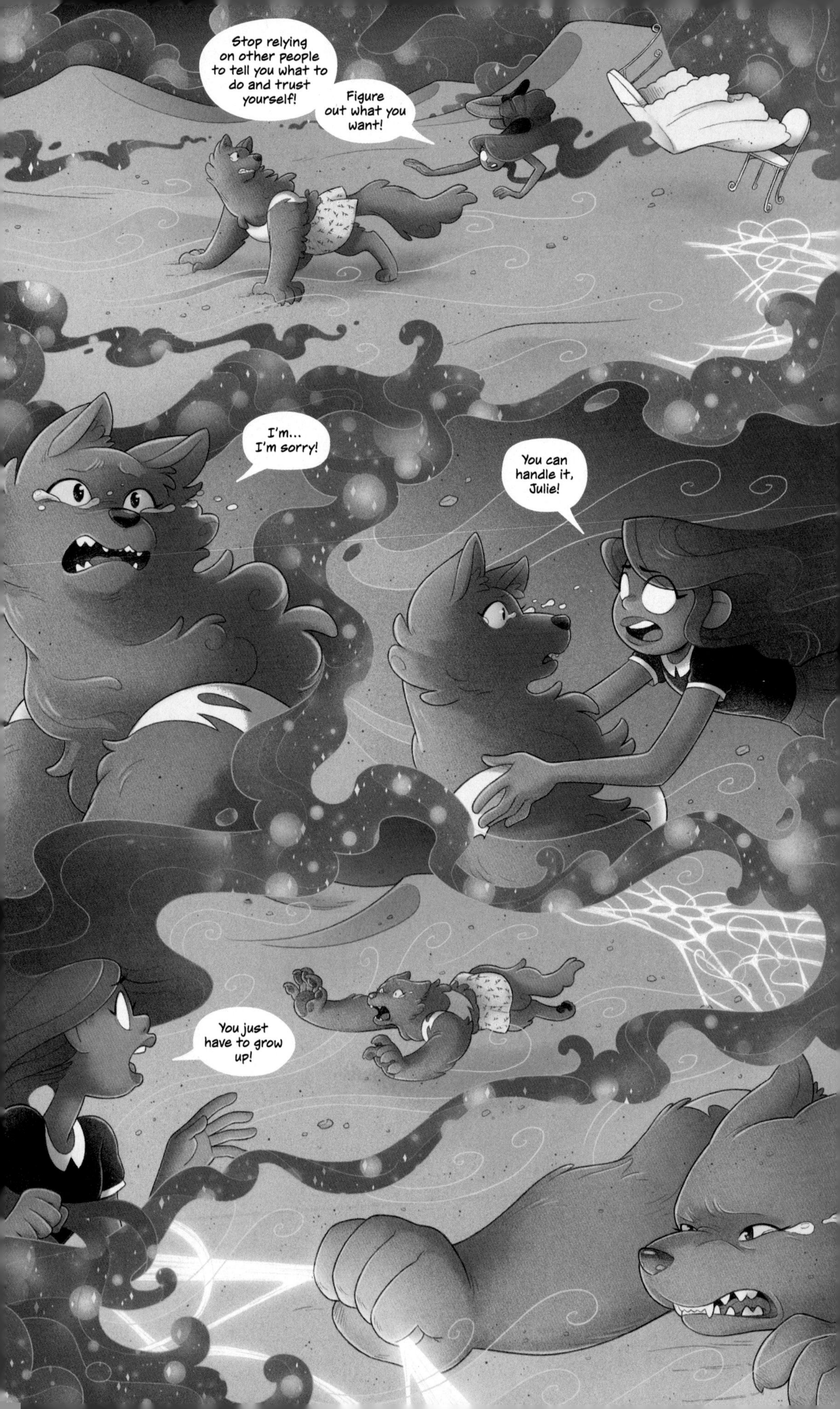
Stop relying on other people to tell you what to do and trust yourself!
Figure out what you want!
I'm... I'm sorry!
You can handle it, Julie!
You just have to grow up!

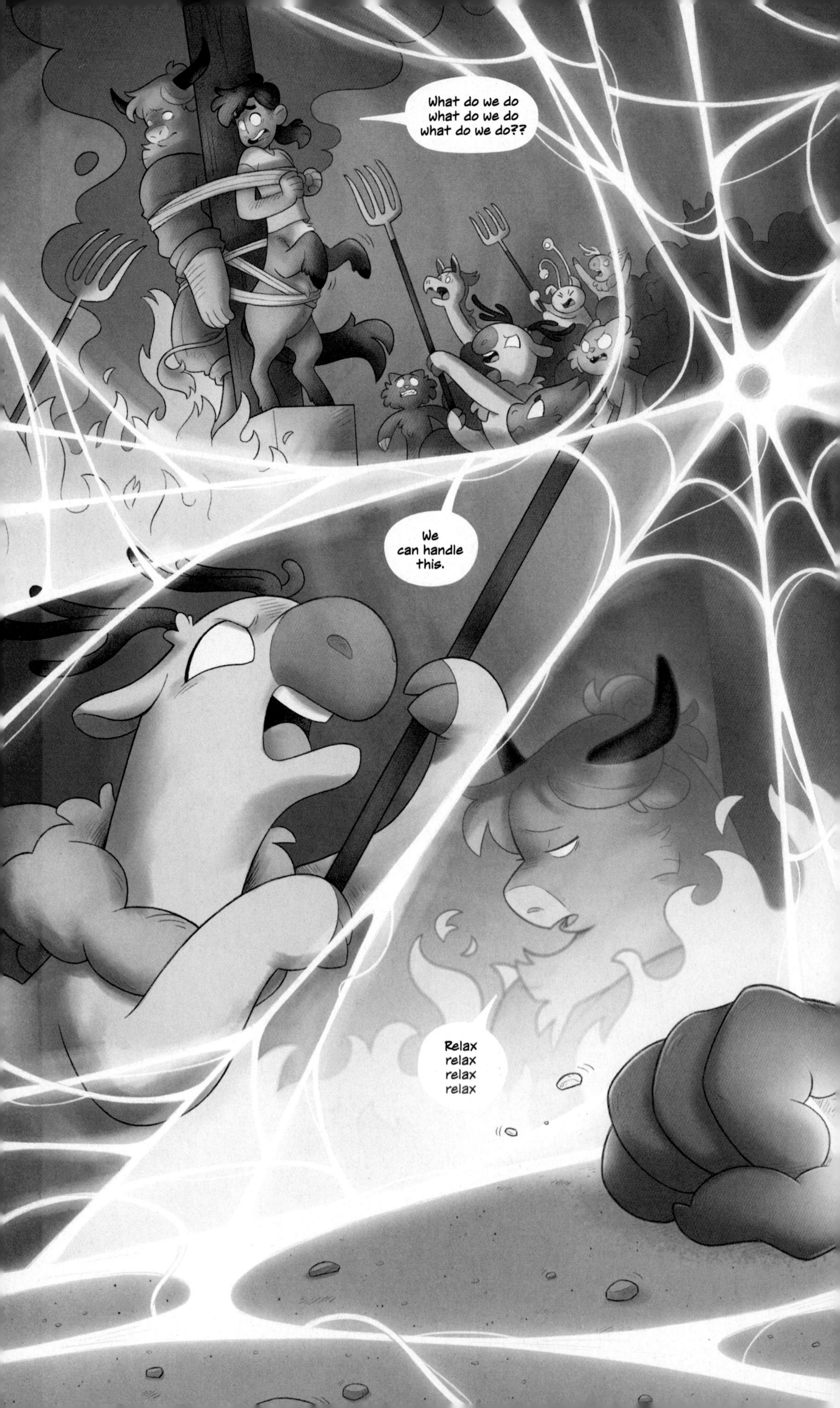
What do we do what do we do what do we do??
We can handle this.
Relax relax relax relax

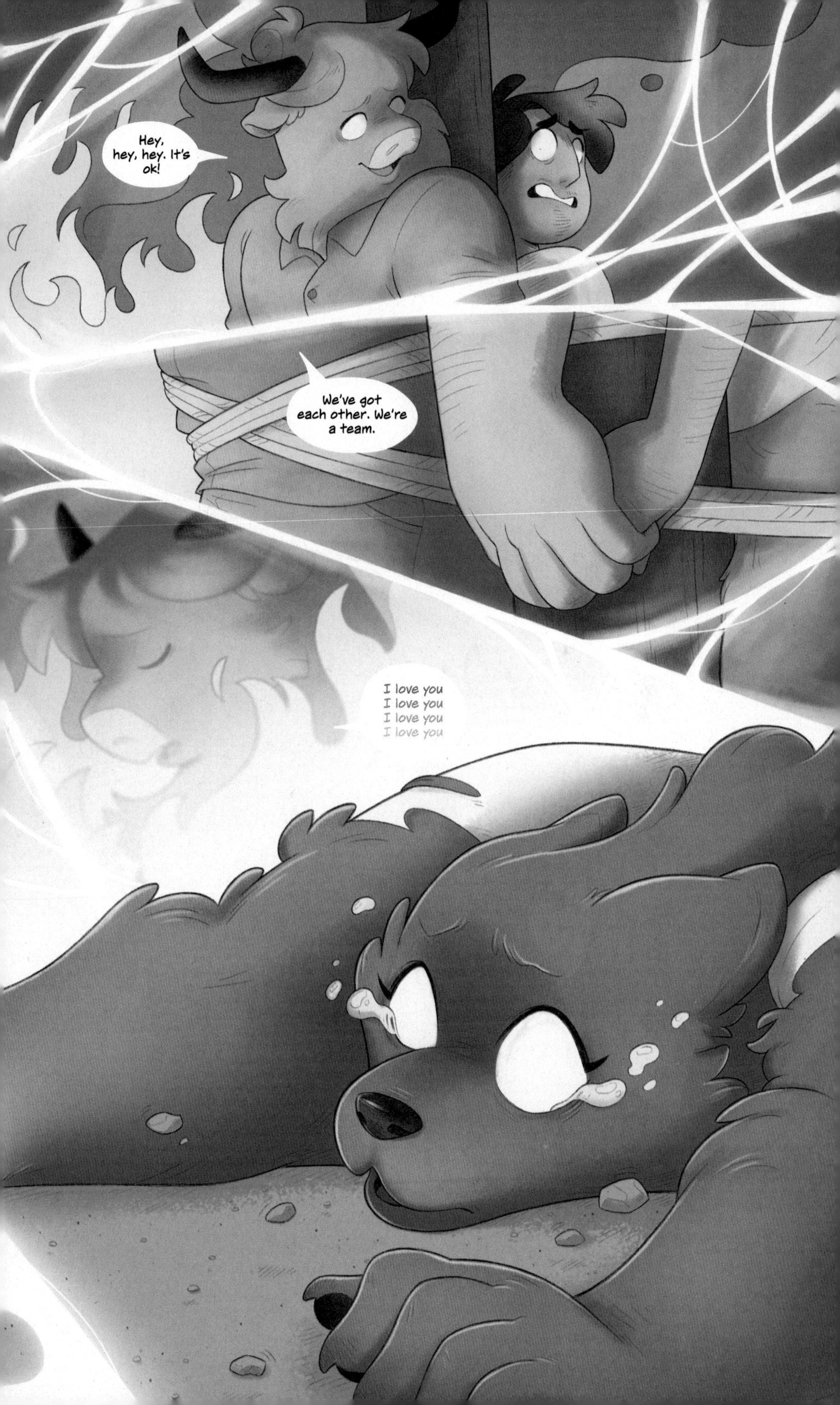
Hey, hey, hey. It's ok!
We've got each other. We're a team.
I love you
I love you
I love you
I love you

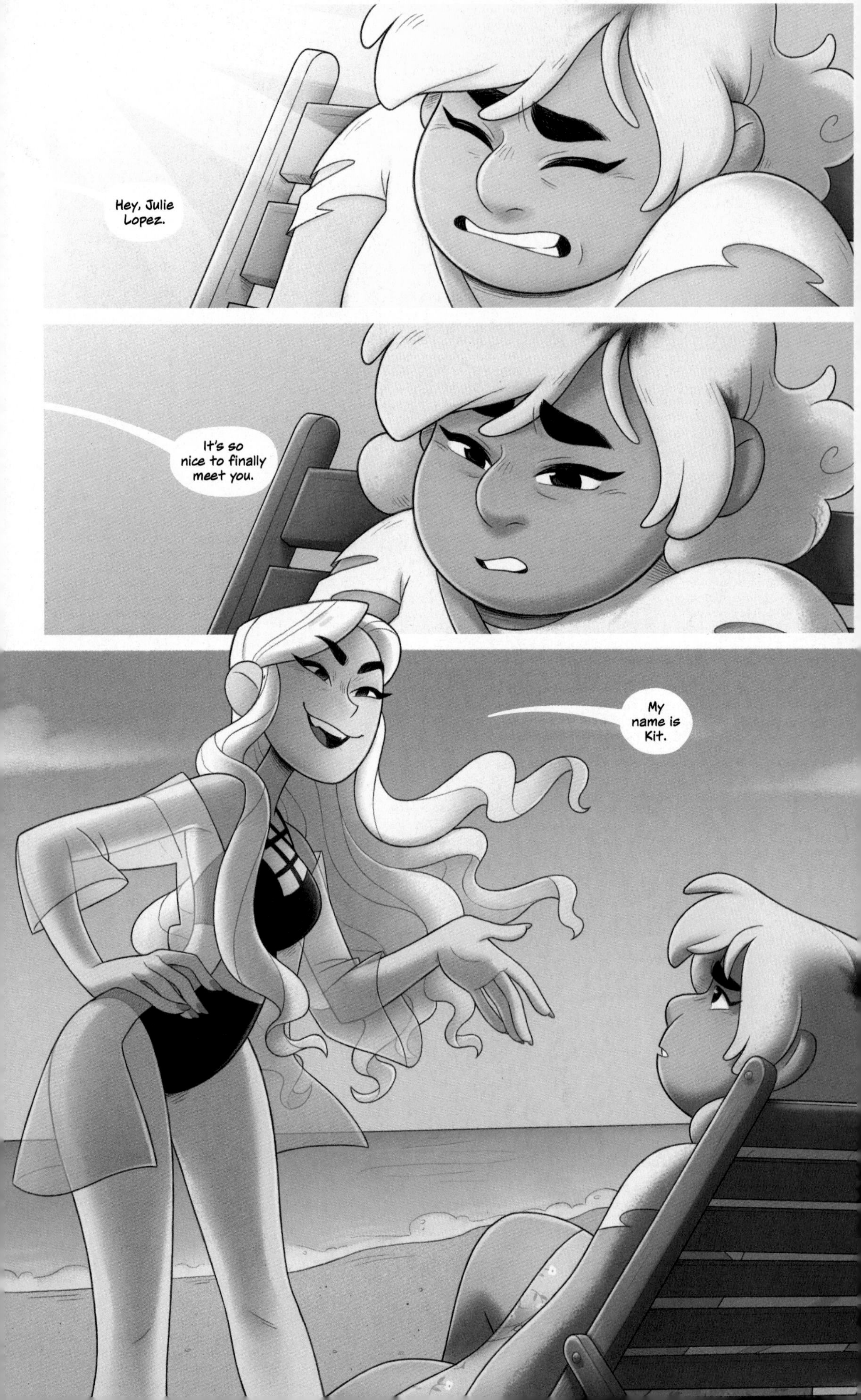

Hey, Julie Lopez.
It's so nice to finally meet you.
My name is Kit.

newPals
Super Fun Pages!

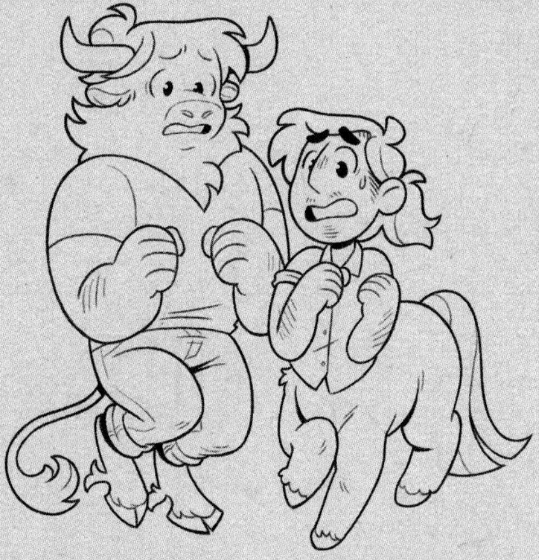

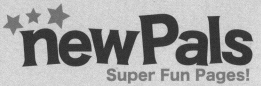

Help Chet and Manuel escape the deranged Newpals!

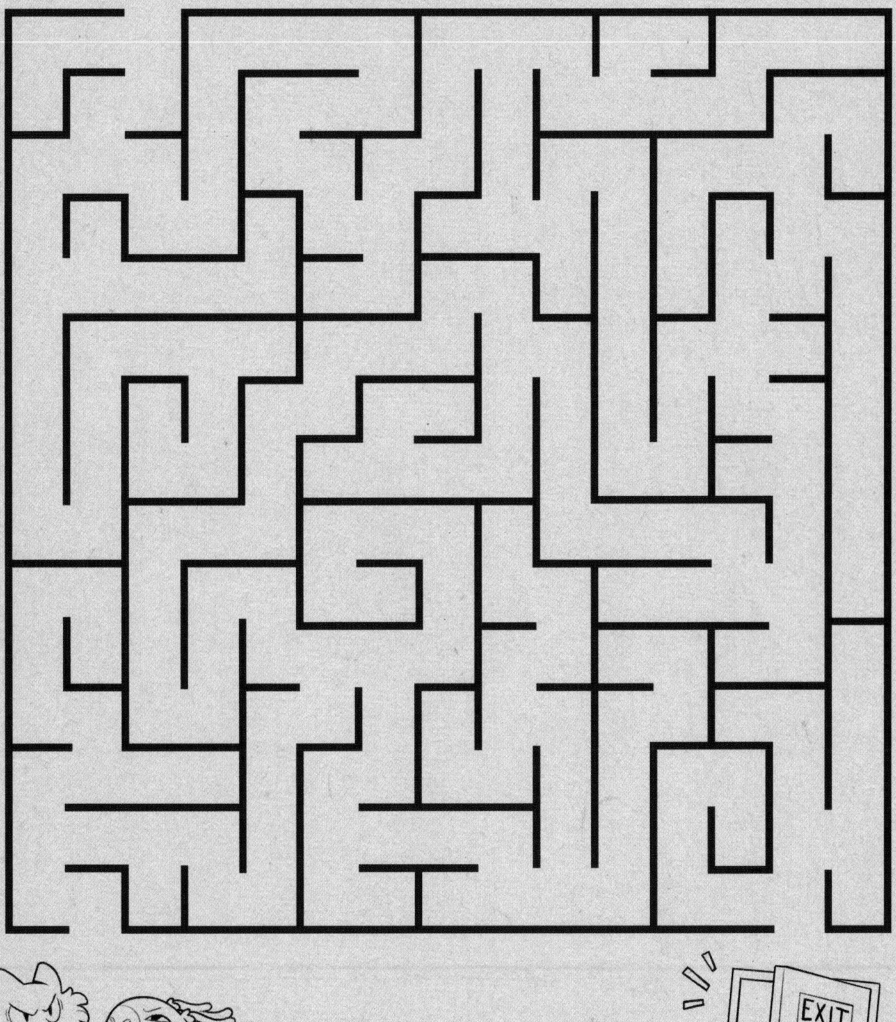

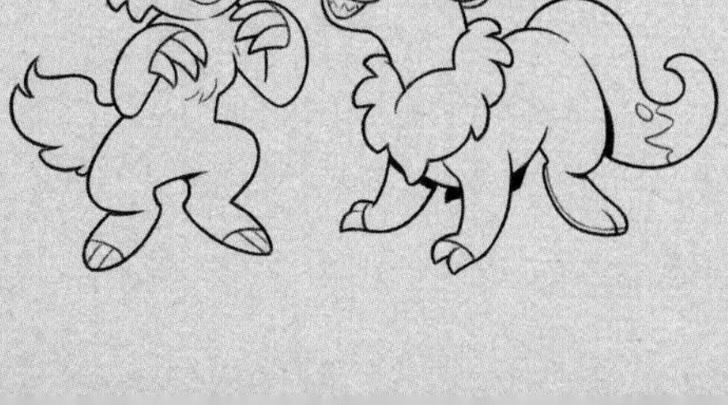

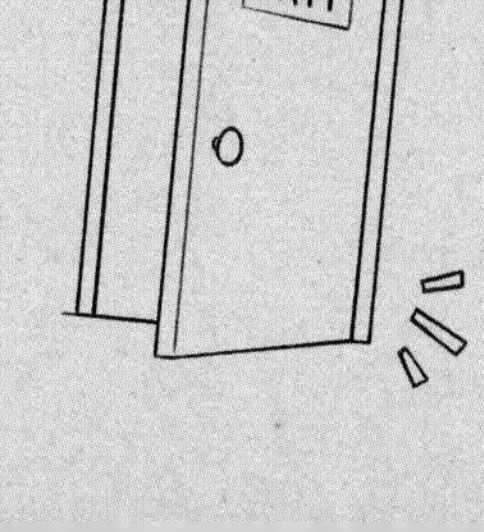
EXIT

CHAPTER FOUR

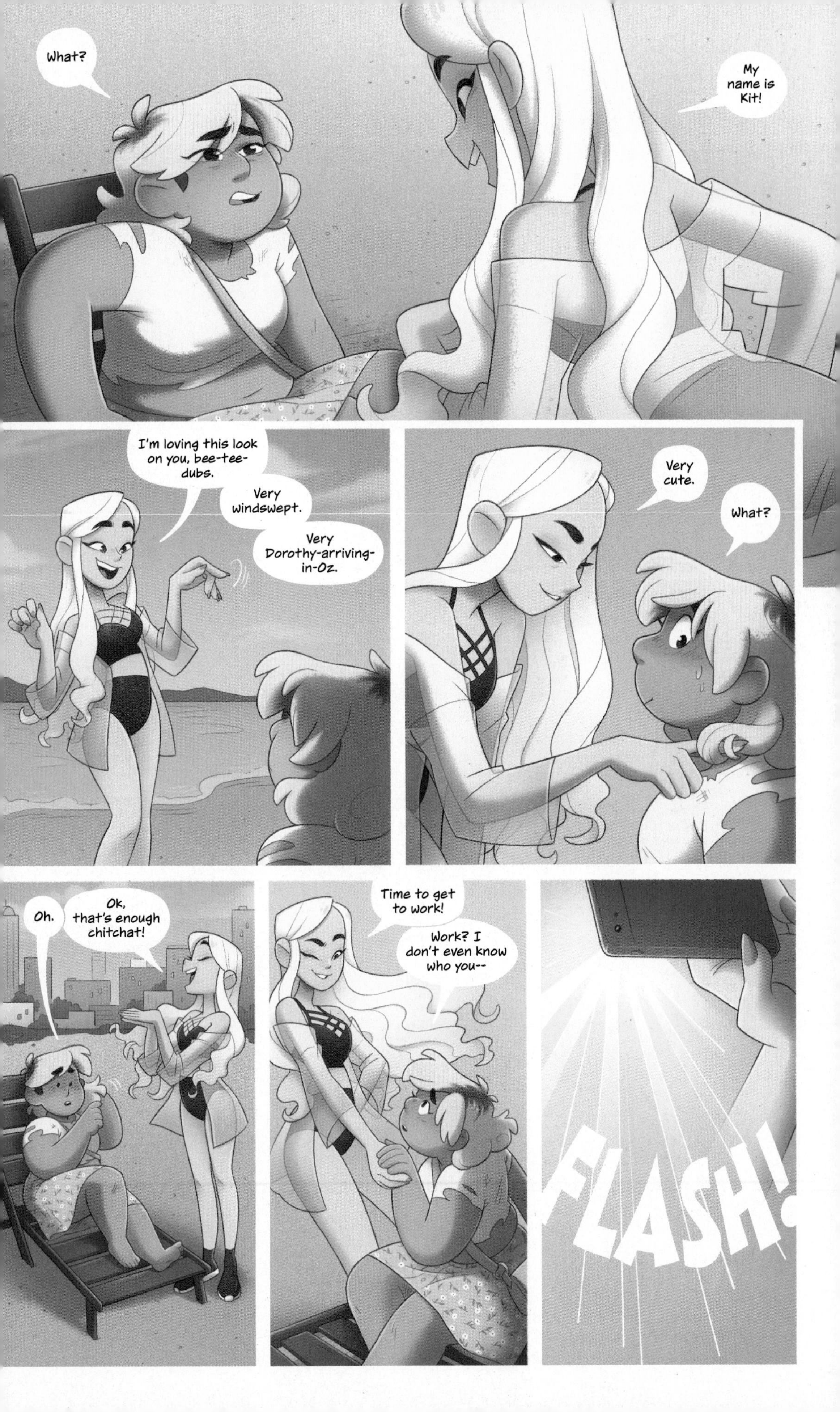
What?
My name is Kit!
I'm loving this look on you, bee-tee-dubs.
Very windswept.
Very Dorothy-arriving-in-Oz.
Very cute.
What?
Oh.
Ok, that's enough chitchat!
Time to get to work!
Work? I don't even know who you--
FLASH!

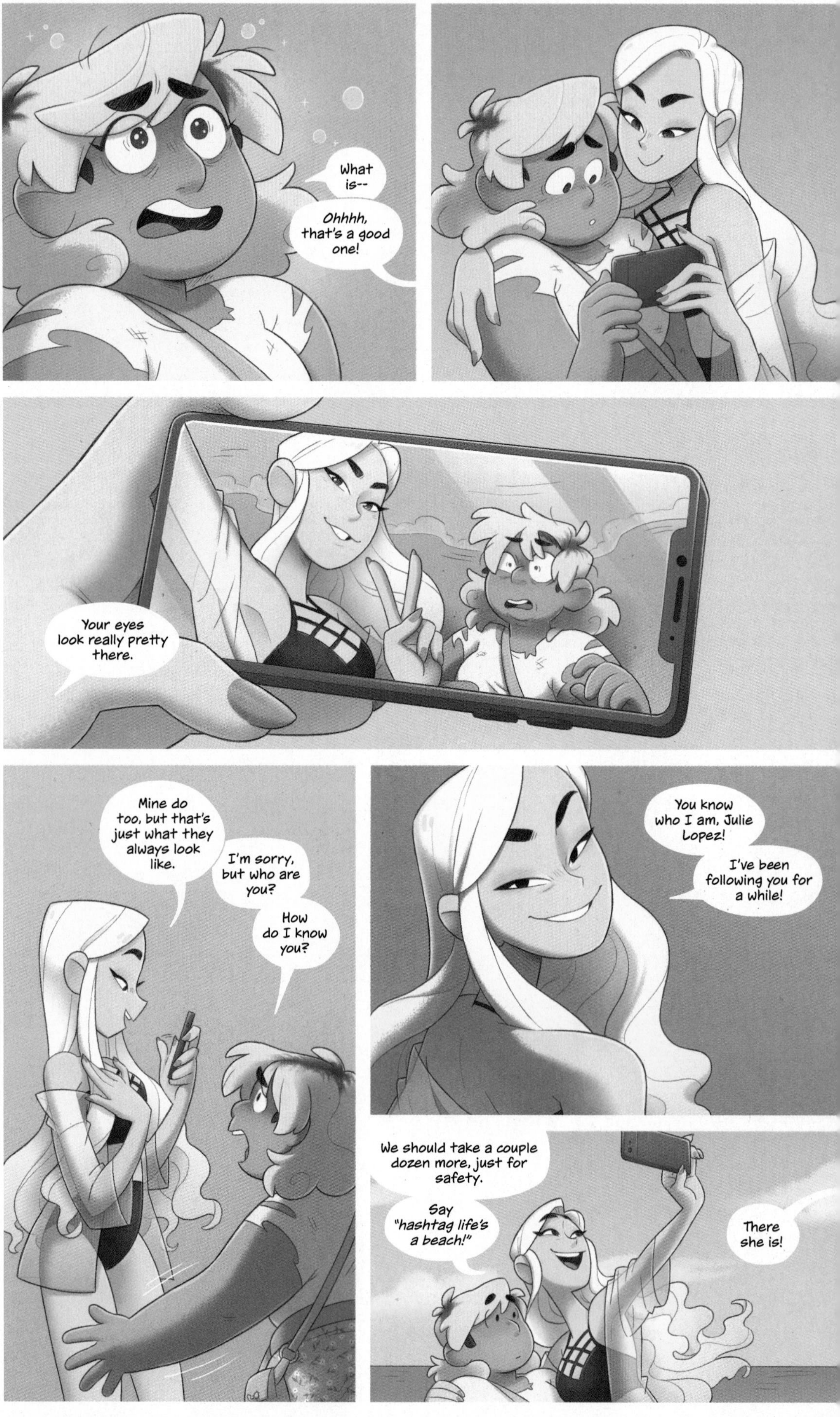
What is--
Ohhhh, that's a good one!
Your eyes look really pretty there.
Mine do too, but that's just what they always look like.
I'm sorry, but who are you?
How do I know you?
You know who I am, Julie Lopez!
I've been following you for a while!
We should take a couple dozen more, just for safety.
Say "hashtag life's a beach!"
There she is!

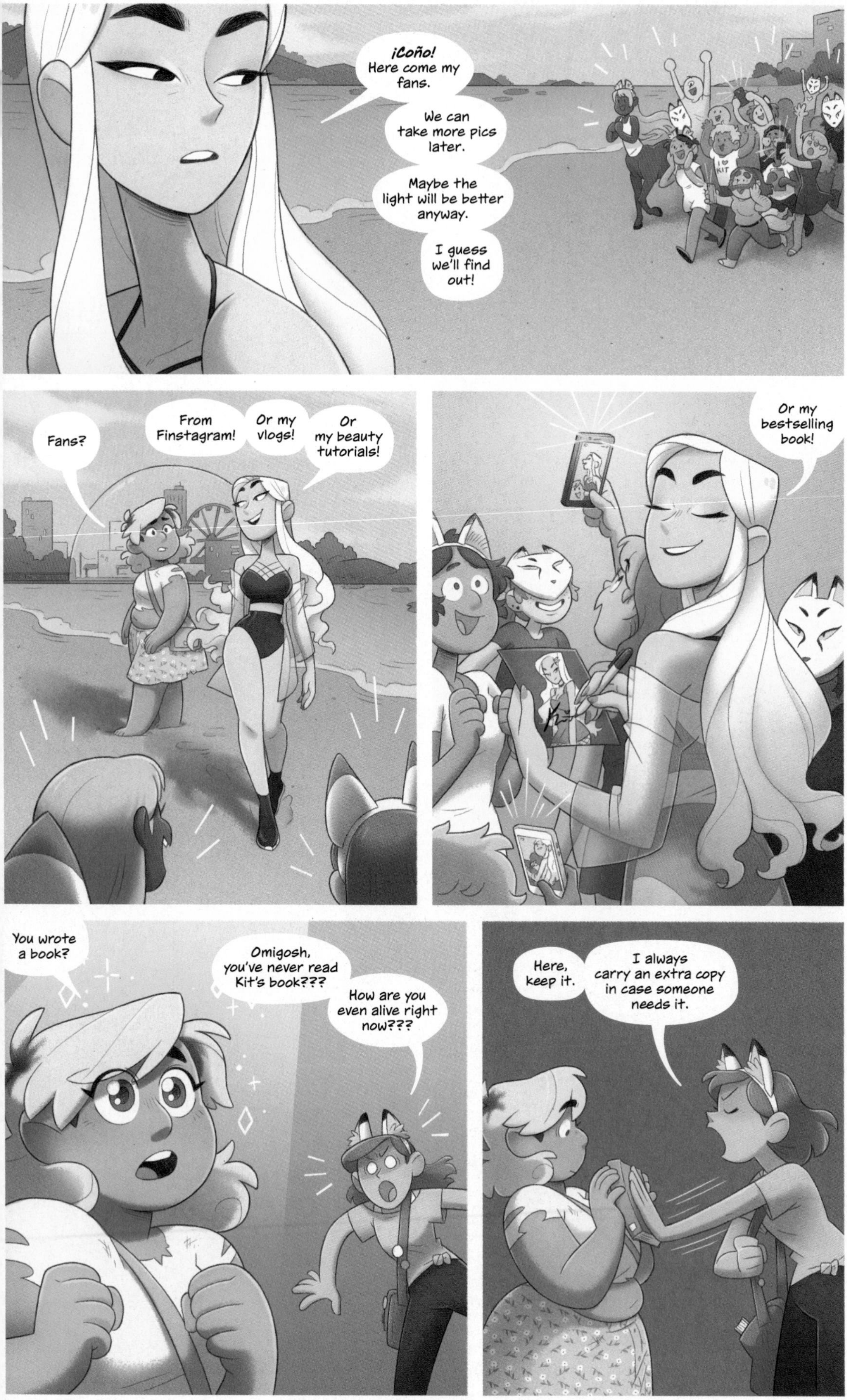

¡Coño!
Here come my fans.
We can take more pics later.
Maybe the light will be better anyway.
I guess we'll find out!
I ♥ KIT
Fans?
From Finstagram!
Or my vlogs!
Or my beauty tutorials!
Or my bestselling book!
You wrote a book?
Omigosh, you've never read Kit's book???
How are you even alive right now???
Here, keep it.
I always carry an extra copy in case someone needs it.

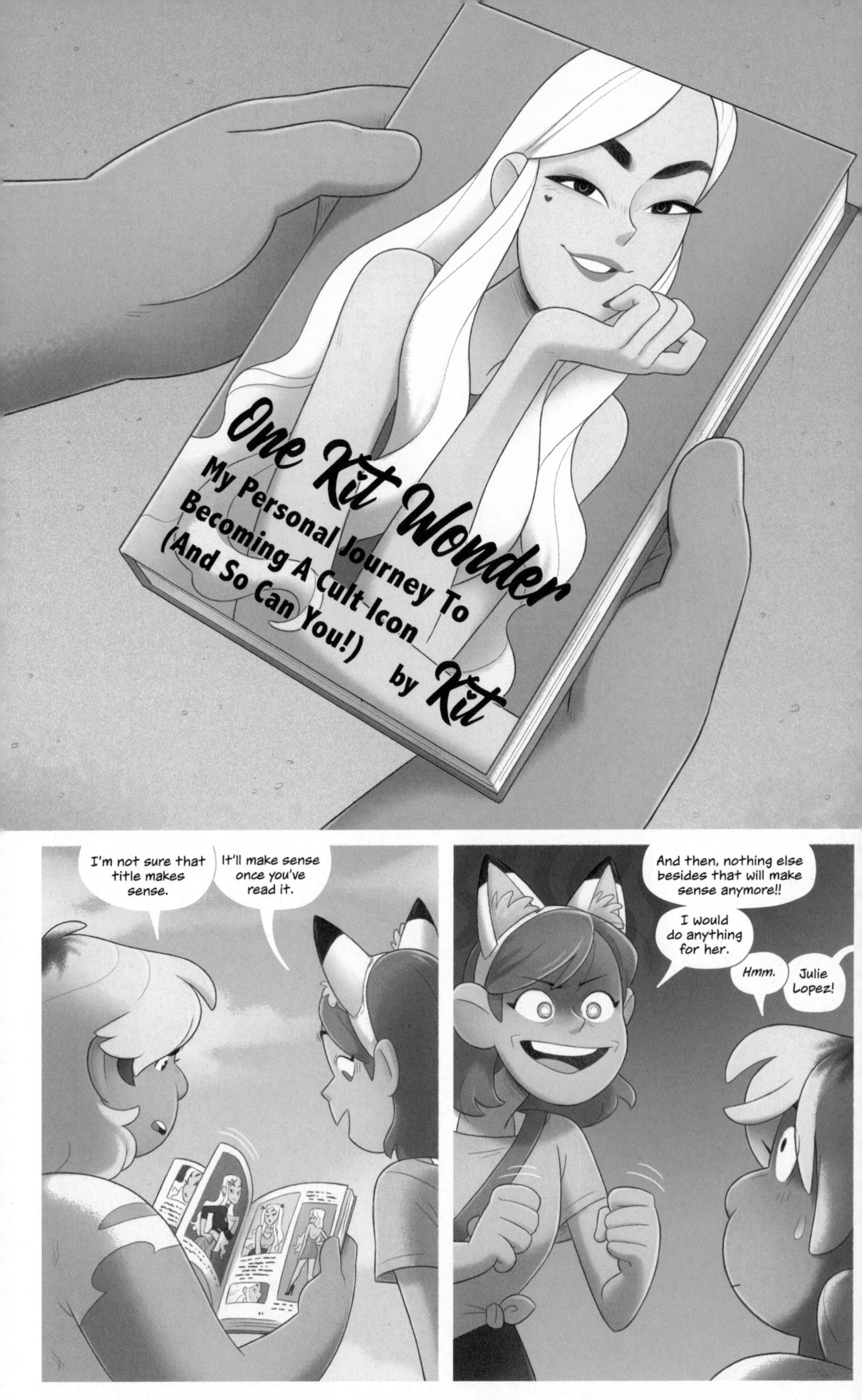
One Kit Wonder
My Personal Journey To Becoming A Cult-Icon (And So Can You!)
by Kit
I'm not sure that title makes sense.
It'll make sense once you've read it.
And then, nothing else besides that will make sense anymore!!
I would do anything for her.
Hmm.
Julie Lopez!

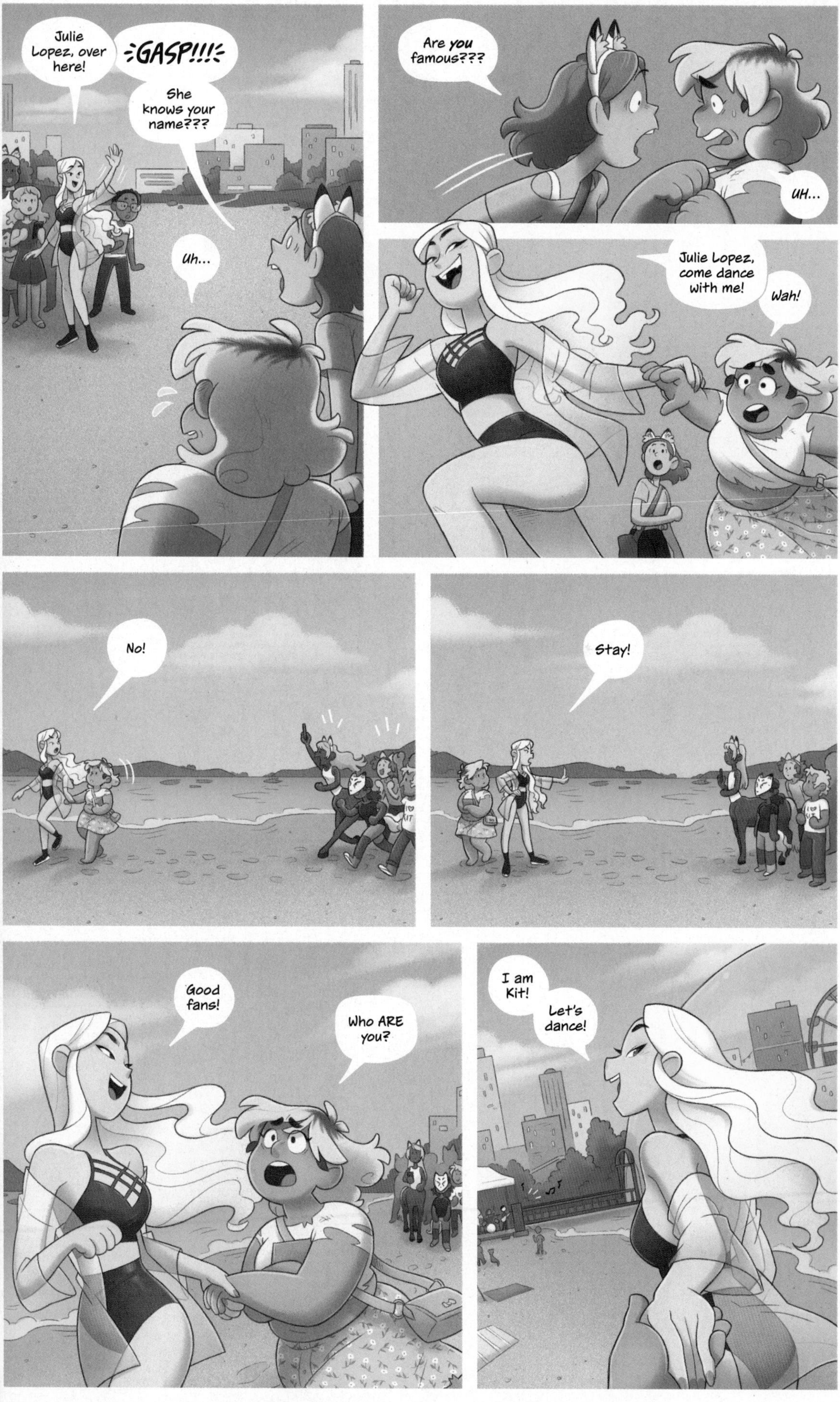
Julie Lopez, over here!
GASP!!!
She knows your name???
Uh...
Are you famous???
UH...
Julie Lopez, come dance with me!
Wah!
No!
Stay!
Good fans!
Who ARE you?
I am Kit!
Let's dance!

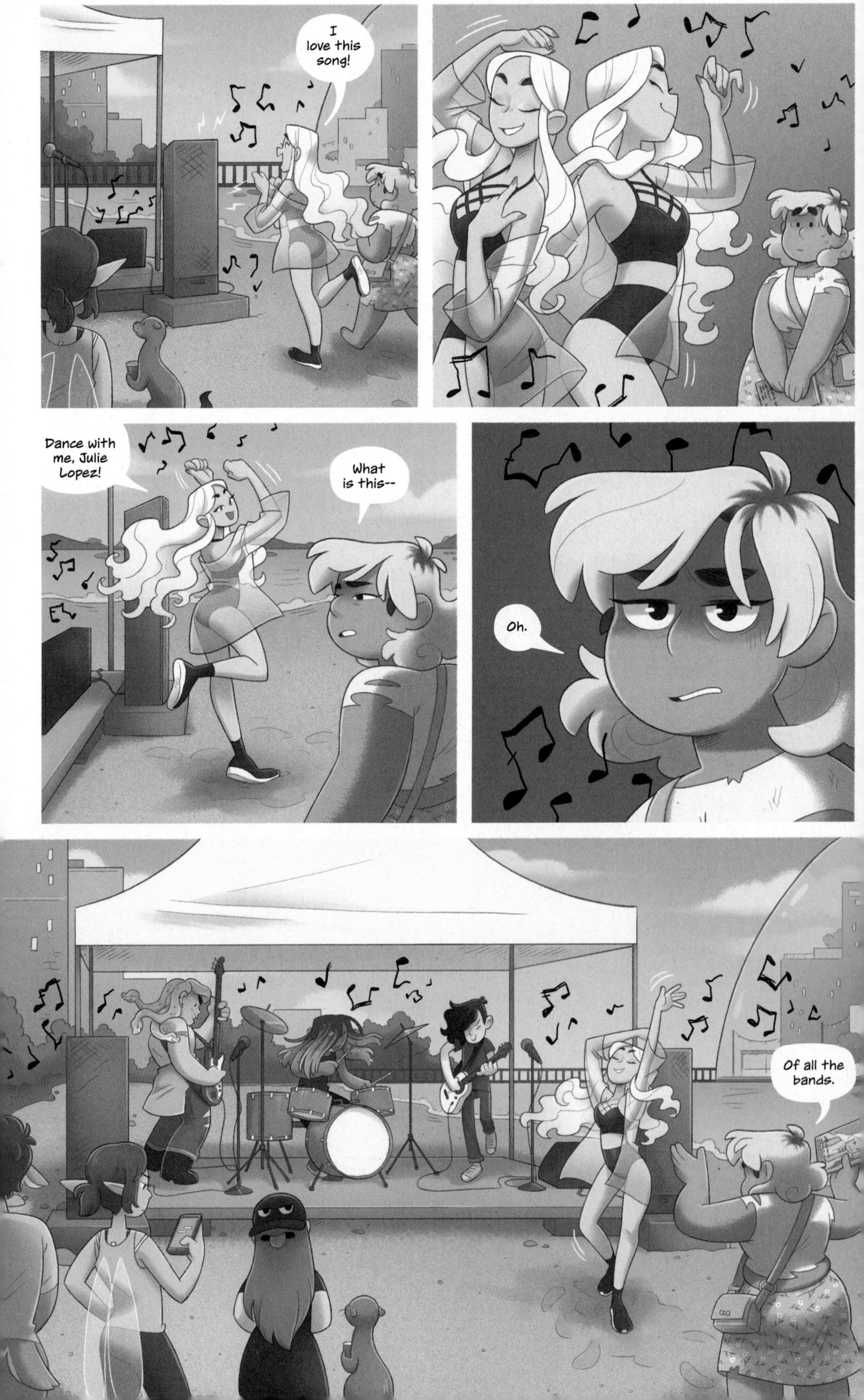
I love this song!
Dance with me, Julie Lopez!
What is this--
Oh.
Of all the bands.

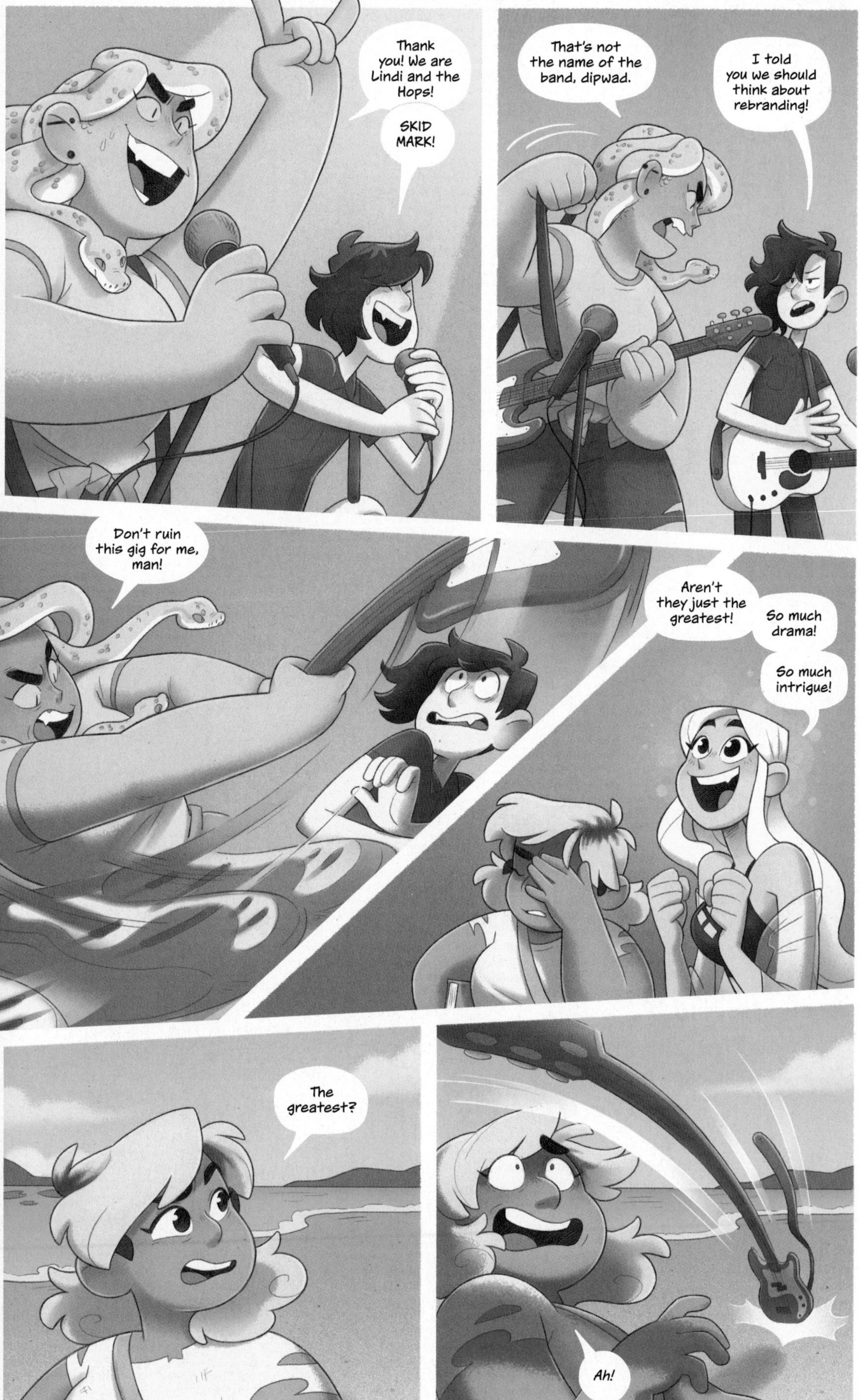
Thank you! We are Lindi and the Hops!
SKID MARK!
That's not the name of the band, dipwad.
I told you we should think about rebranding!
Don't ruin this gig for me, man!
Aren't they just the greatest!
So much drama!
So much intrigue!
The greatest?
Ah!

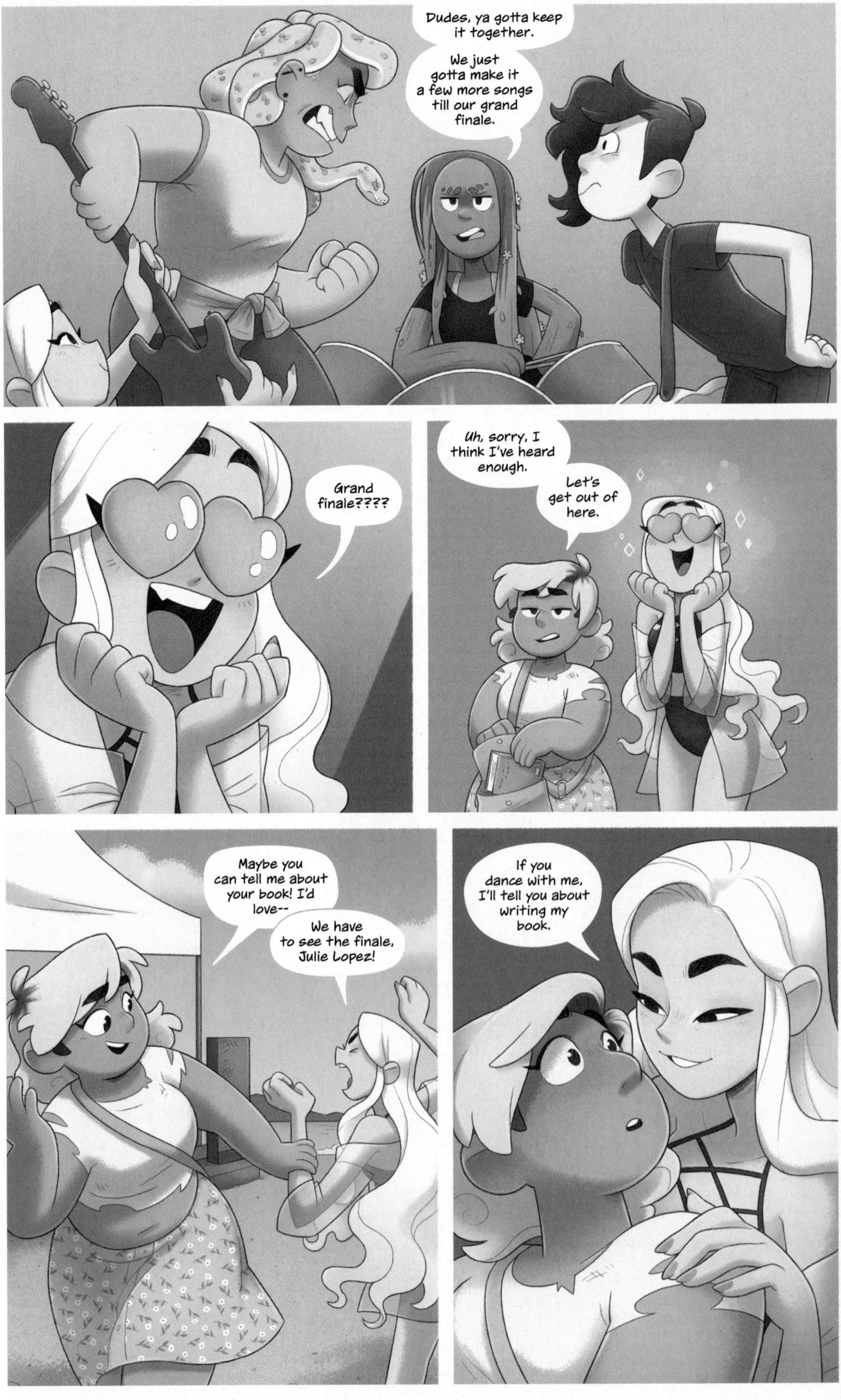
Dudes, ya gotta keep it together.
We just gotta make it a few more songs till our grand finale.
Grand finale????
Uh, sorry, I think I've heard enough.
Let's get out of here.
Maybe you can tell me about your book! I'd love--
We have to see the finale, Julie Lopez!
If you dance with me, I'll tell you about writing my book.

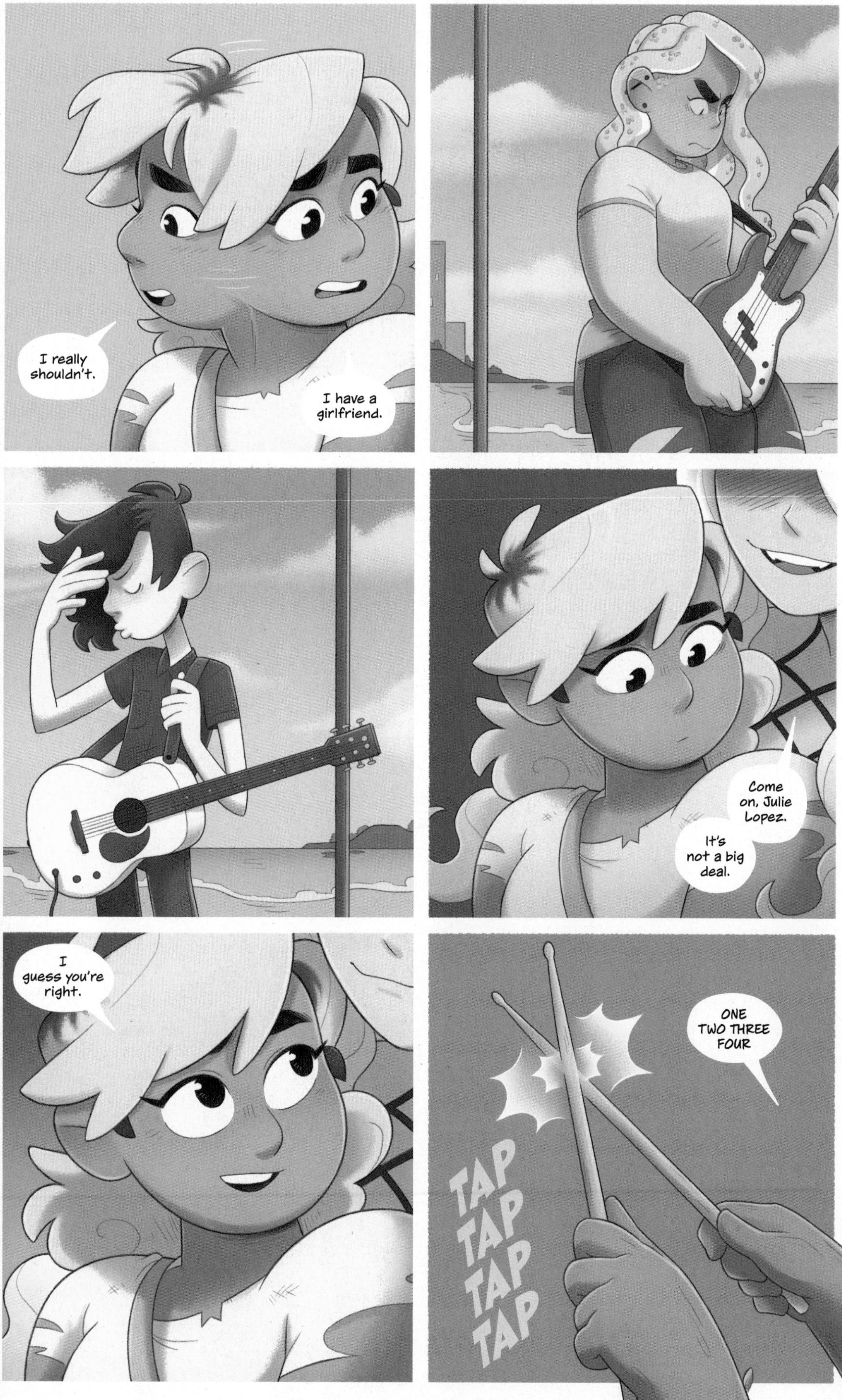
I really shouldn't.
I have a girlfriend.
Come on, Julie Lopez.
It's not a big deal.
I guess you're right.
ONE TWO THREE FOUR
TAP TAP TAP TAP

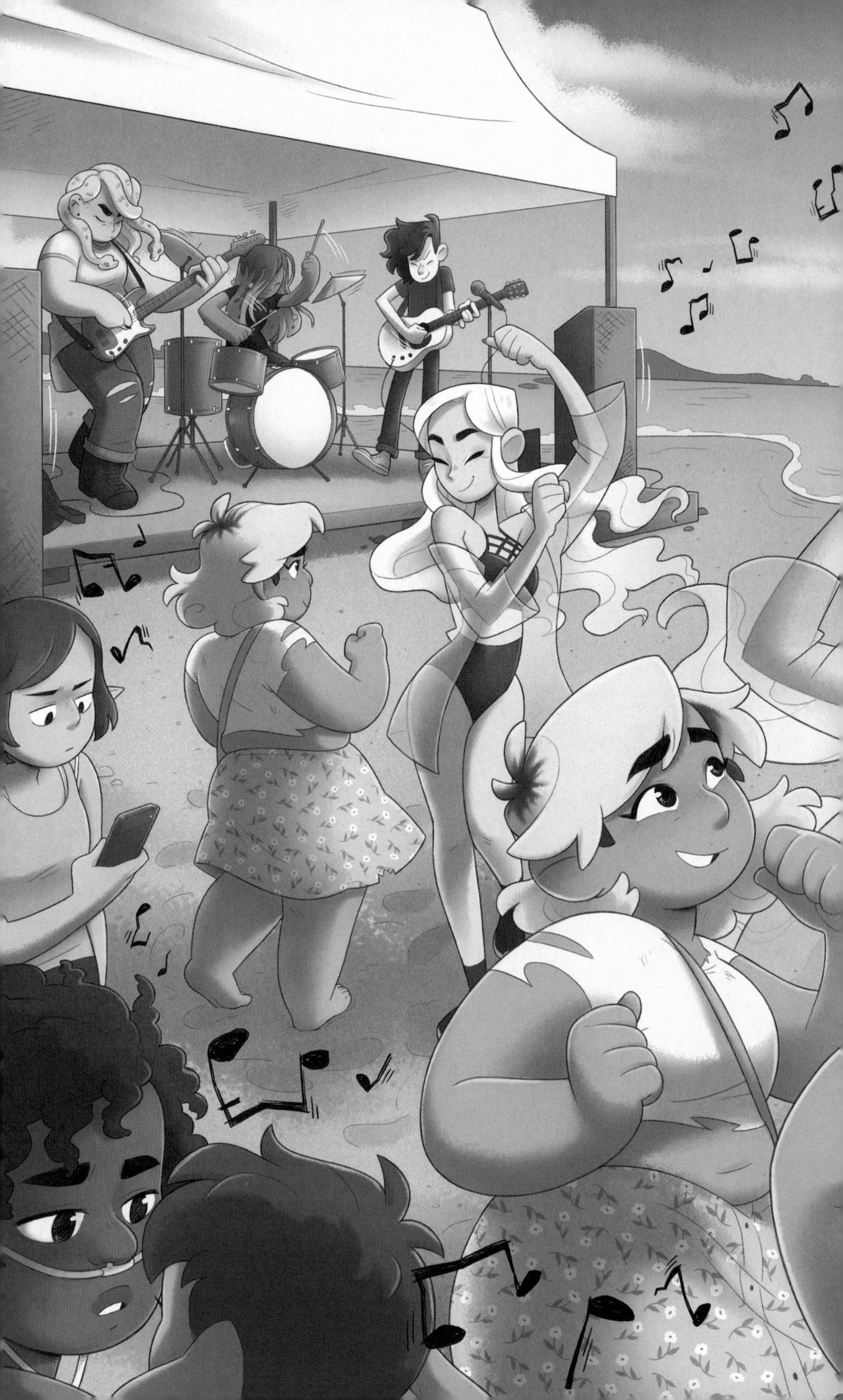

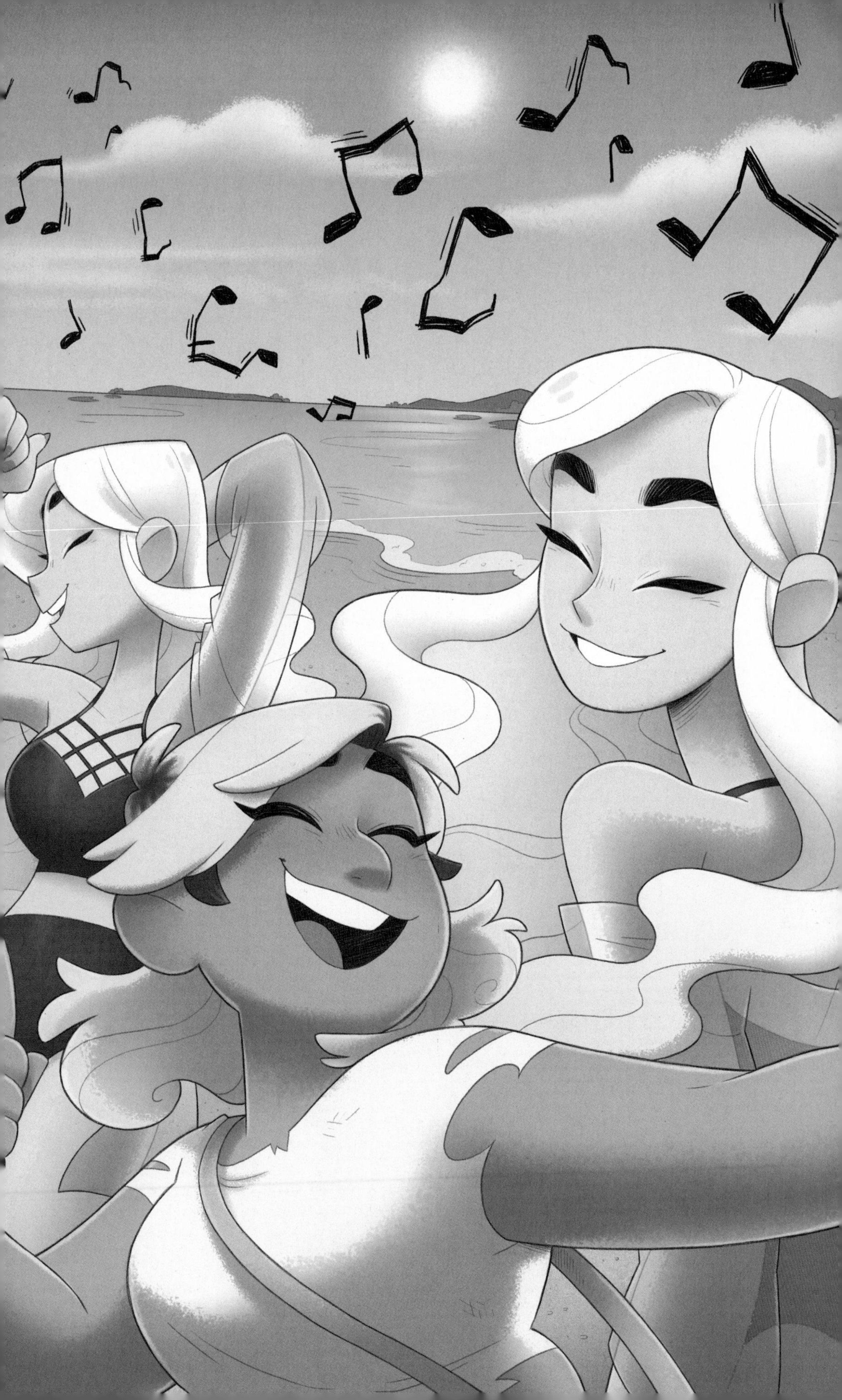

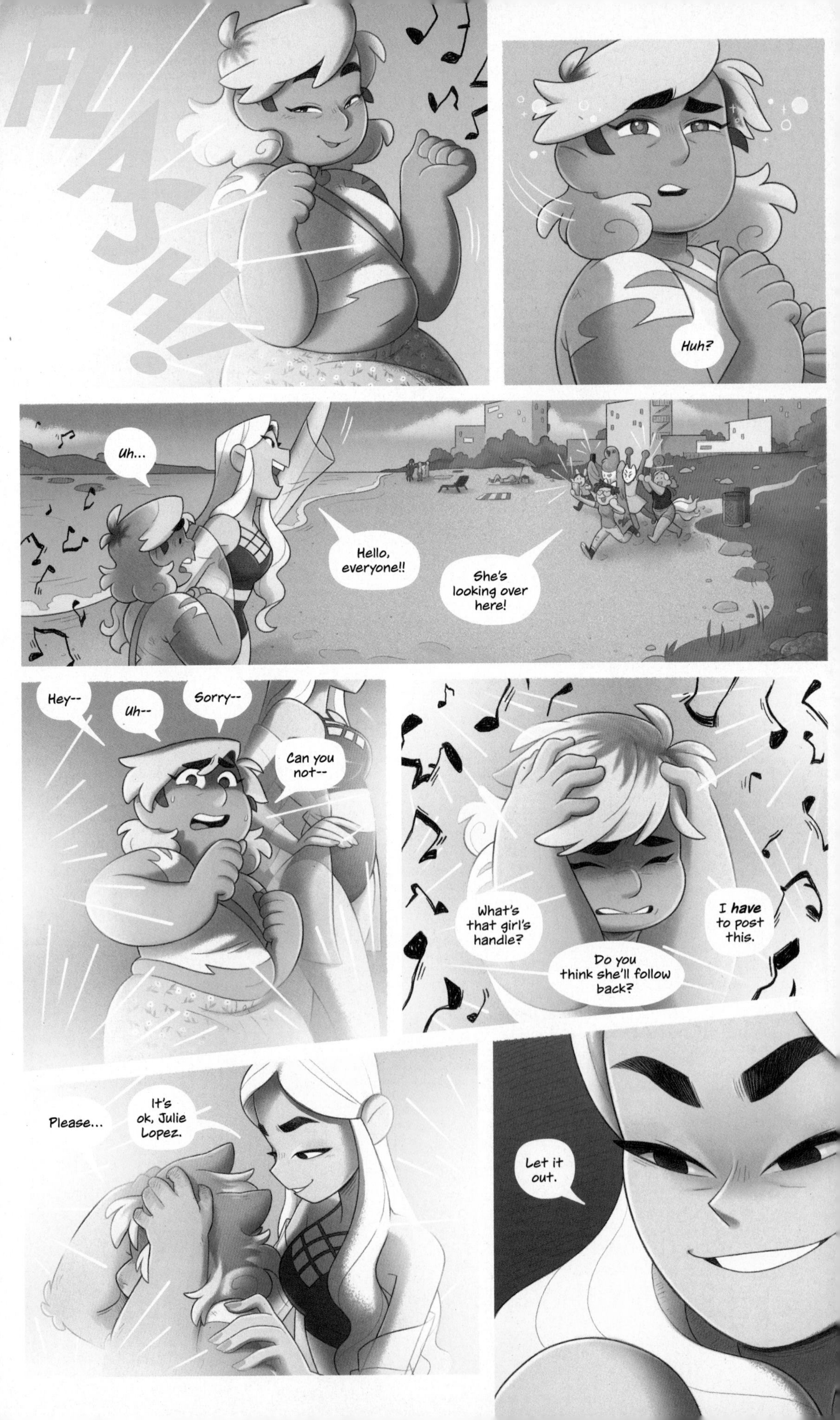
FLASH!!
Huh?
Uh...
Hello, everyone!!
She's looking over here!
Hey--
Uh--
Sorry--
Can you not--
What's that girl's handle?
I *have* to post this.
Do you think she'll follow back?
Please...
It's ok, Julie Lopez.
Let it out.

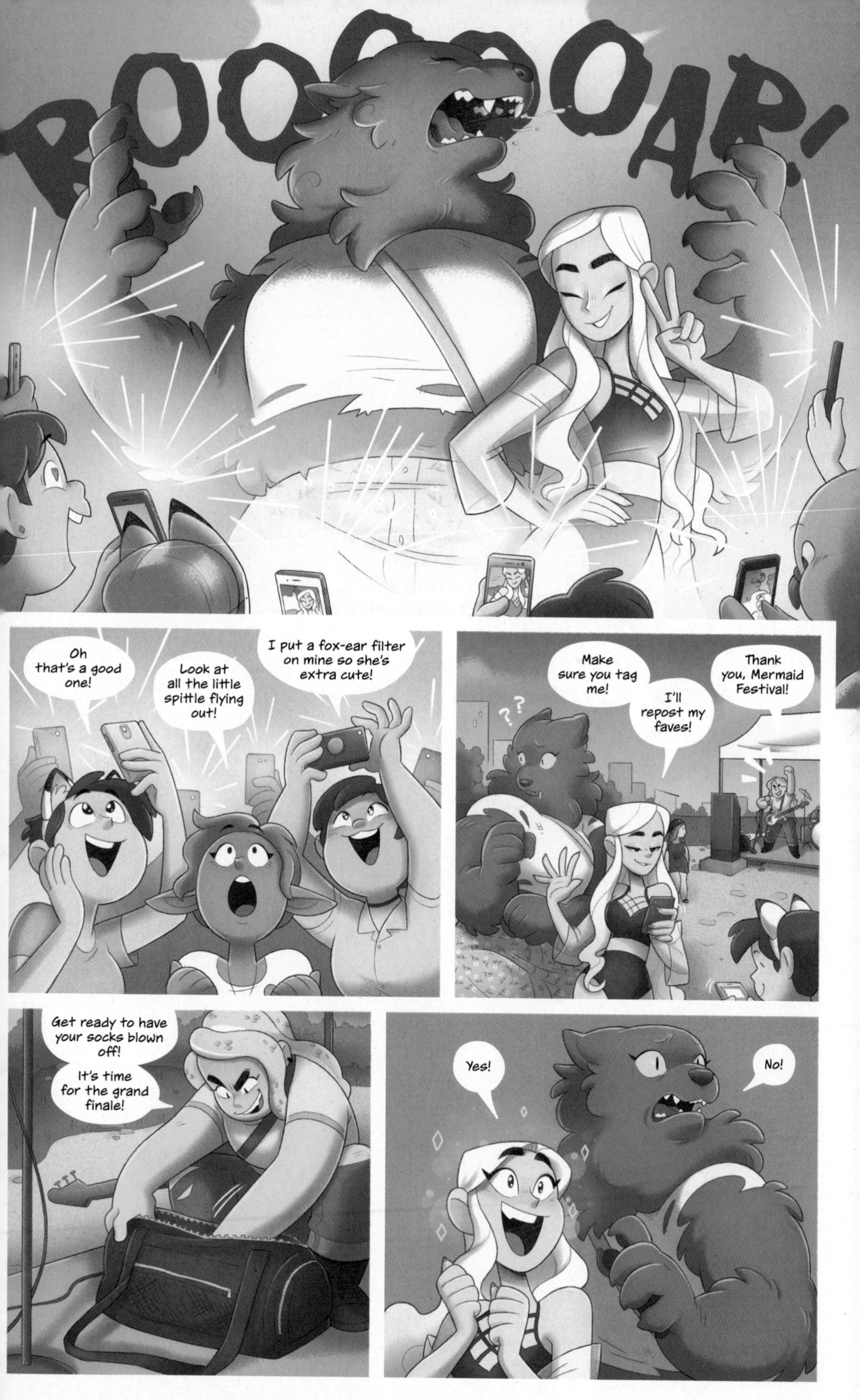
ROOOOOAR!
Oh that's a good one!
Look at all the little spittle flying out!
I put a fox-ear filter on mine so she's extra cute!
Make sure you tag me!
I'll repost my faves!
Thank you, Mermaid Festival!
Get ready to have your socks blown off!
It's time for the grand finale!
Yes!
No!

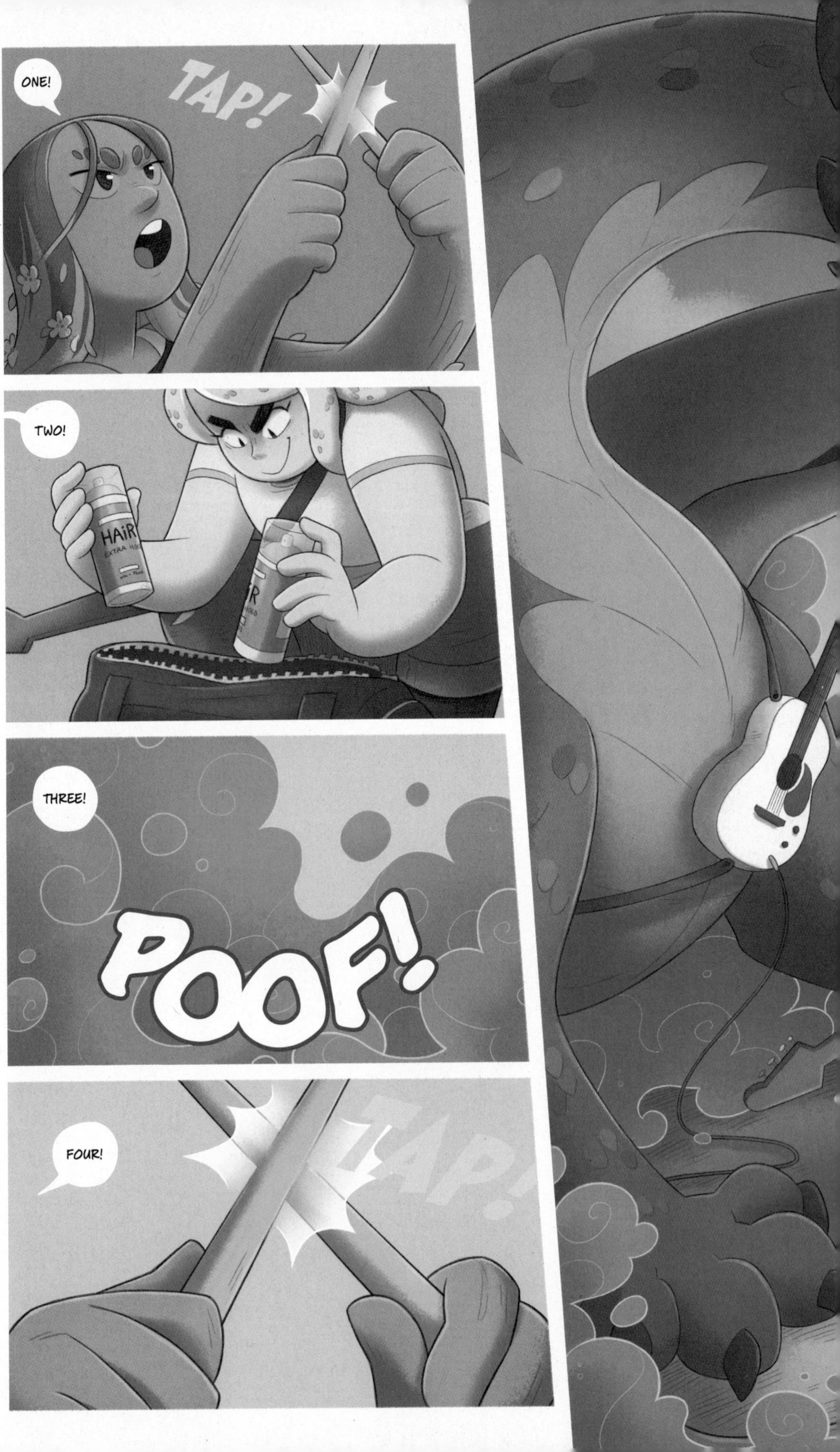
ONE!
TAP!
TWO!
THREE!
POOF!
FOUR!
TAP!

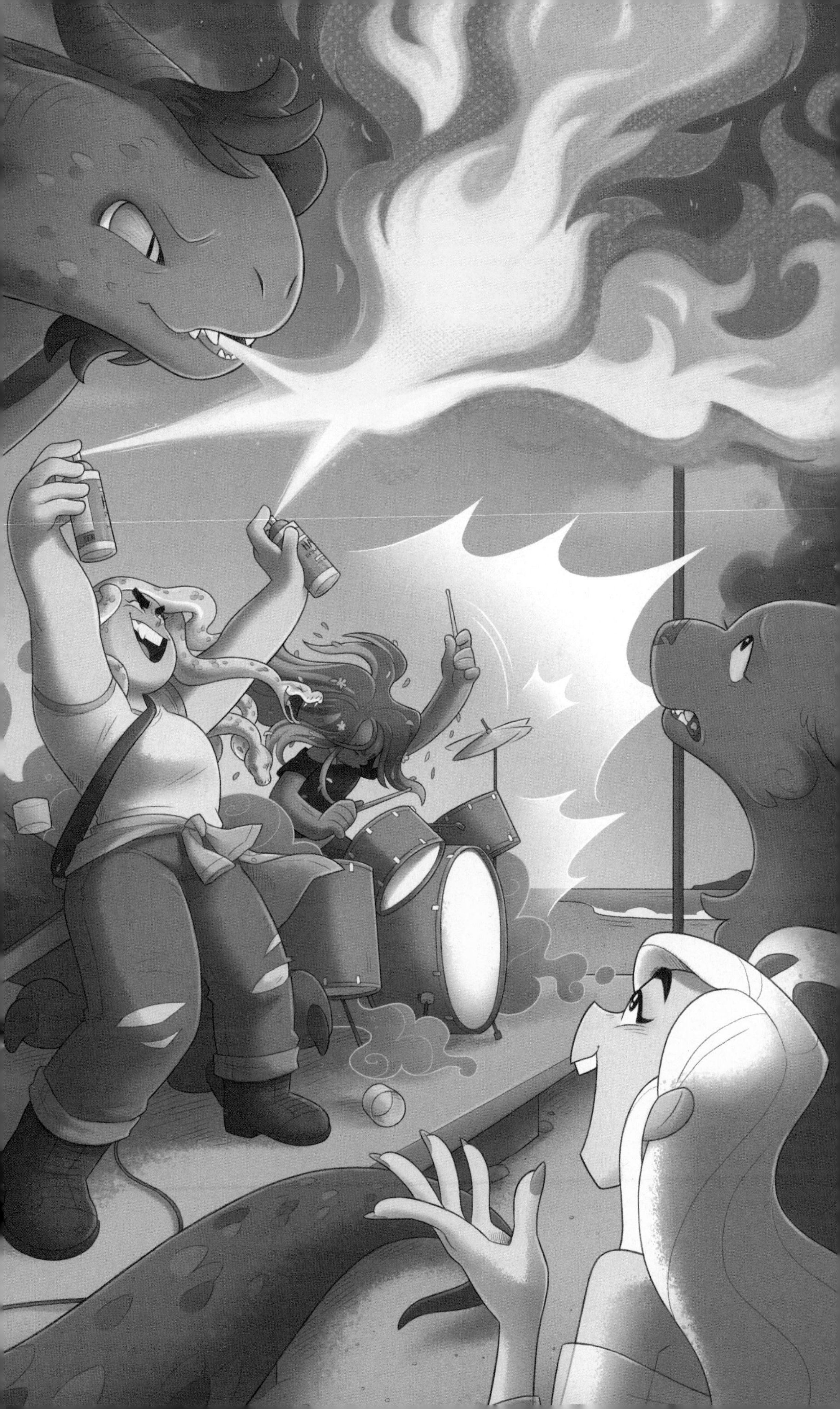

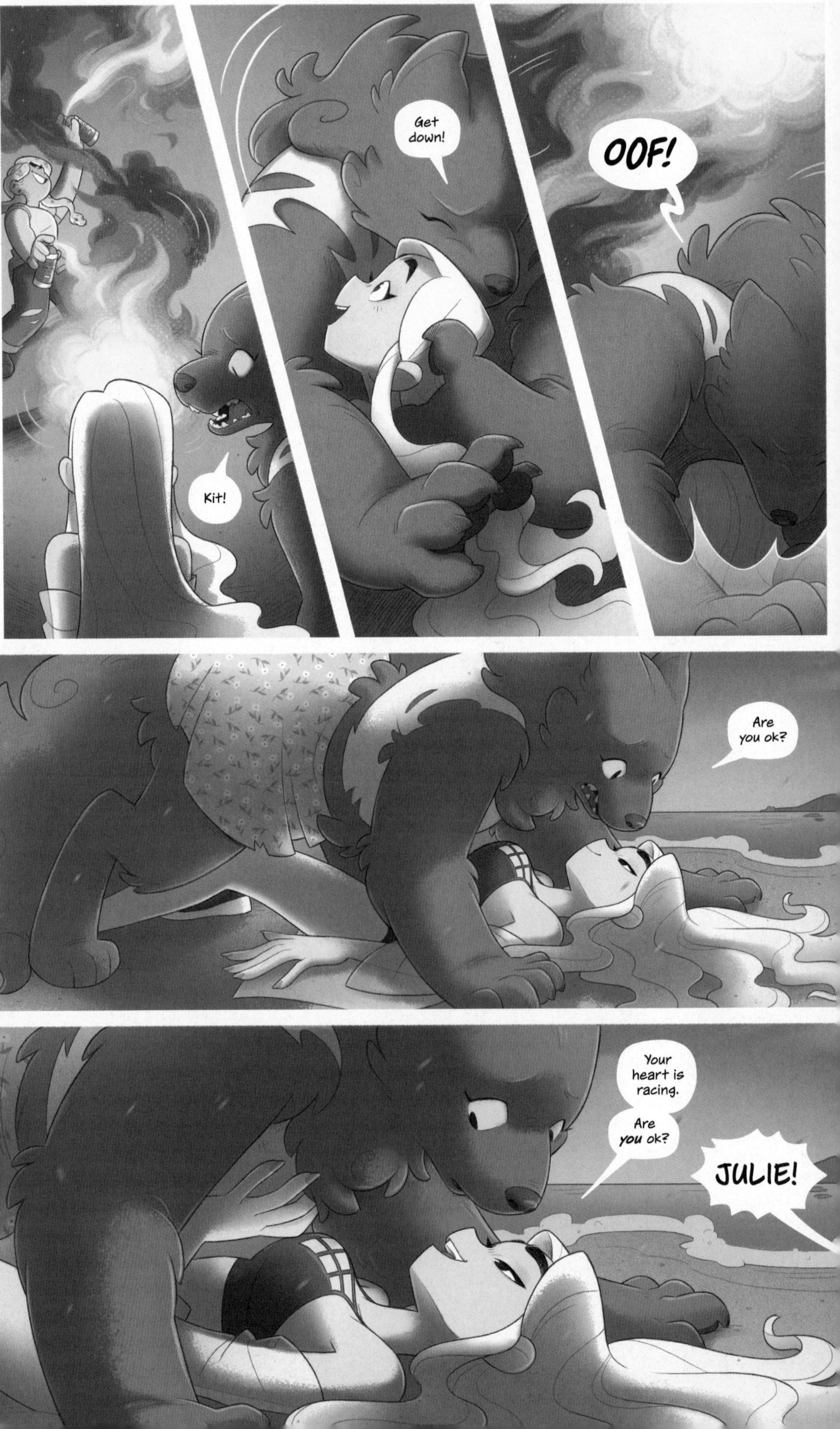
Kit!
Get down!
OOF!
Are you ok?
Your heart is racing.
Are *you* ok?
JULIE!

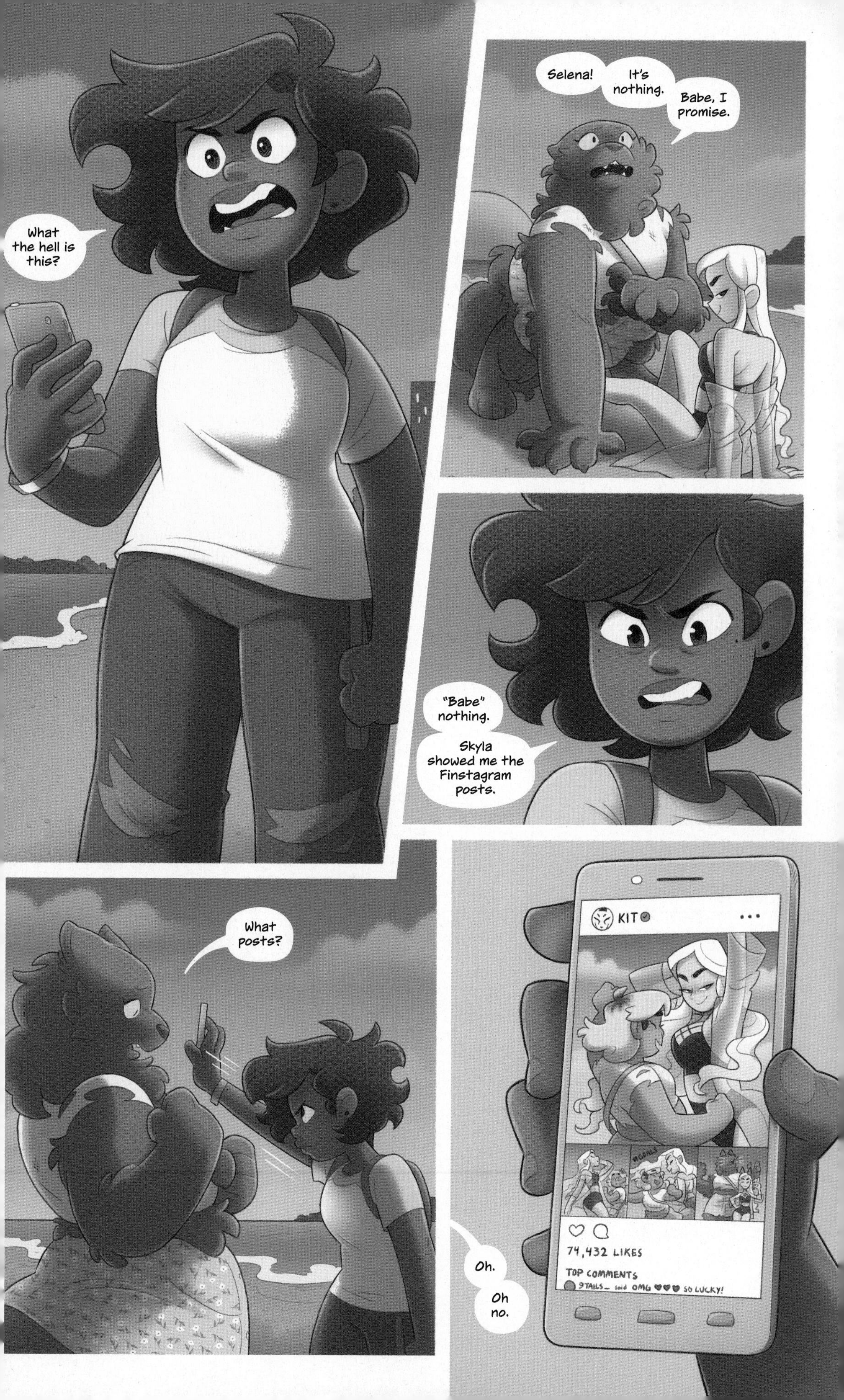
What the hell is this?
Selena!
It's nothing.
Babe, I promise.
"Babe" nothing.
Skyla showed me the Finstagram posts.
What posts?
KIT
74,432 LIKES
TOP COMMENTS
9TAILS_ said OMG ♥♥♥ SO LUCKY!
Oh.
Oh no.

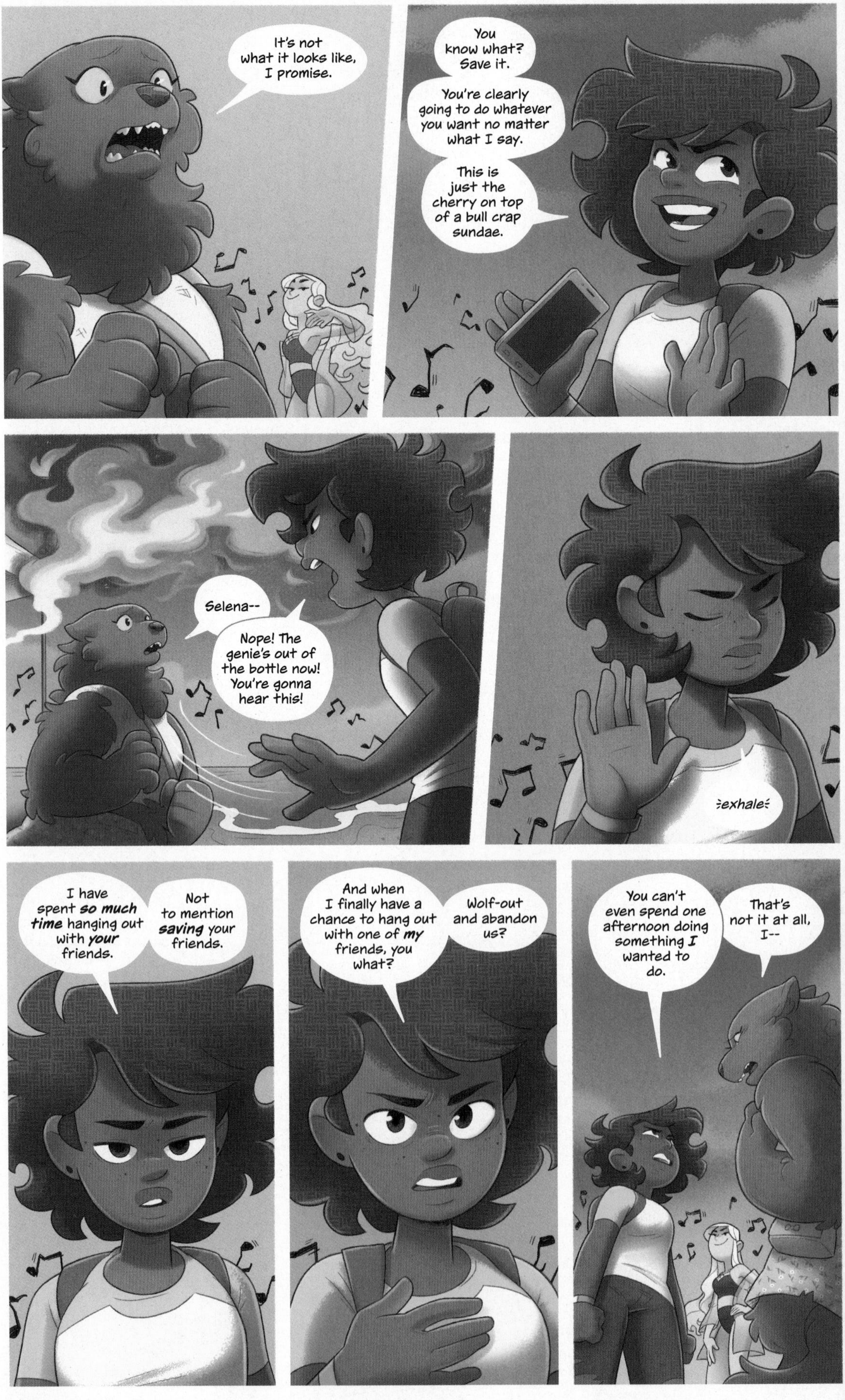
It's not what it looks like, I promise.
You know what? Save it.
You're clearly going to do whatever you want no matter what I say.
This is just the cherry on top of a bull crap sundae.
Selena--
Nope! The genie's out of the bottle now! You're gonna hear this!
exhale
I have spent so much time hanging out with your friends.
Not to mention saving your friends.
And when I finally have a chance to hang out with one of my friends, you what?
Wolf-out and abandon us?
You can't even spend one afternoon doing something I wanted to do.
That's not it at all, I--

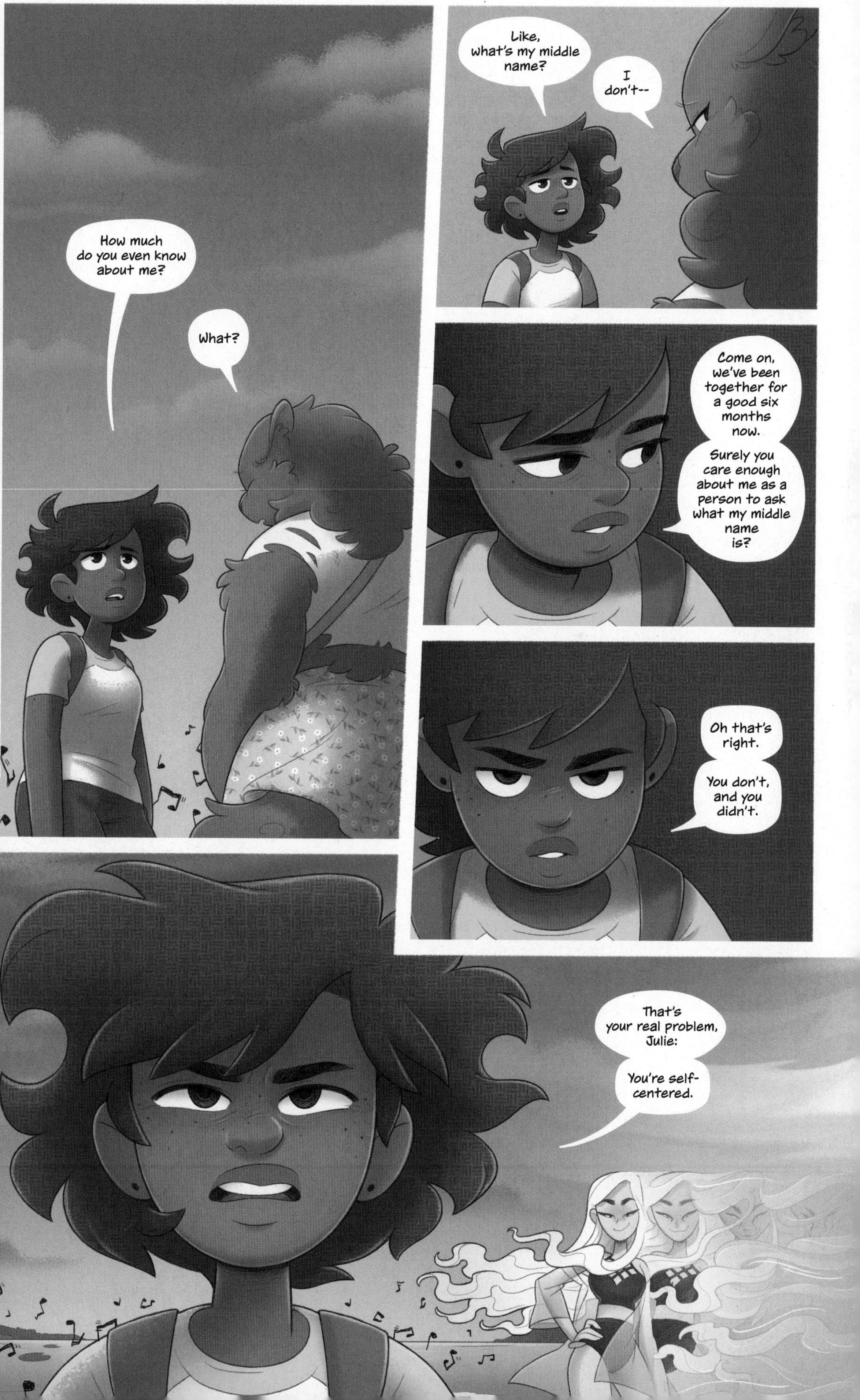
How much do you even know about me?
What?
Like, what's my middle name?
I don't--
Come on, we've been together for a good six months now.
Surely you care enough about me as a person to ask what my middle name is?
Oh that's right.
You don't, and you didn't.
That's your real problem, Julie:
You're self-centered.

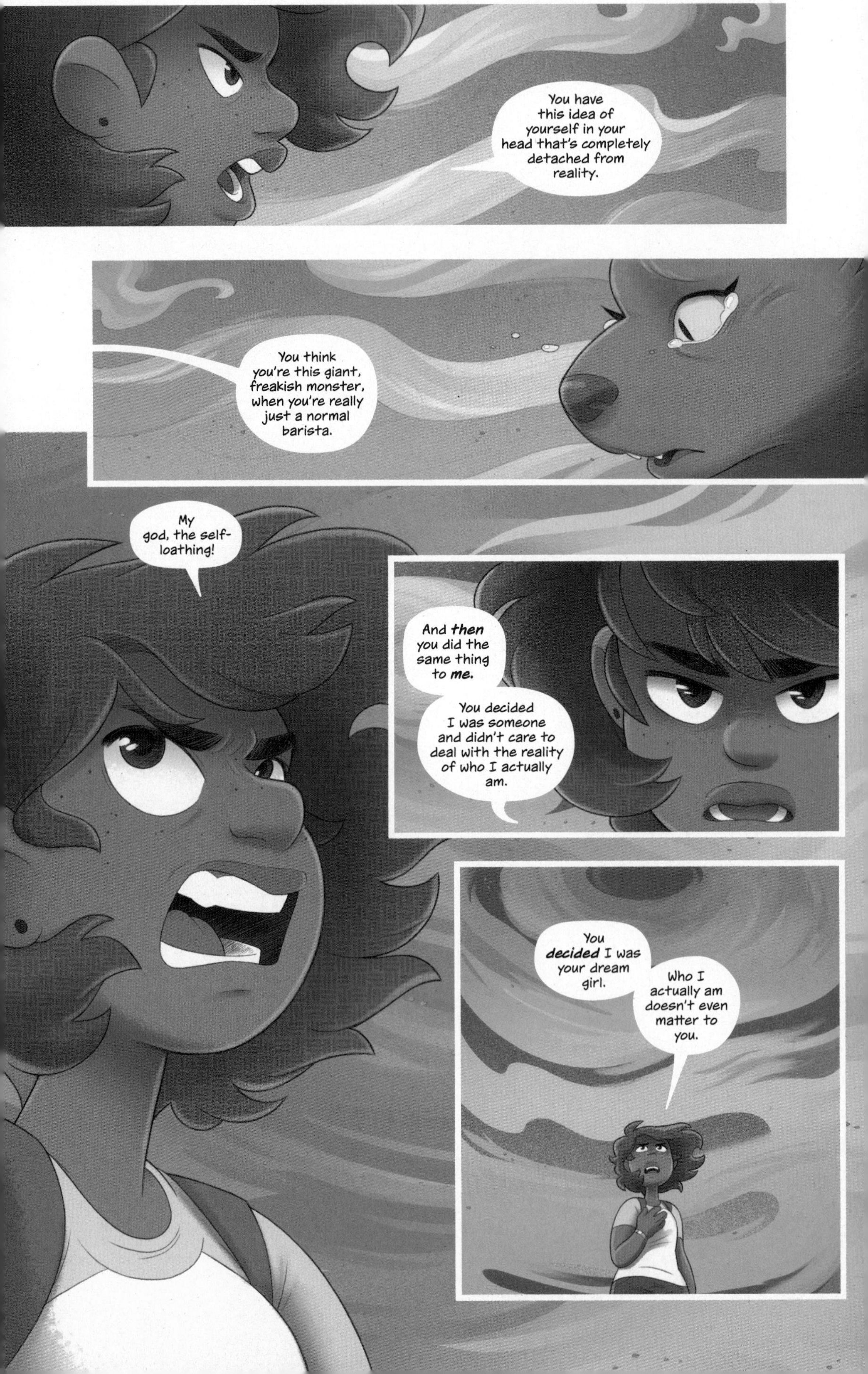
You have this idea of yourself in your head that's completely detached from reality.
You think you're this giant, freakish monster, when you're really just a normal barista.
My god, the self-loathing!
And **then** you did the same thing to **me.**
You decided I was someone and didn't care to deal with the reality of who I actually am.
You **decided** I was your dream girl.
Who I actually am doesn't even matter to you.

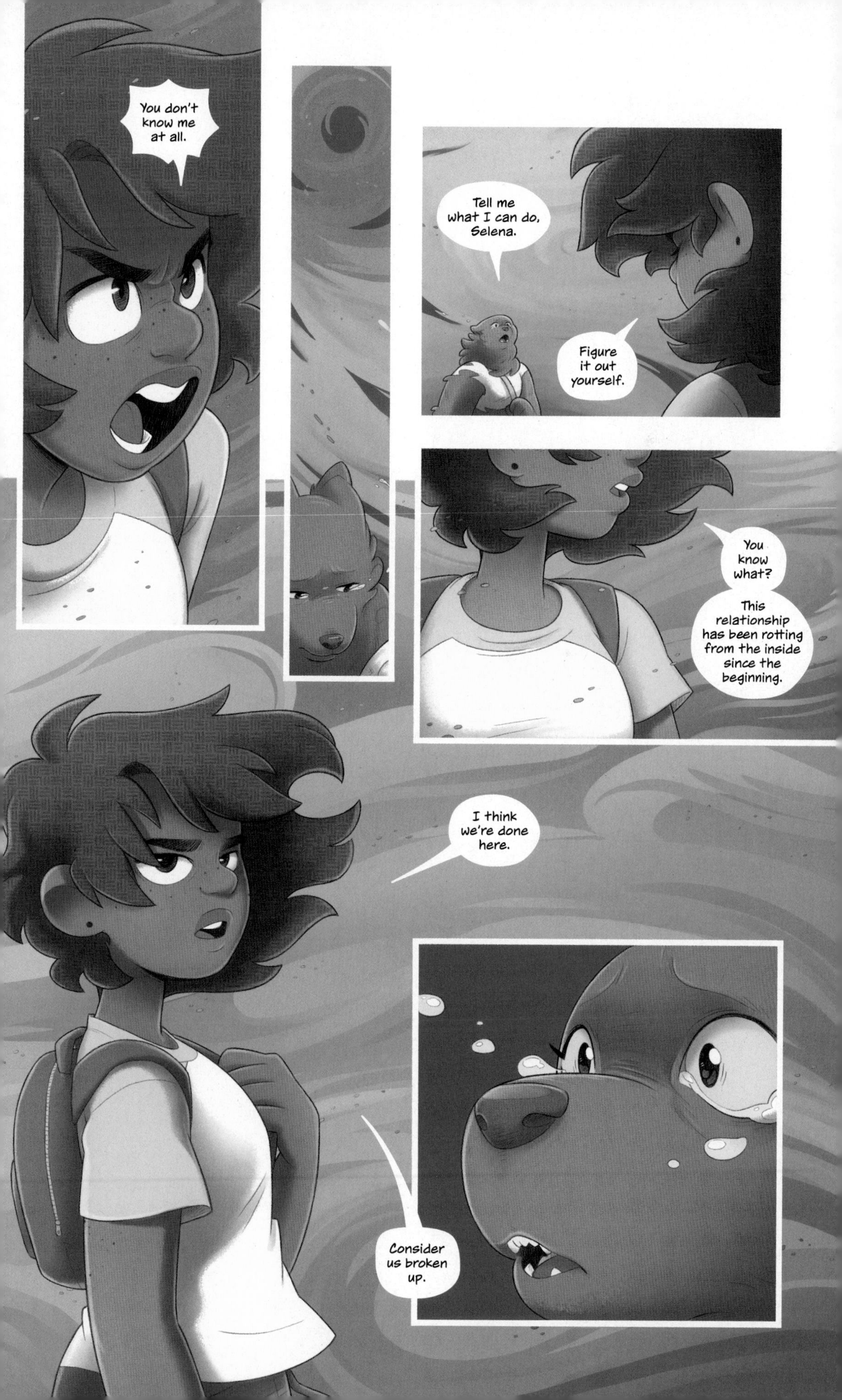

You don't know me at all.
Tell me what I can do, Selena.
Figure it out yourself.
You know what?
This relationship has been rotting from the inside since the beginning.
I think we're done here.
Consider us broken up.

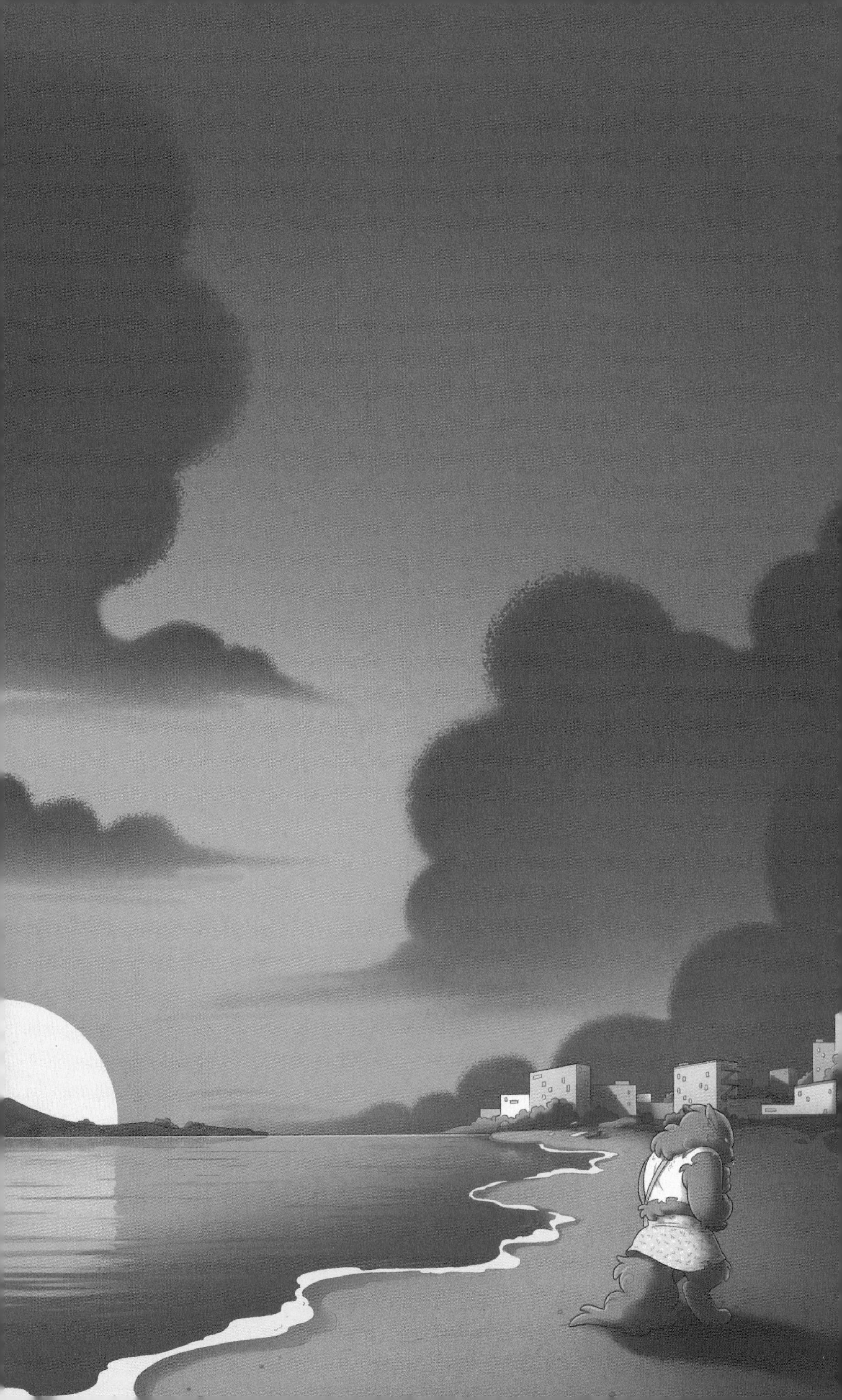

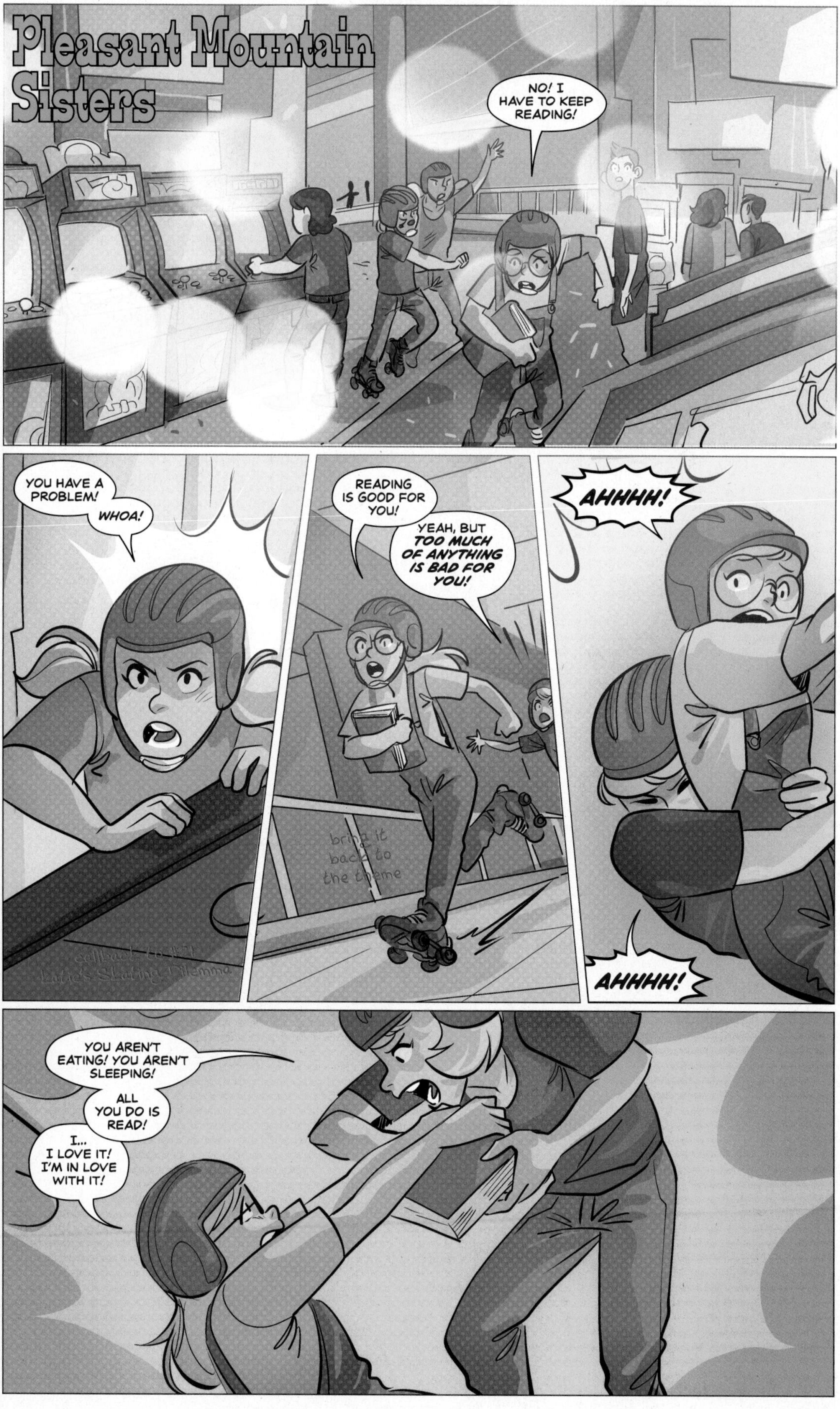
Pleasant Mountain Sisters
NO! I HAVE TO KEEP READING!
YOU HAVE A PROBLEM!
WHOA!
READING IS GOOD FOR YOU!
YEAH, BUT TOO MUCH OF ANYTHING IS BAD FOR YOU!
bring it back to the theme
AHHHH!
AHHHH!
YOU AREN'T EATING! YOU AREN'T SLEEPING!
ALL YOU DO IS READ!
I... I LOVE IT! I'M IN LOVE WITH IT!

newPals
Super Fun Pages!

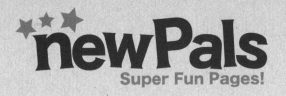

Help Chet and Manuel!
Please, please help them!!

LESAEP	P _ _ _ _ _
YDSBMEOO	S _ _ _ _ _ _ _
DAYONBY	A _ _ _ _ _ _
ESPWALN	N _ _ _ _ _ _
BDIRA	R _ _ _ _
DESN	S _ _ _
SEINNREMFETORC	R _ _ _ _ _ _ _ _ _ _ _ _ _
ODWLR	W _ _ _ _
DMOIIOATNN	D _ _ _ _ _ _ _ _ _
MTIMNENI	I _ _ _ _ _ _ _

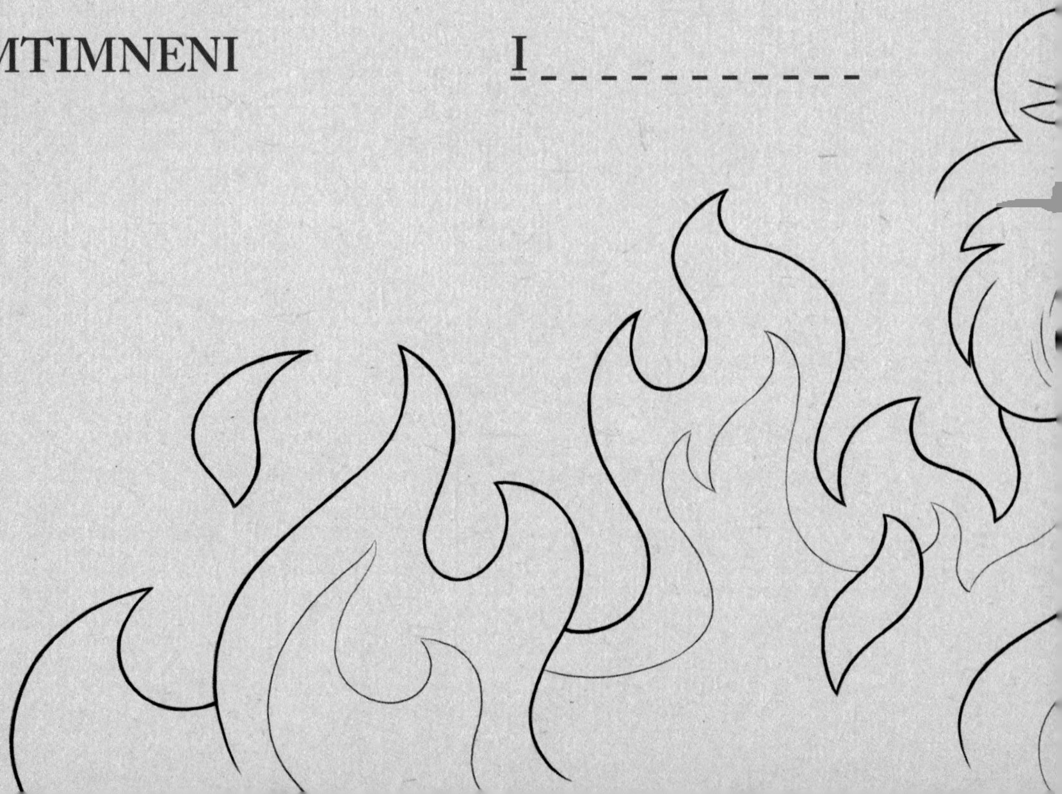

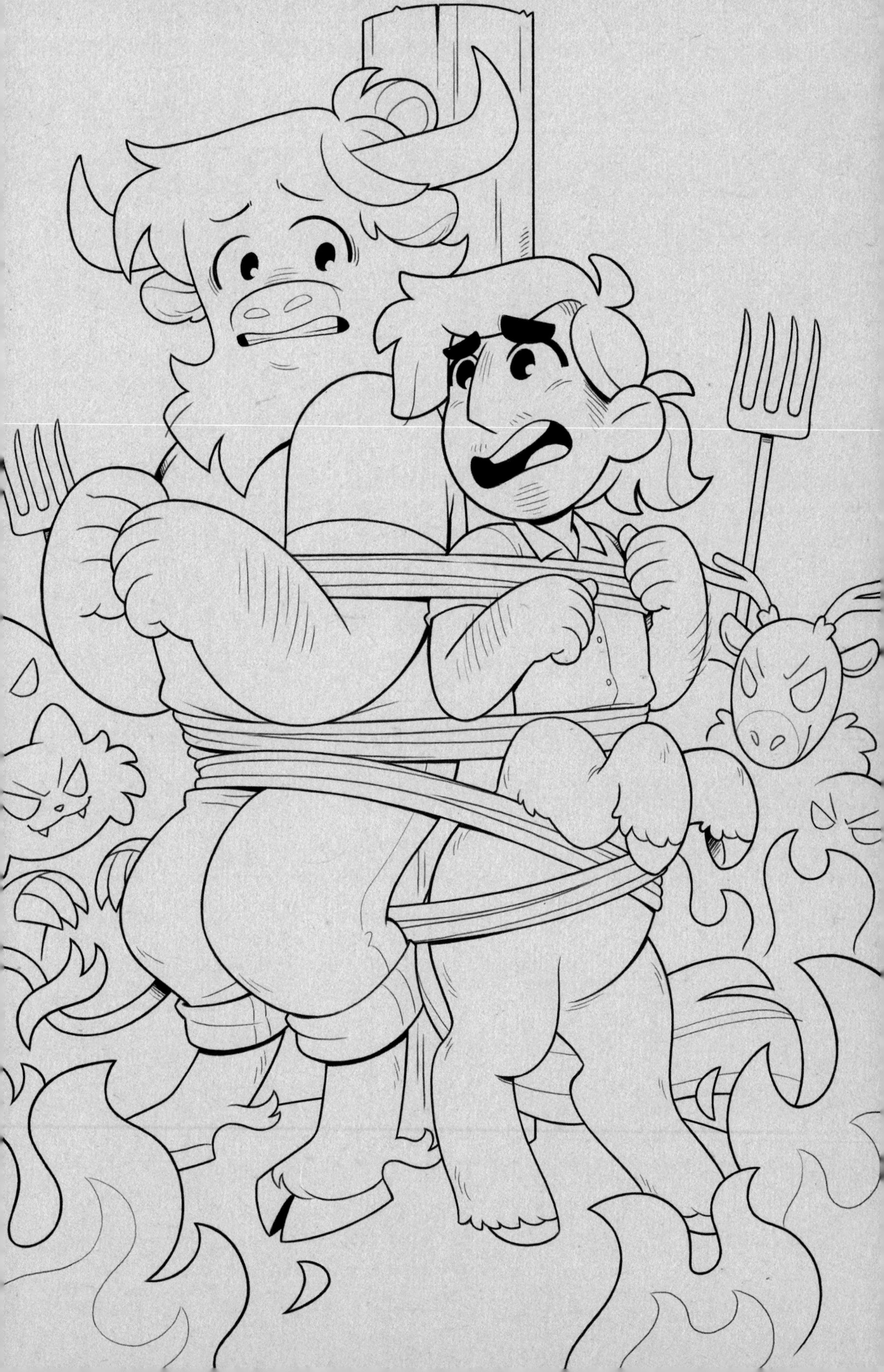

CHAPTER FIVE

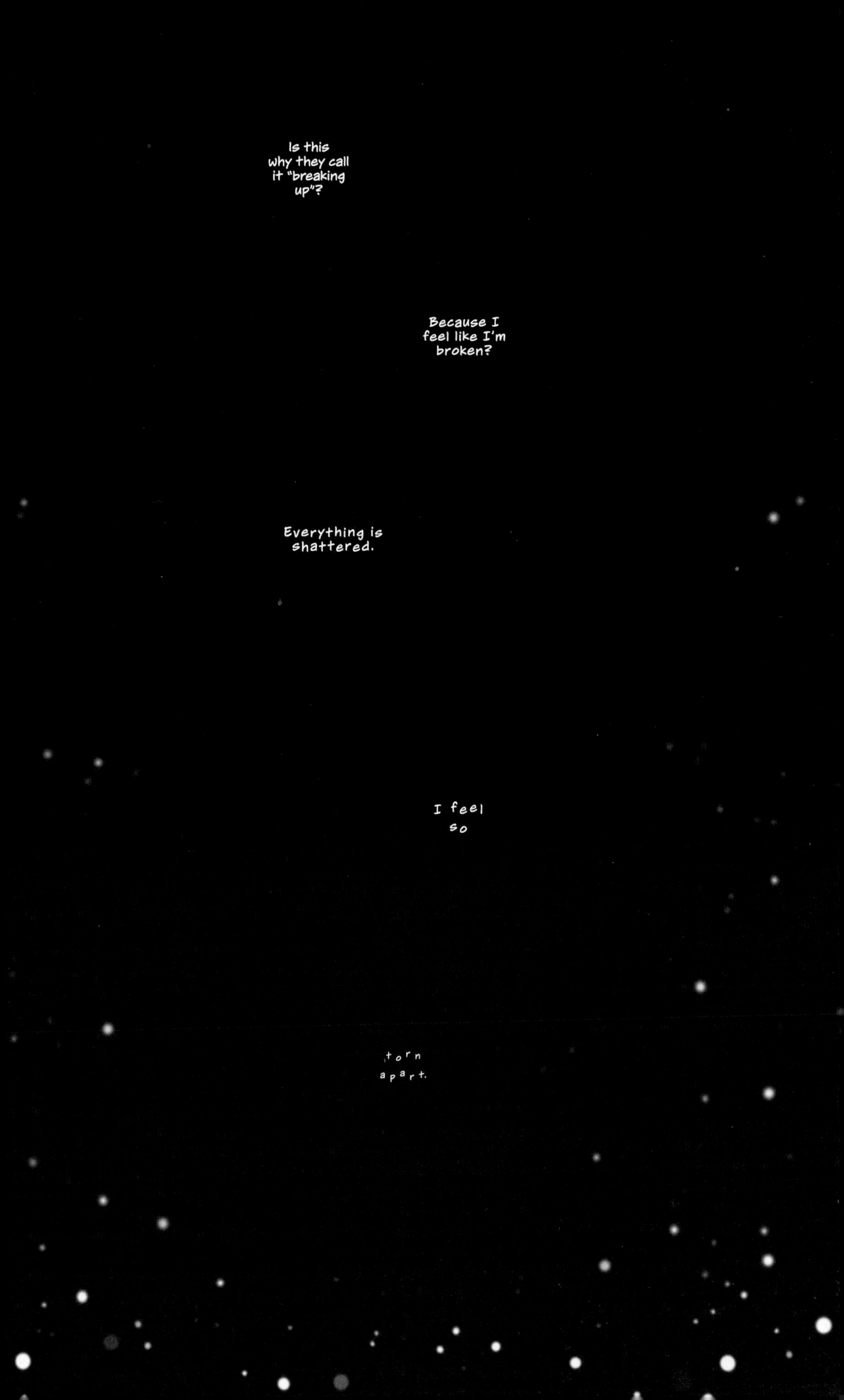
Is this why they call it "breaking up"?
Because I feel like I'm broken?
Everything is shattered.
I feel so
torn apart.

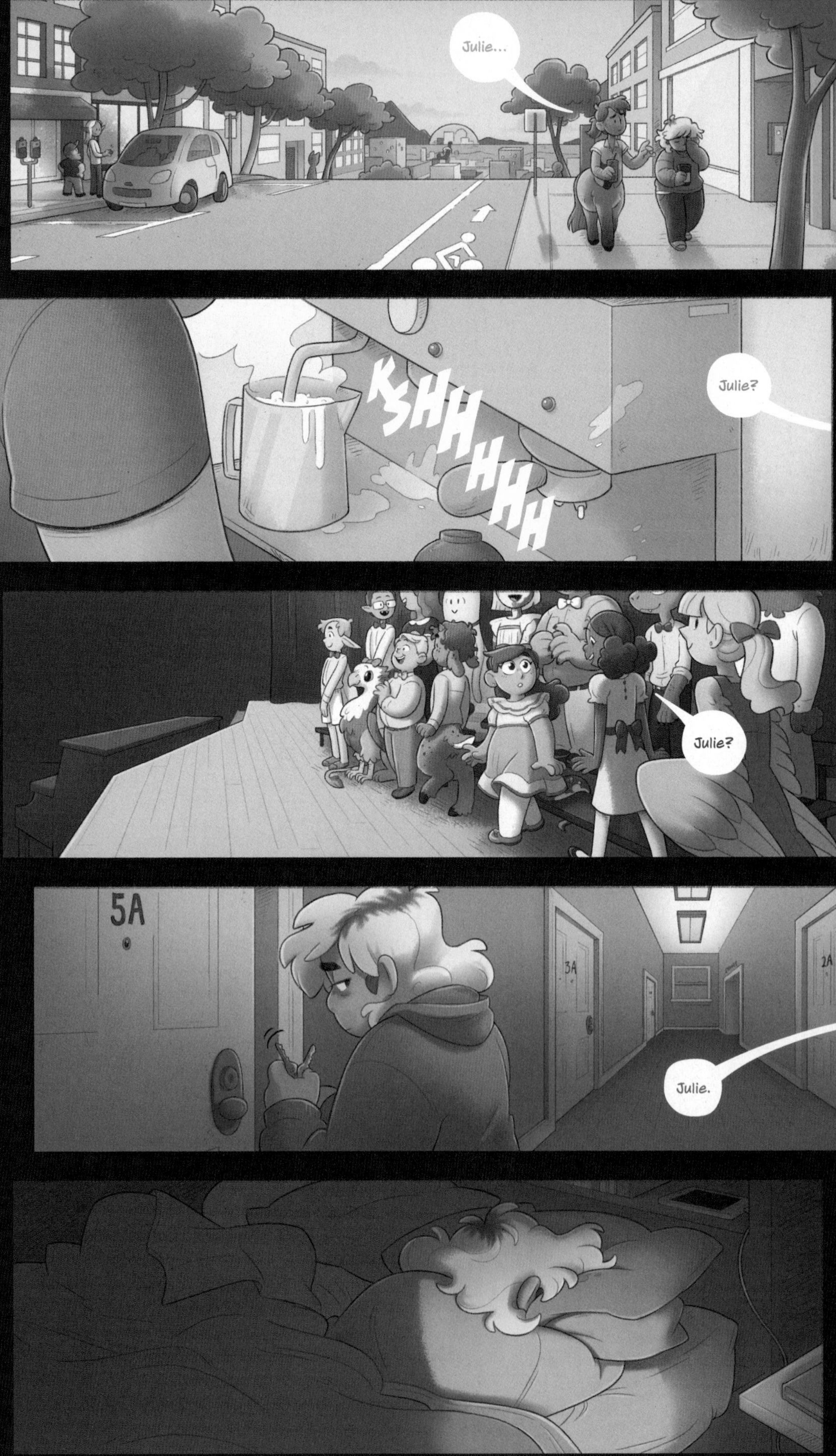
Julie...
Julie?
KSHHHHHH
Julie?
5A
3A
2A
Julie.

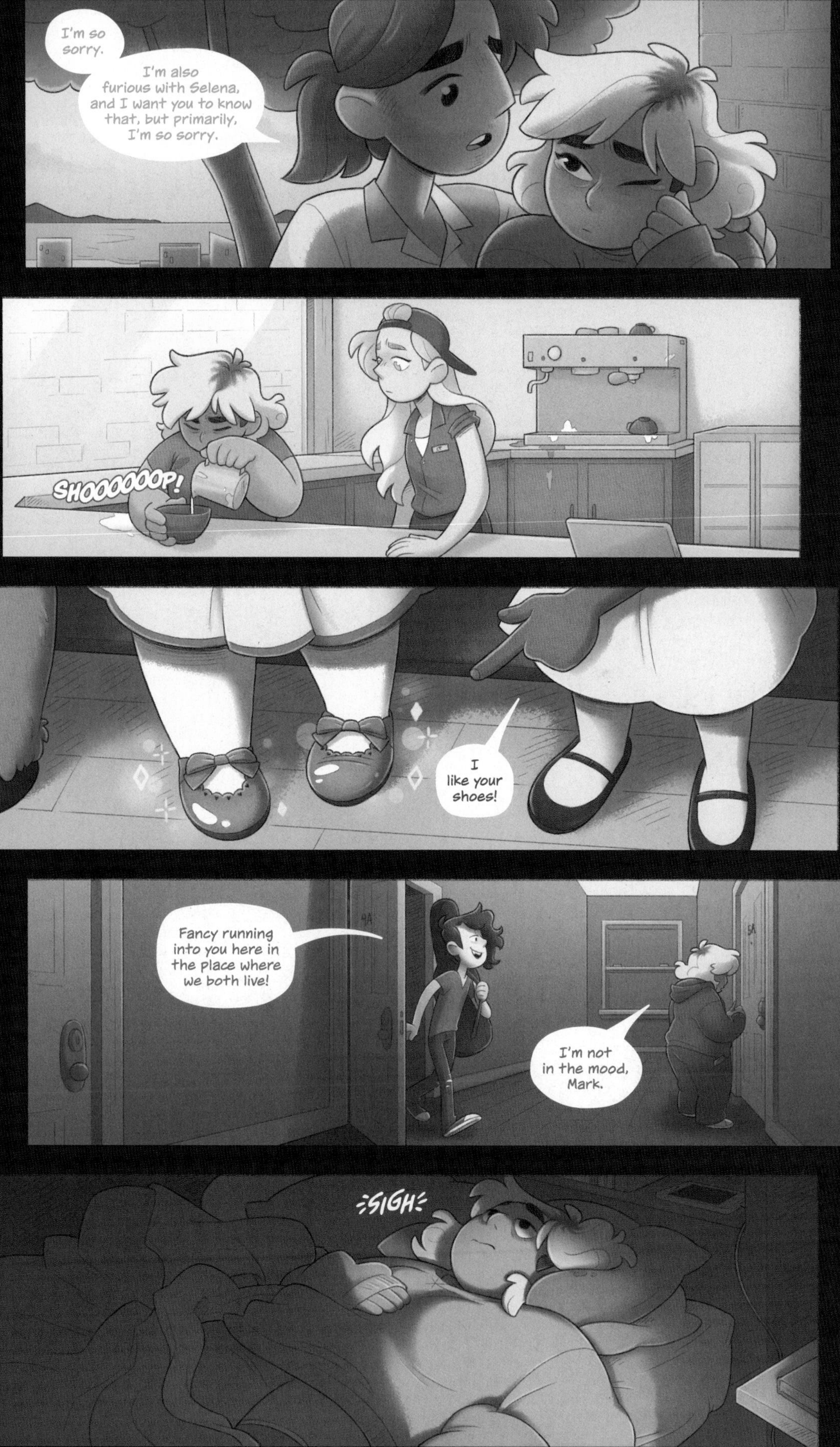
I'm so sorry.
I'm also furious with Selena, and I want you to know that, but primarily, I'm so sorry.
SHOOOOOOP!
I like your shoes!
Fancy running into you here in the place where we both live!
I'm not in the mood, Mark.
SIGH

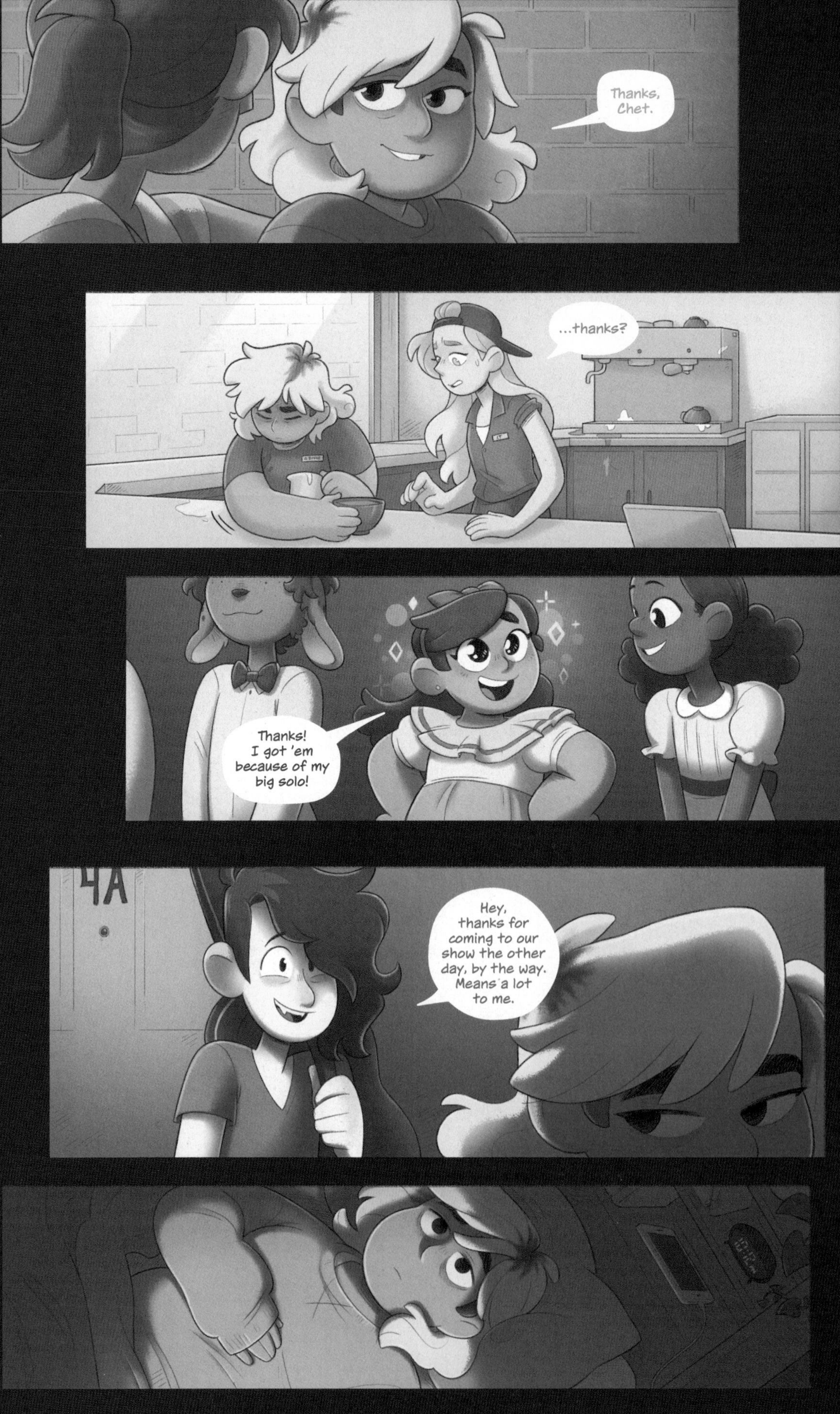
Thanks, Chet.
...thanks?
Thanks! I got 'em because of my big solo!
4A
Hey, thanks for coming to our show the other day, by the way. Means a lot to me.

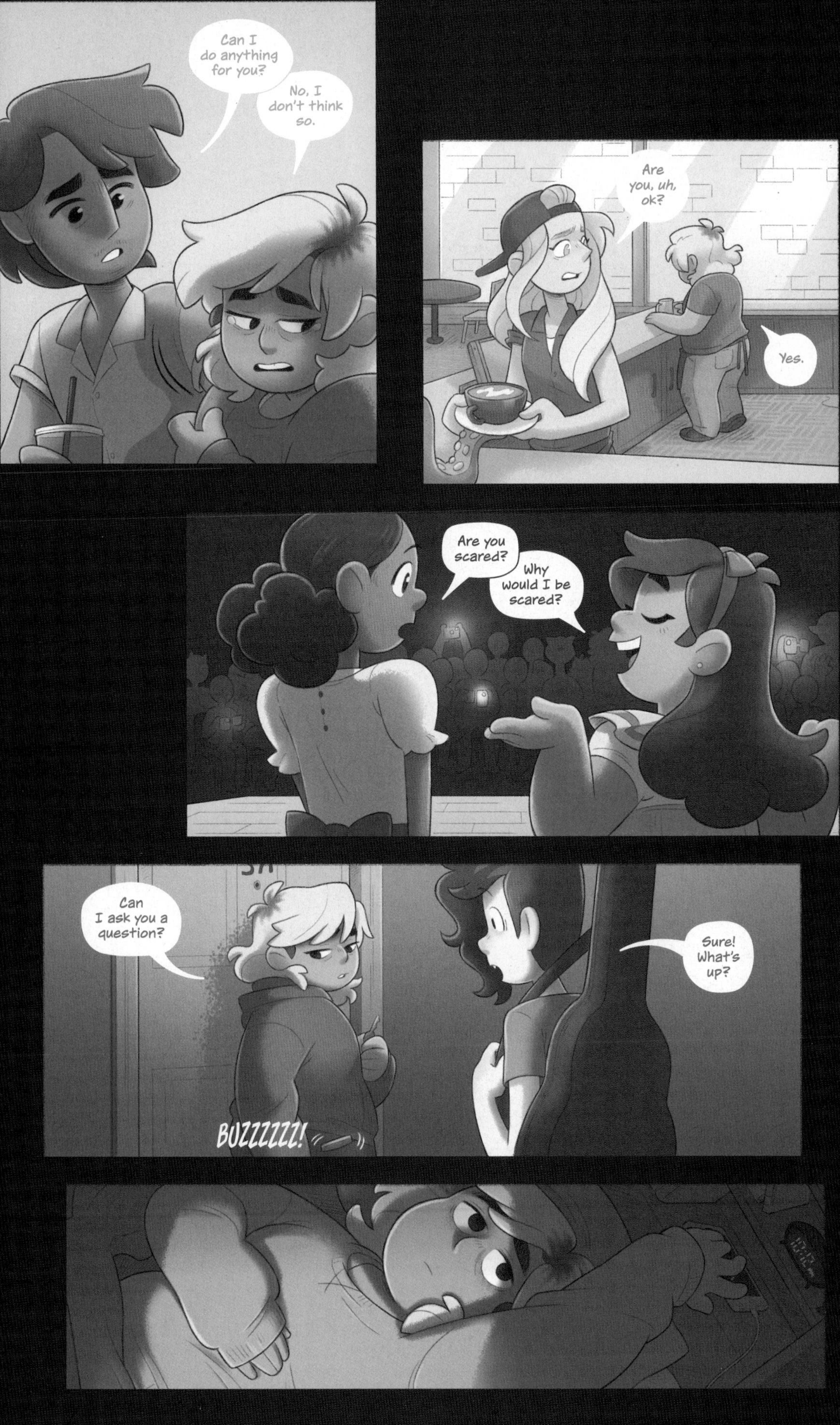
Can I do anything for you?
No, I don't think so.
Are you, uh, ok?
Yes.
Are you scared?
Why would I be scared?
Can I ask you a question?
Sure! What's up?
BUZZZZZZ!

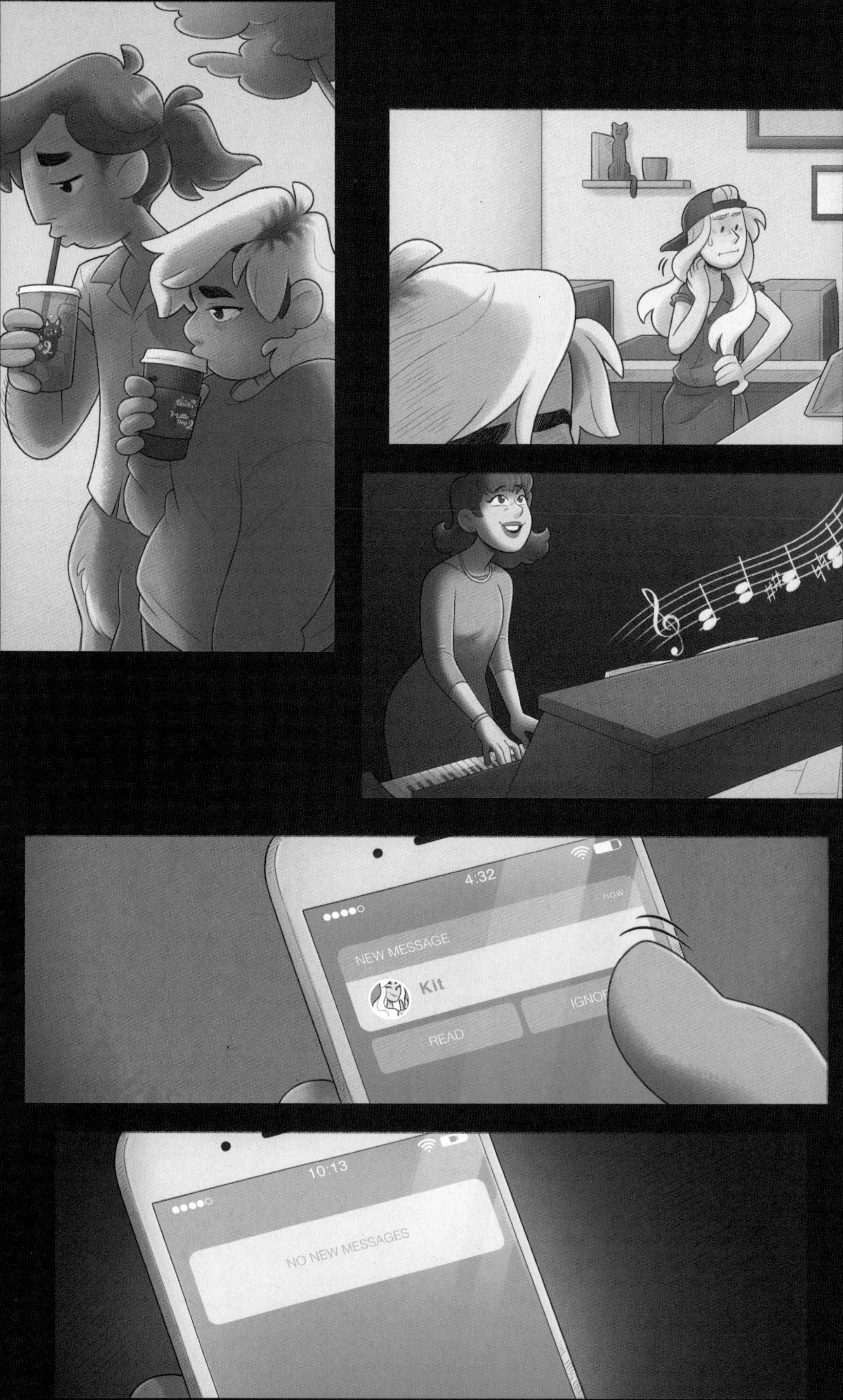
4:32
now
NEW MESSAGE
Kit
READ
IGNOR
10:13
NO NEW MESSAGES

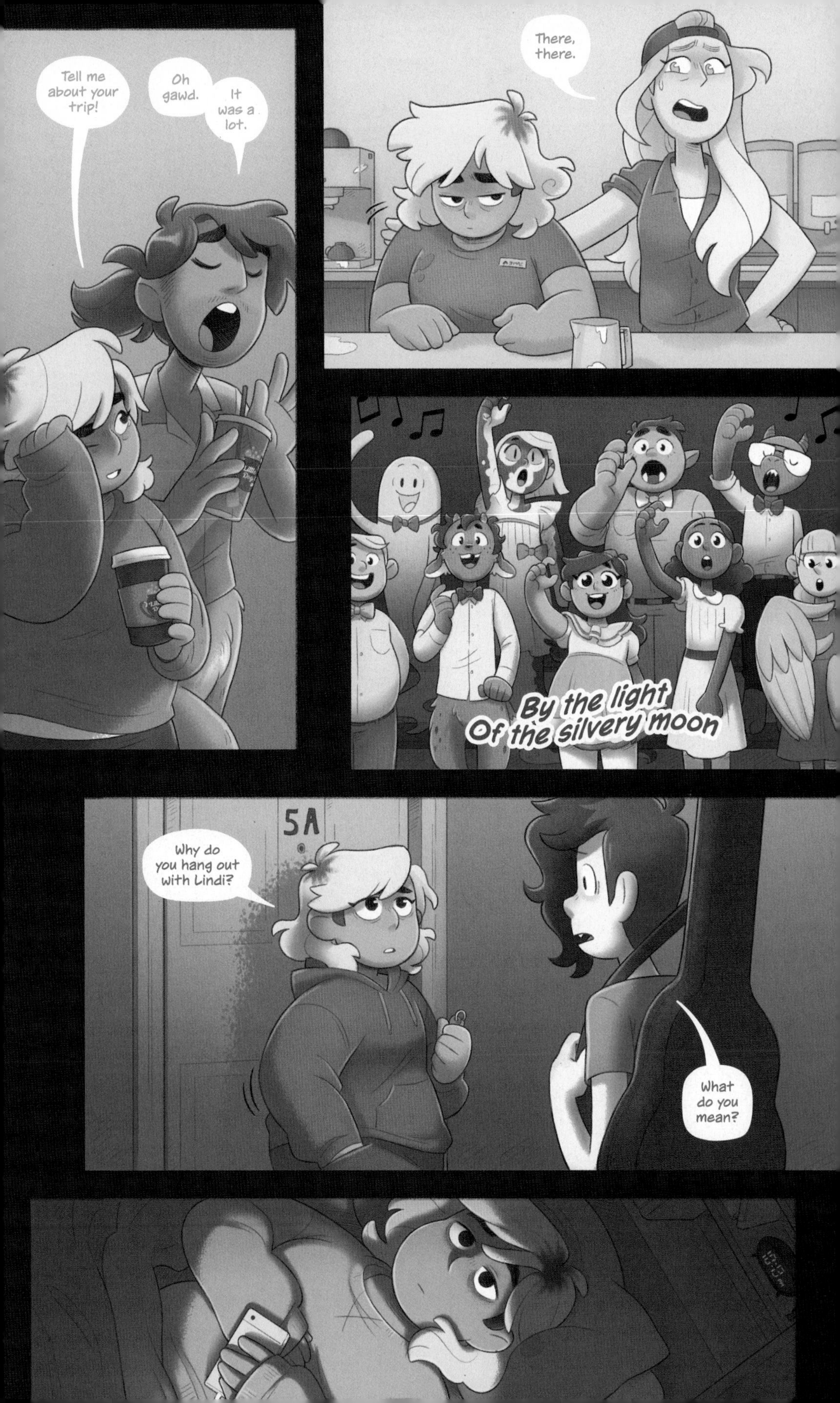
Tell me about your trip!
Oh gawd.
It was a lot.
There, there.
By the light Of the silvery moon
5A
Why do you hang out with Lindi?
What do you mean?

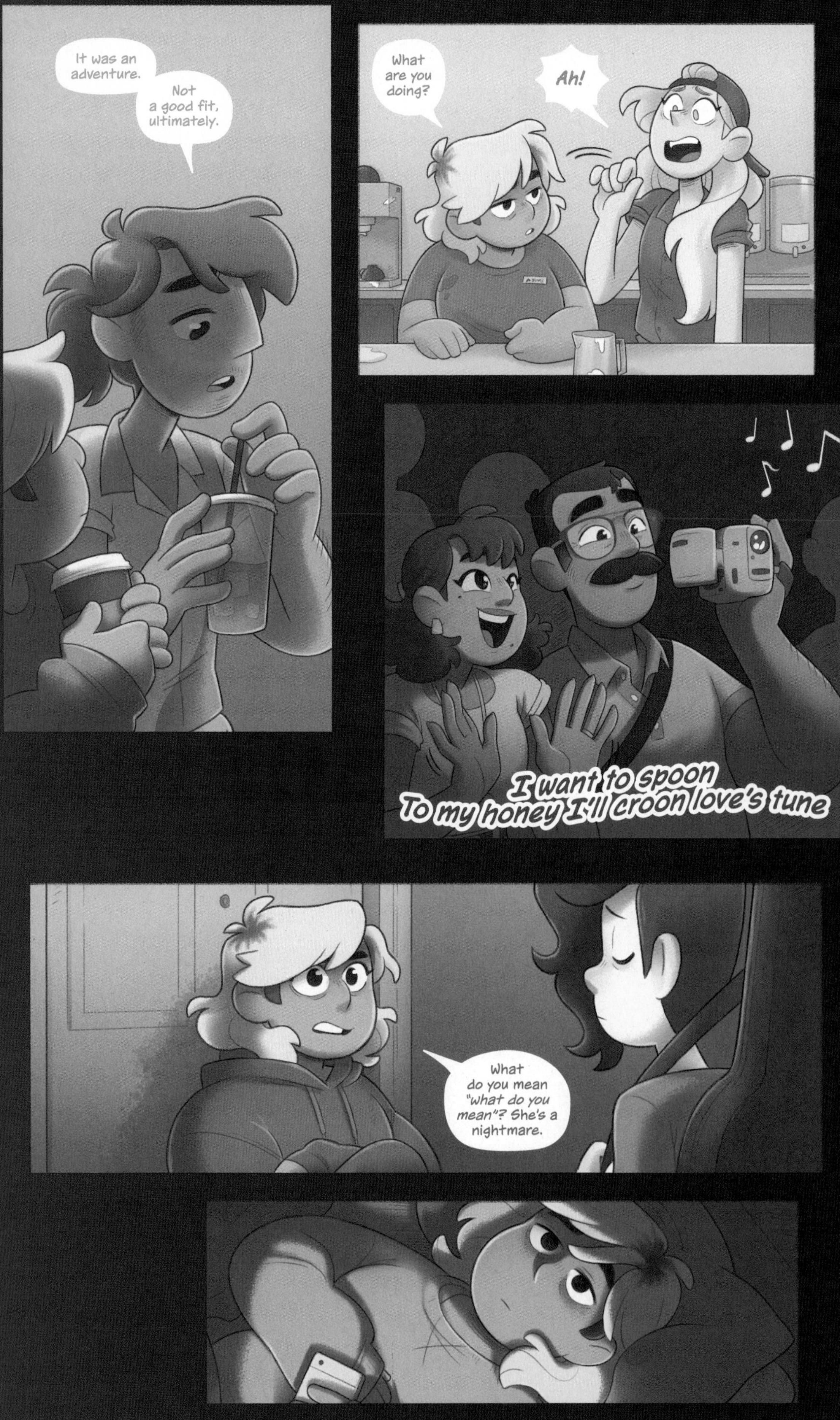
It was an adventure.
Not a good fit, ultimately.
What are you doing?
Ah!
I want to spoon
To my honey I'll croon love's tune
What do you mean "what do you mean"? She's a nightmare.

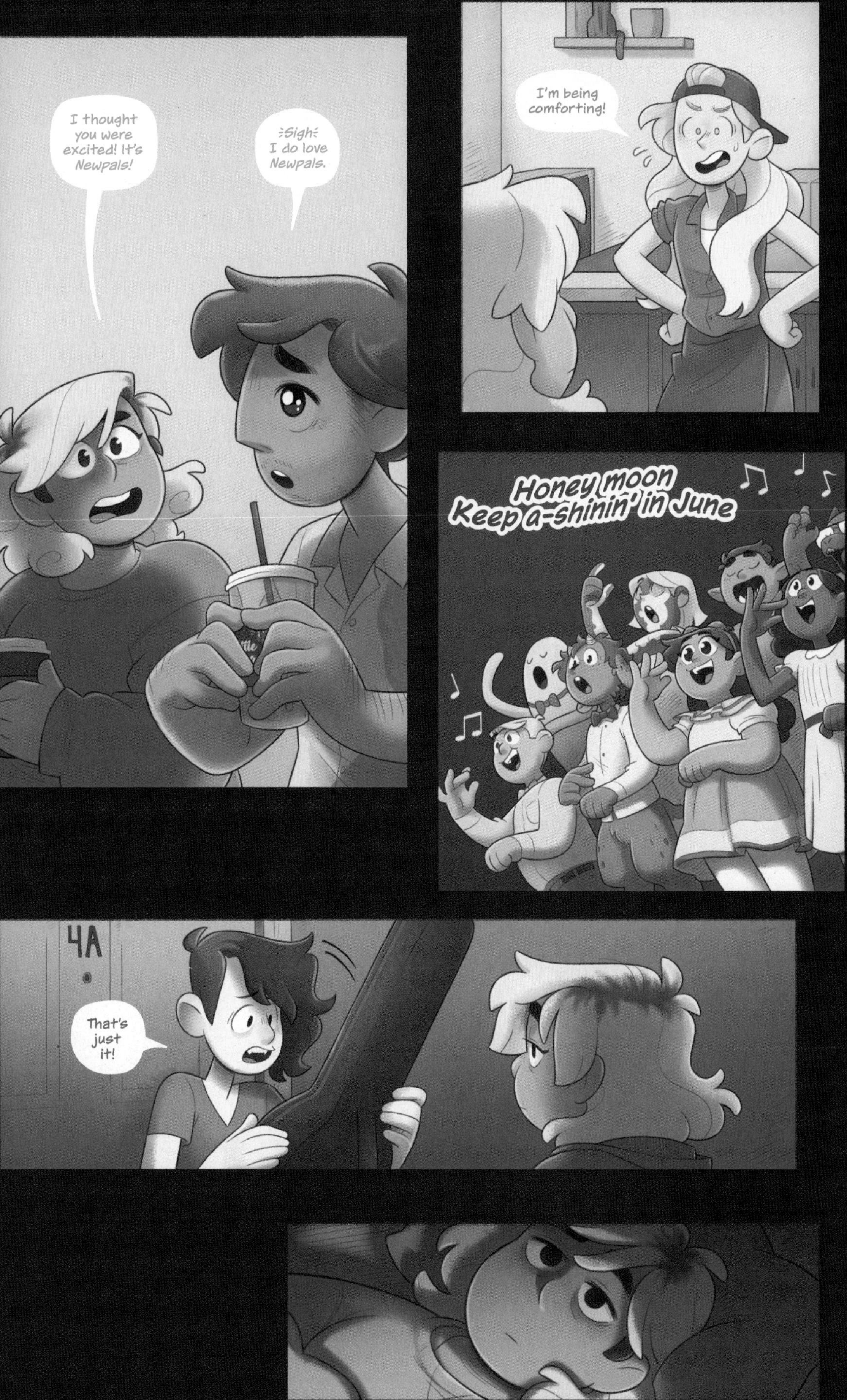
I thought you were excited! It's Newpals!
≠Sigh≠ I do love Newpals.
I'm being comforting!
Honey moon
Keep a-shinin' in June
4A
That's just it!

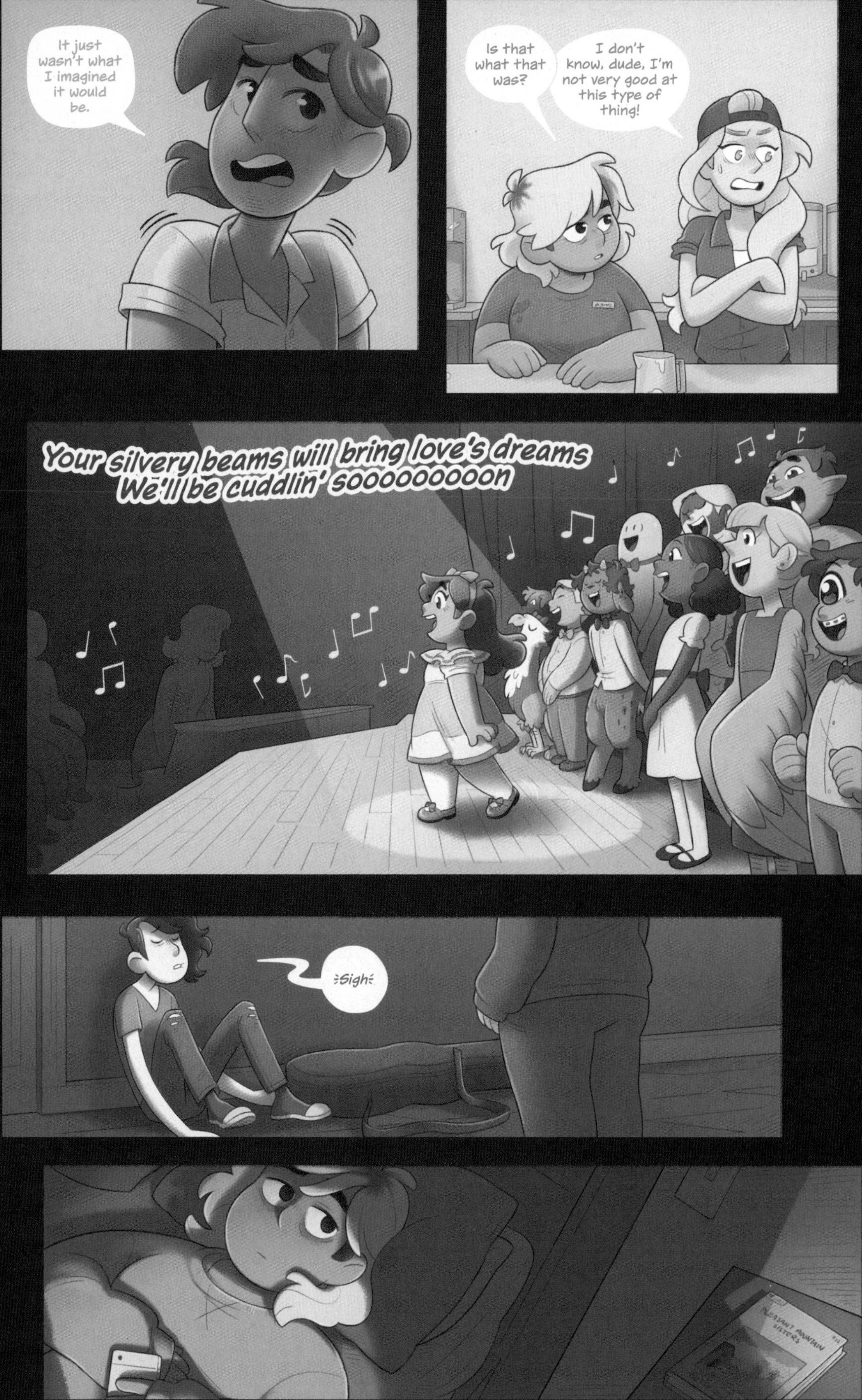
It just wasn't what I imagined it would be.
Is that what that was?
I don't know, dude, I'm not very good at this type of thing!
Your silvery beams will bring love's dreams
We'll be cuddlin' soooooooooon
Sigh
PLEASANT MOUNTAIN SISTERS

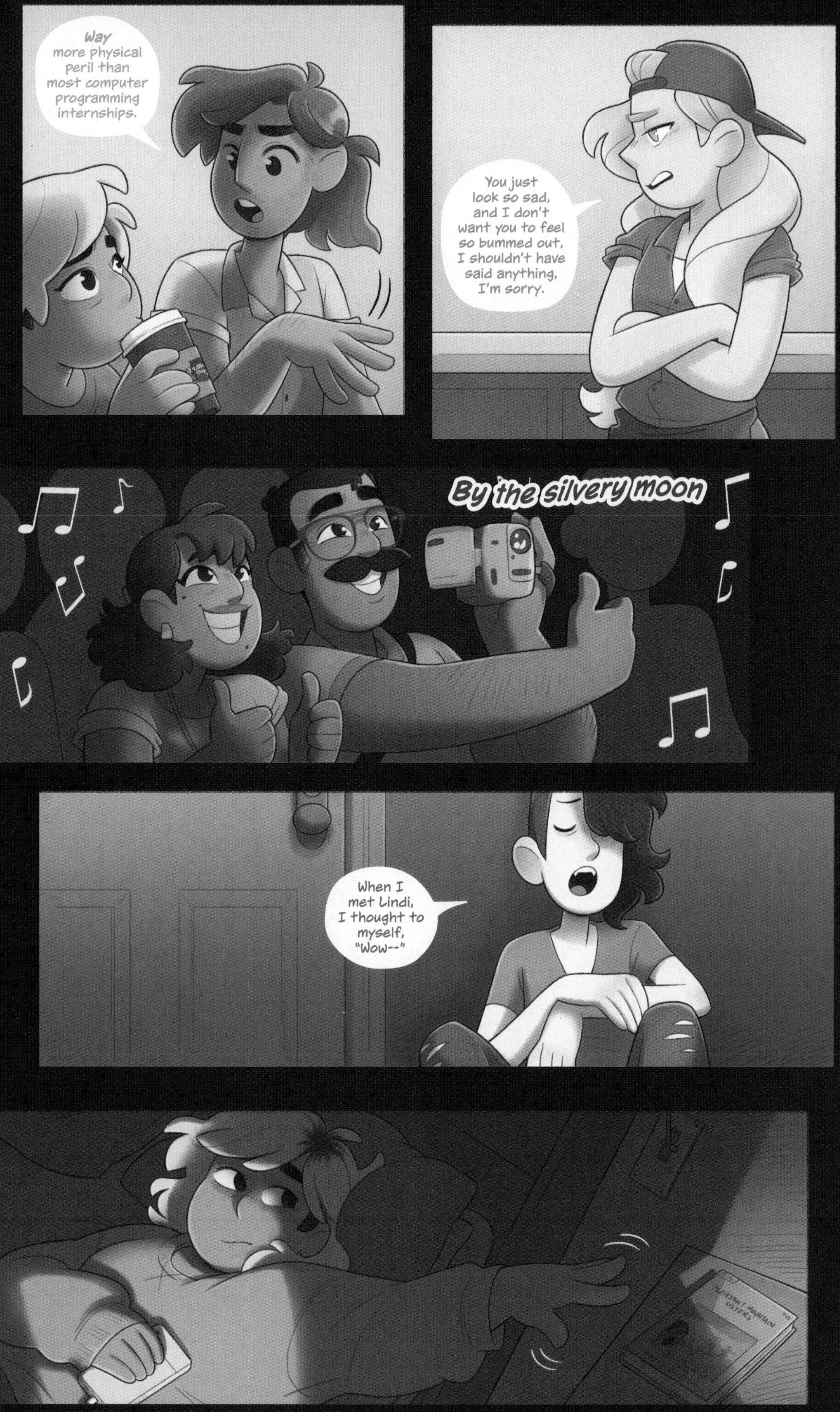
Way more physical peril than most computer programming internships.
You just look so sad, and I don't want you to feel so bummed out, I shouldn't have said anything, I'm sorry.
By the silvery moon
When I met Lindi, I thought to myself, "Wow--"
PLEASANT MOUNTAIN SISTERS

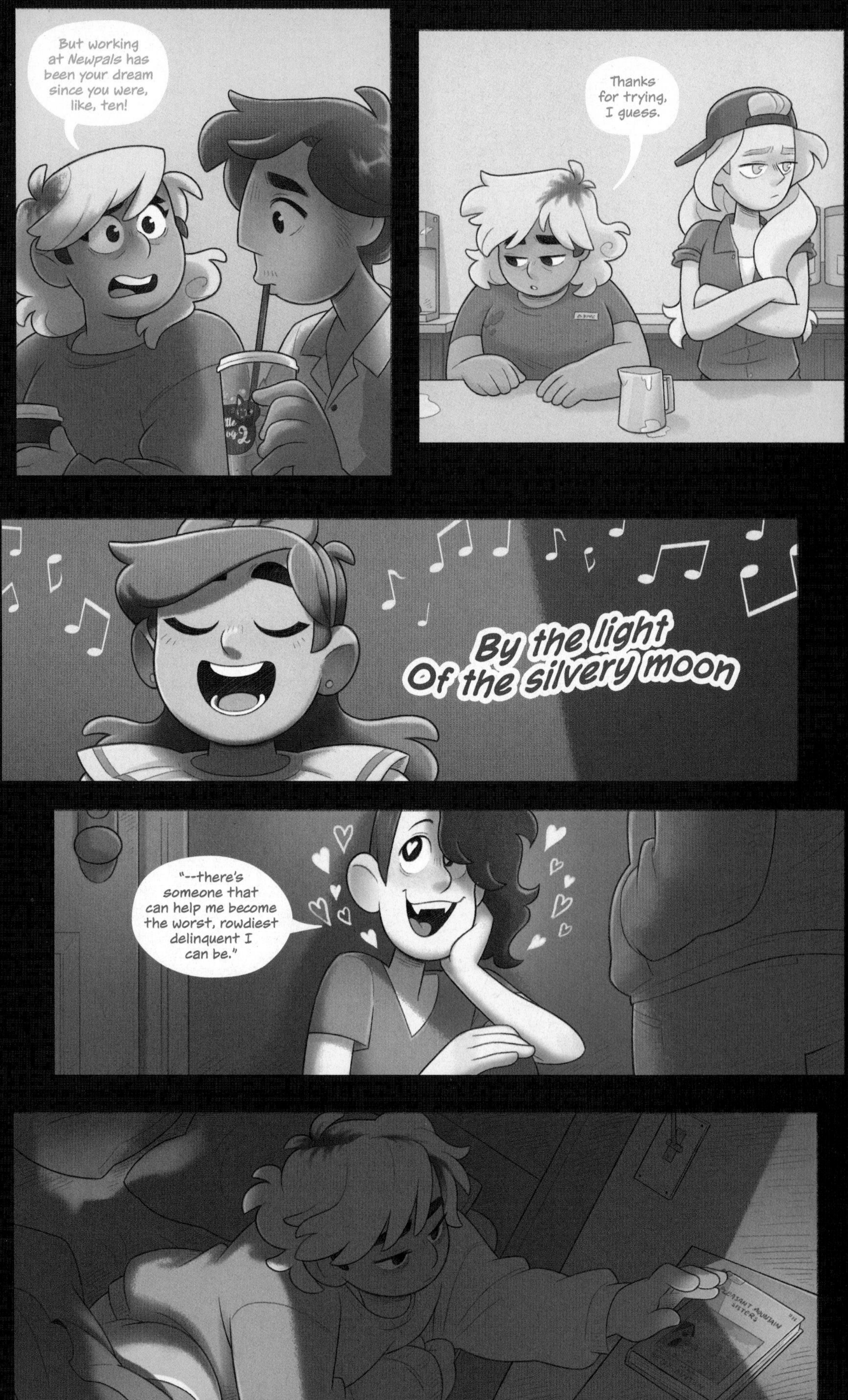
But working at Newpals has been your dream since you were, like, ten!
Thanks for trying, I guess.
By the light Of the silvery moon
"--there's someone that can help me become the worst, rowdiest delinquent I can be."

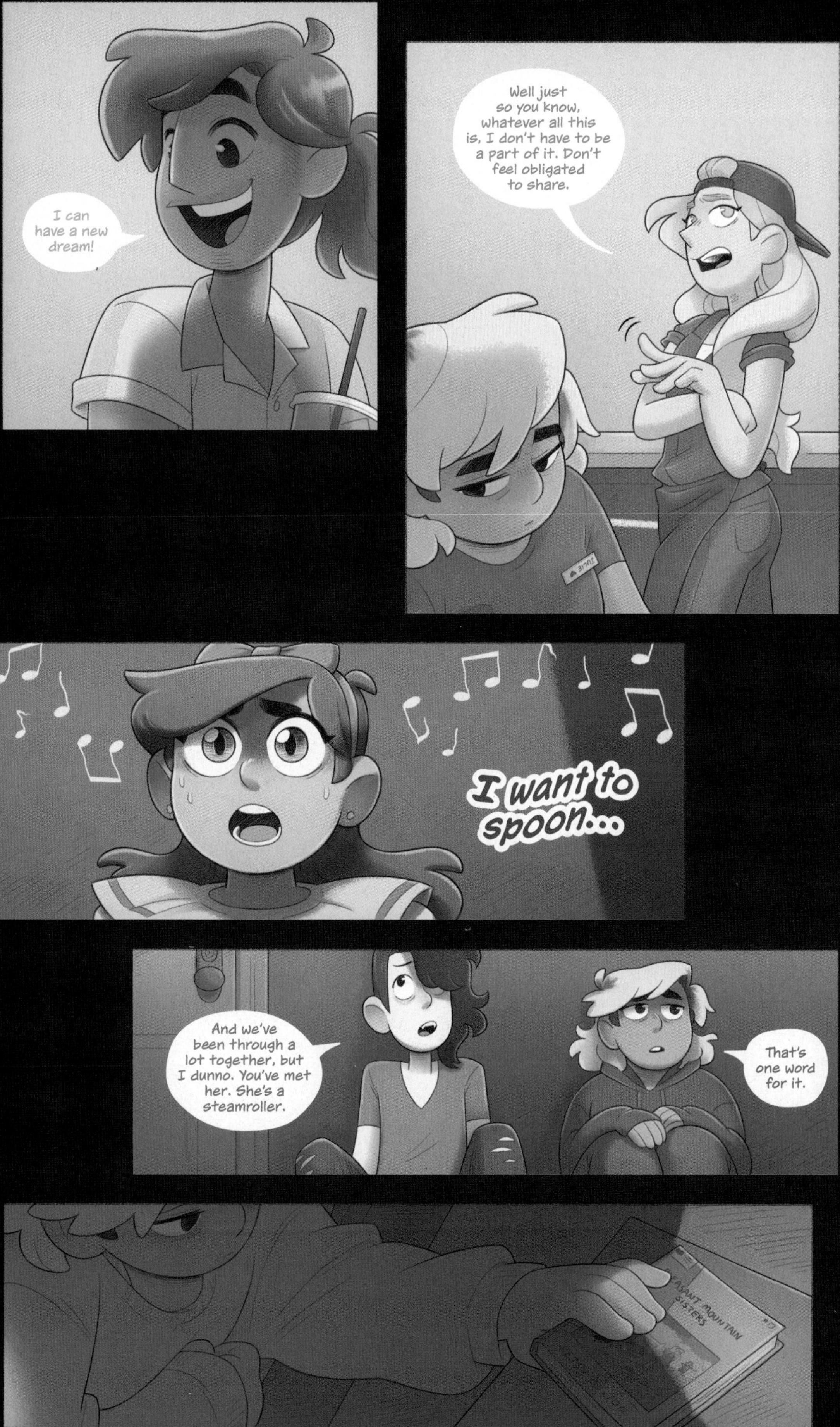
I can have a new dream!
Well just so you know, whatever all this is, I don't have to be a part of it. Don't feel obligated to share.
I want to spoon...
And we've been through a lot together, but I dunno. You've met her. She's a steamroller.
That's one word for it.

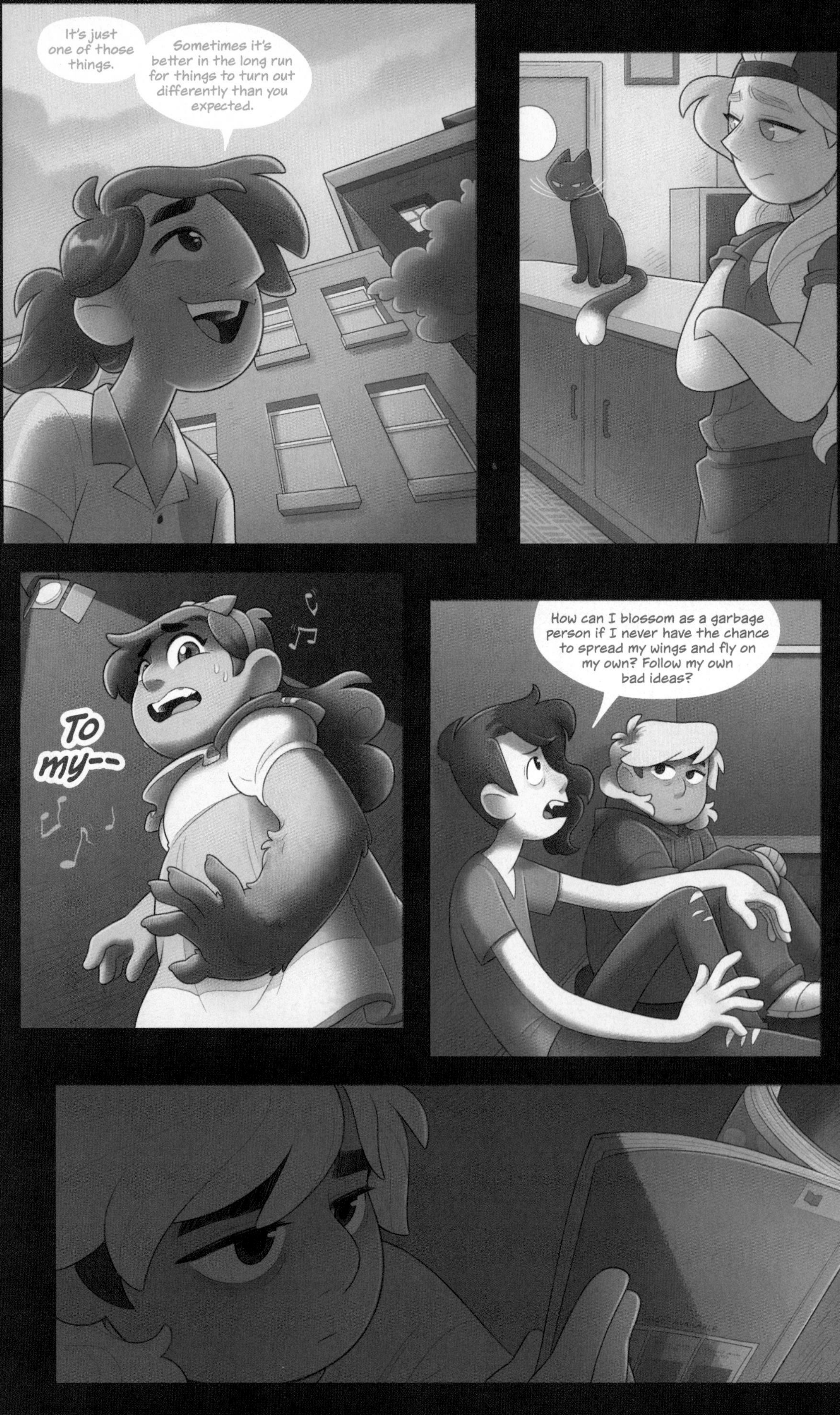
It's just one of those things.
Sometimes it's better in the long run for things to turn out differently than you expected.
To my--
How can I blossom as a garbage person if I never have the chance to spread my wings and fly on my own? Follow my own bad ideas?

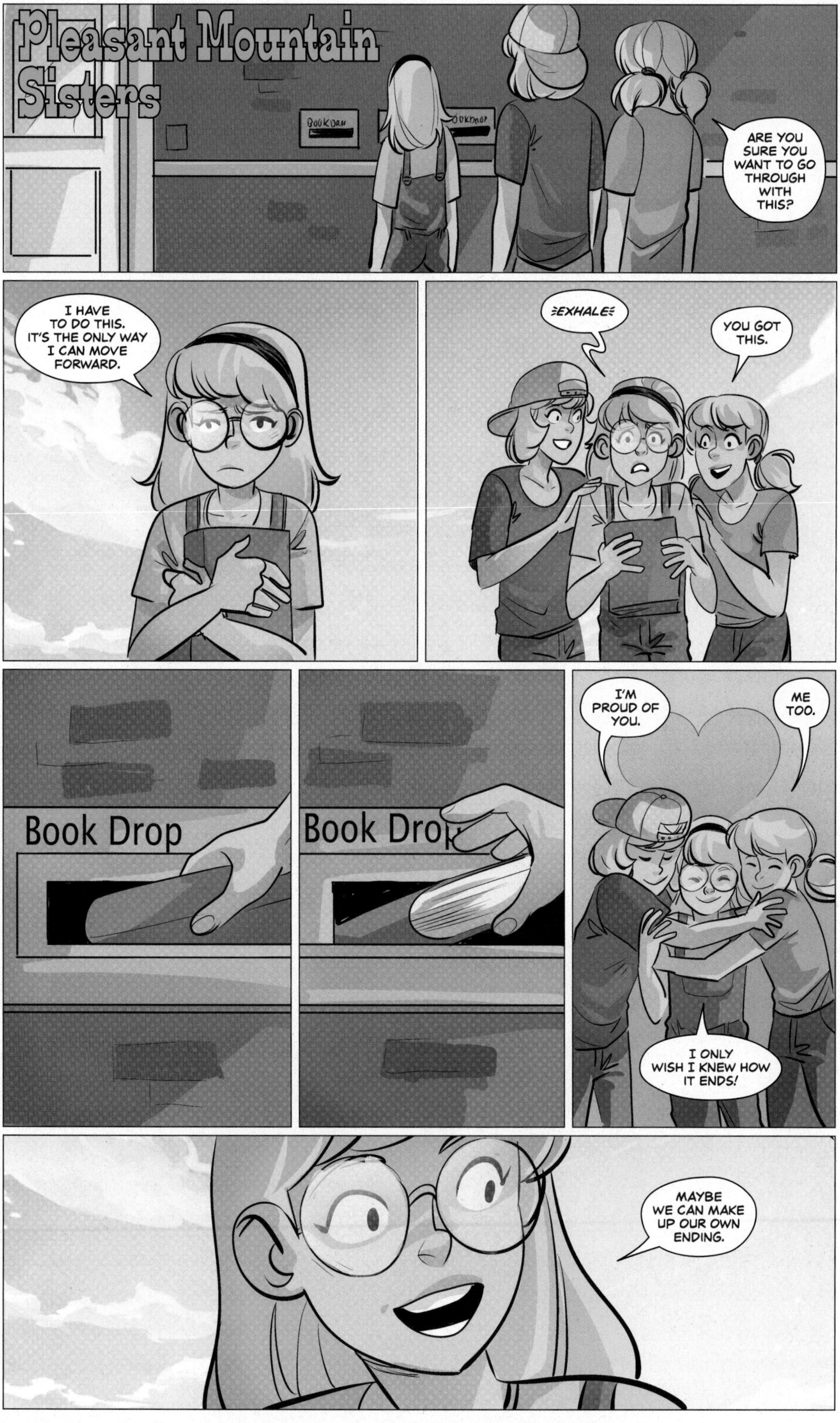
Pleasant Mountain Sisters
ARE YOU SURE YOU WANT TO GO THROUGH WITH THIS?
I HAVE TO DO THIS. IT'S THE ONLY WAY I CAN MOVE FORWARD.
EXHALE
YOU GOT THIS.
Book Drop
Book Drop
I'M PROUD OF YOU.
ME TOO.
I ONLY WISH I KNEW HOW IT ENDS!
MAYBE WE CAN MAKE UP OUR OWN ENDING.

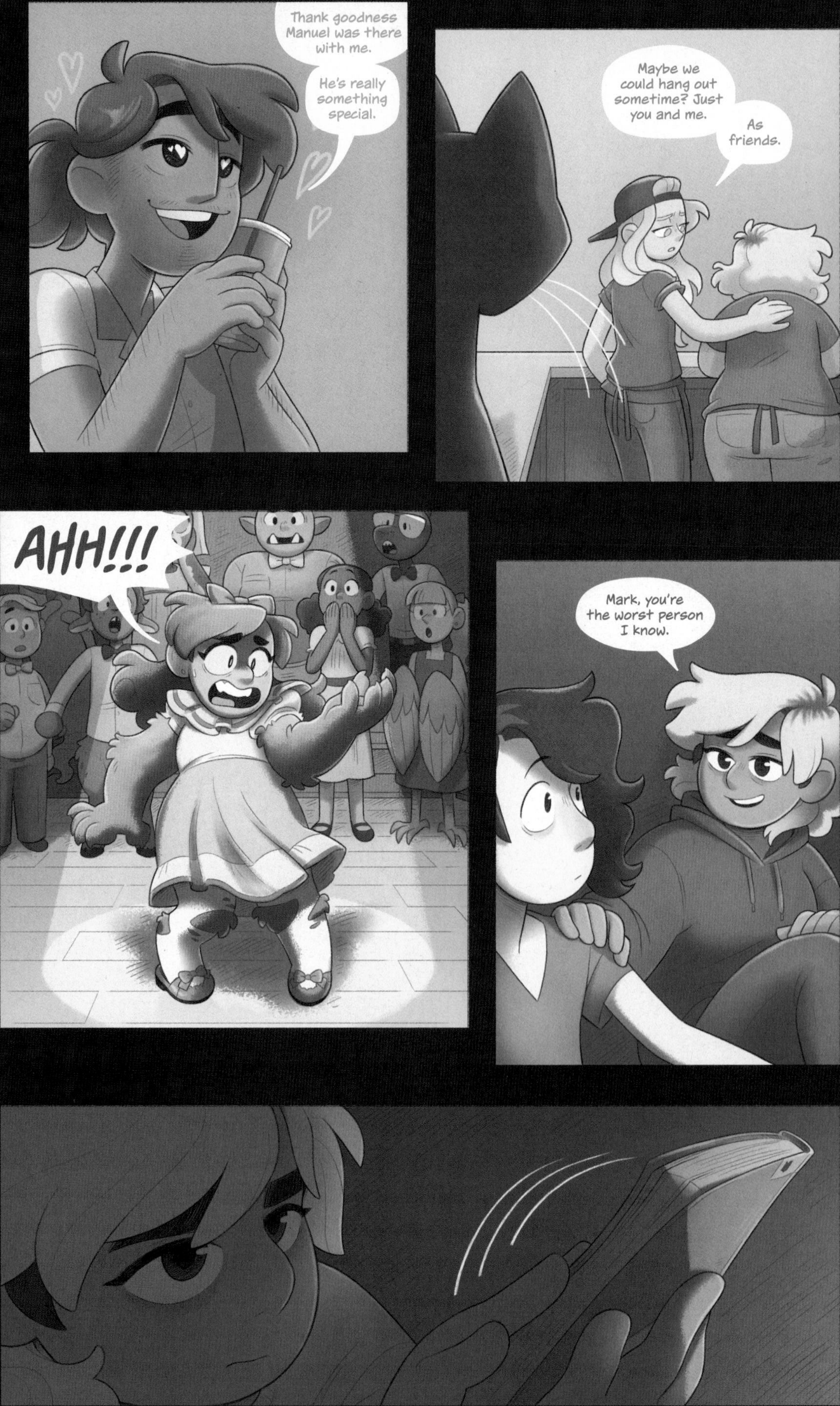
Thank goodness Manuel was there with me.
He's really something special.
Maybe we could hang out sometime? Just you and me.
As friends.
AHH!!!
Mark, you're the worst person I know.

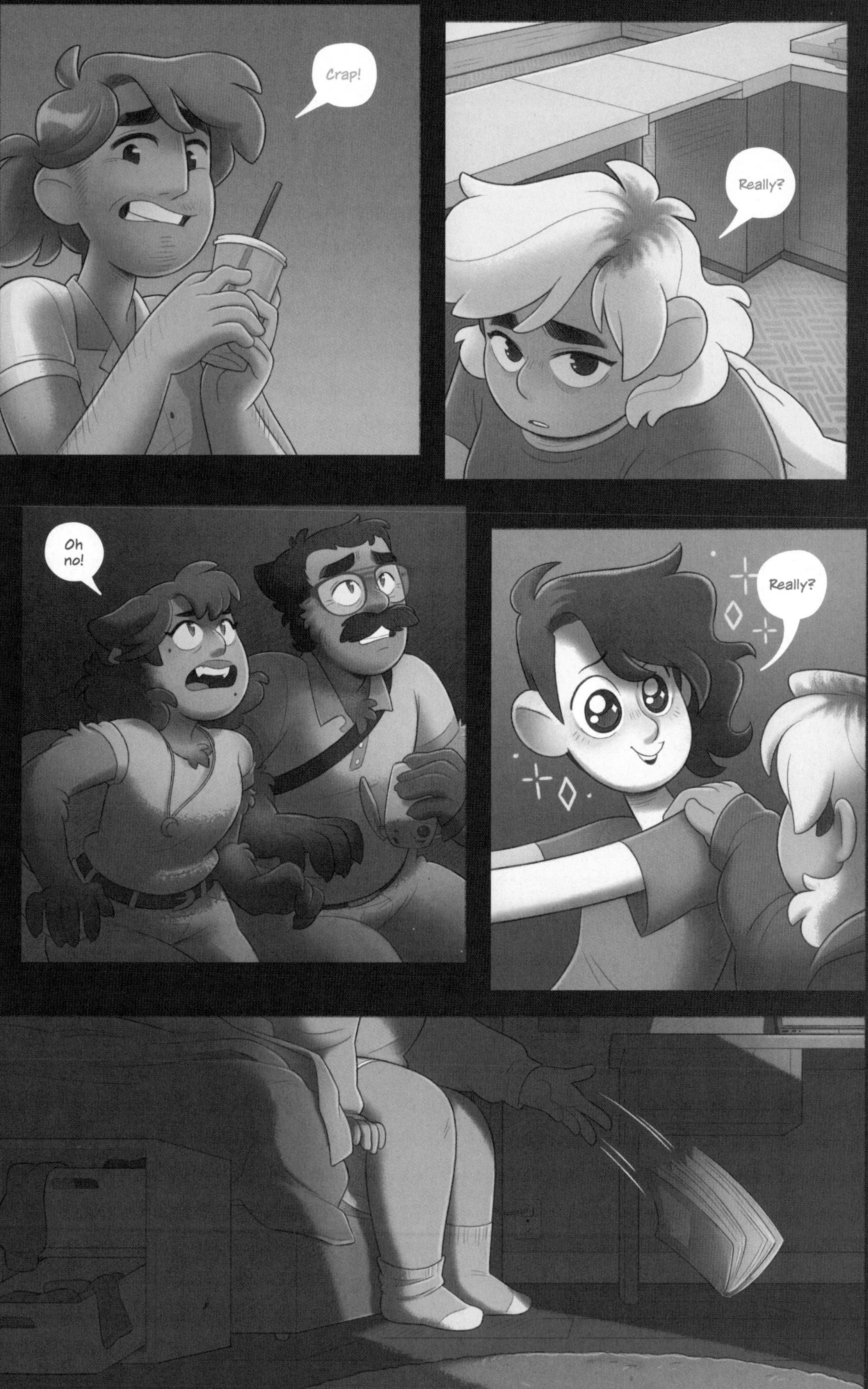
Crap!
Really?
Oh no!
Really?

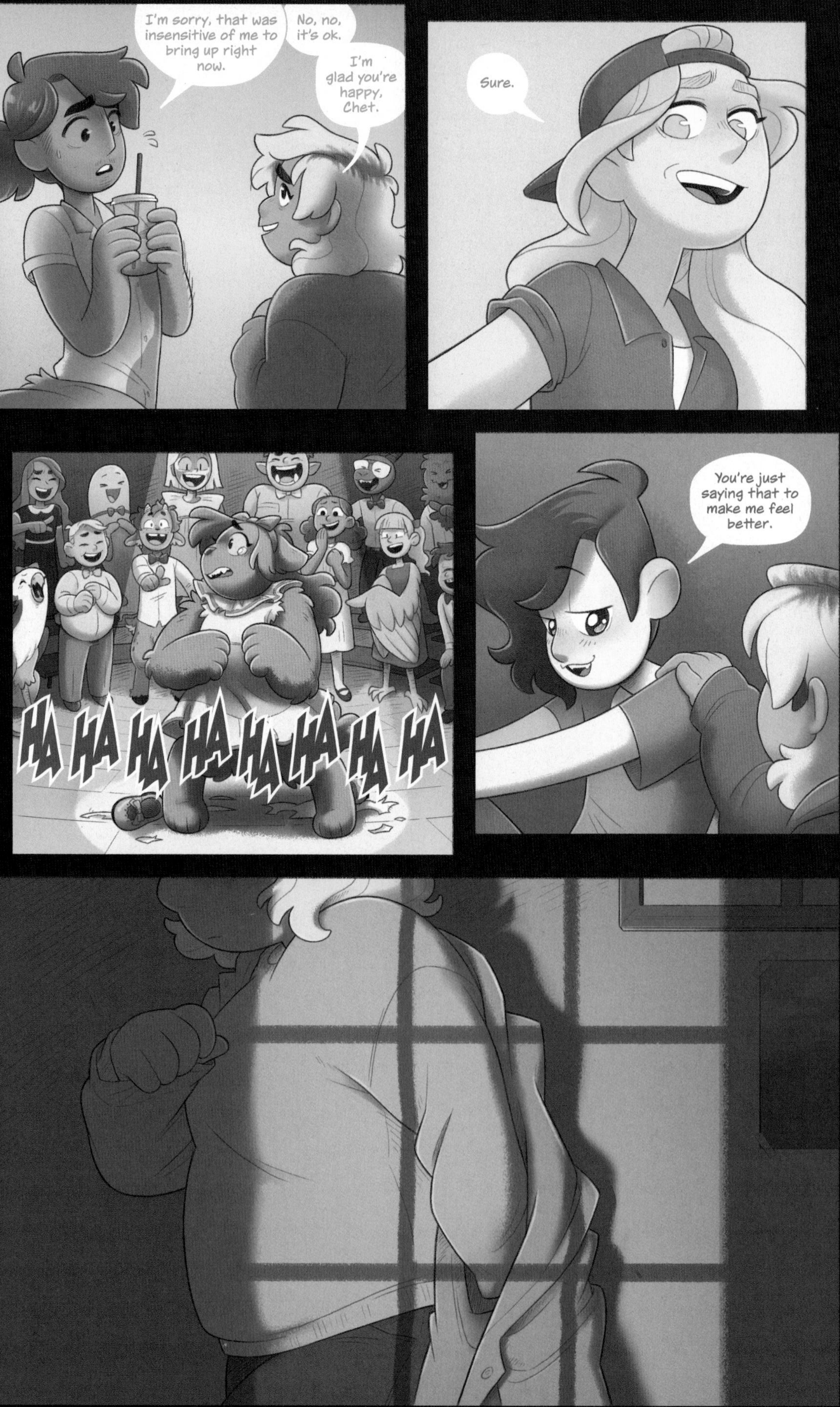

I'm sorry, that was insensitive of me to bring up right now.
No, no, it's ok.
I'm glad you're happy, Chet.
Sure.
HA HA HA HA HA HA HA HA
You're just saying that to make me feel better.

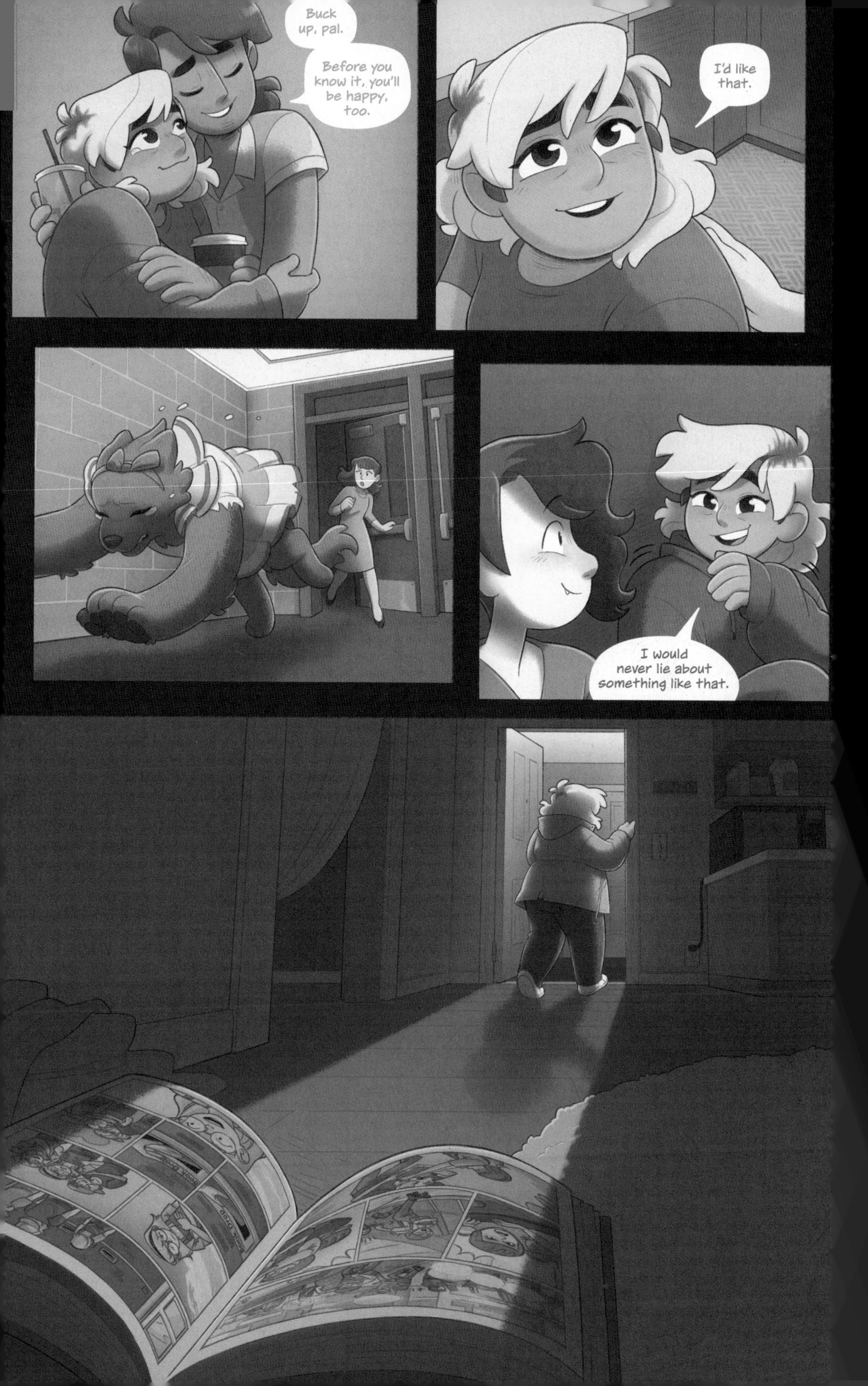
Buck up, pal.
Before you know it, you'll be happy, too.
I'd like that.
I would never lie about something like that.

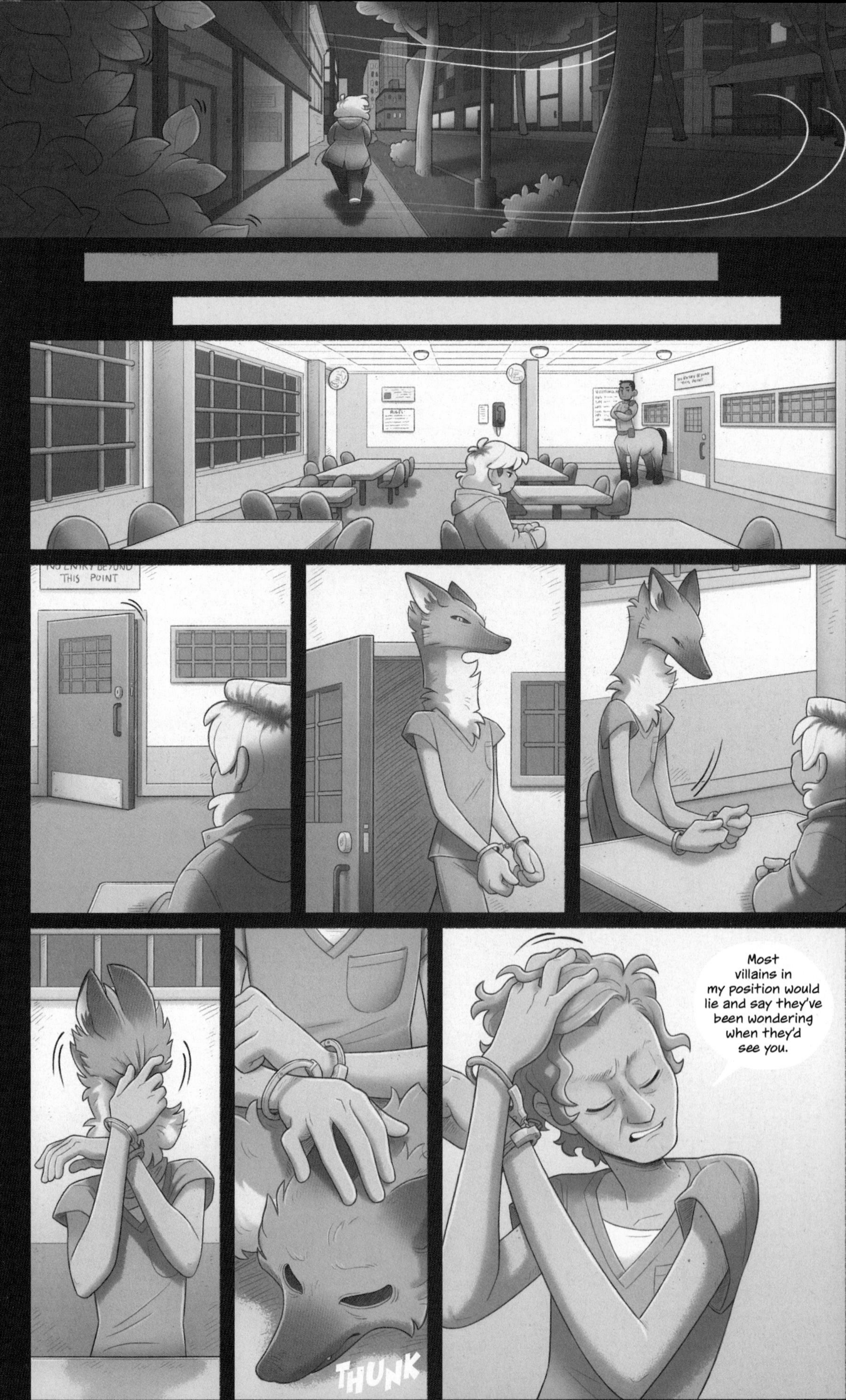

NO ENTRY BEYOND THIS POINT
Most villains in my position would lie and say they've been wondering when they'd see you.
THUNK

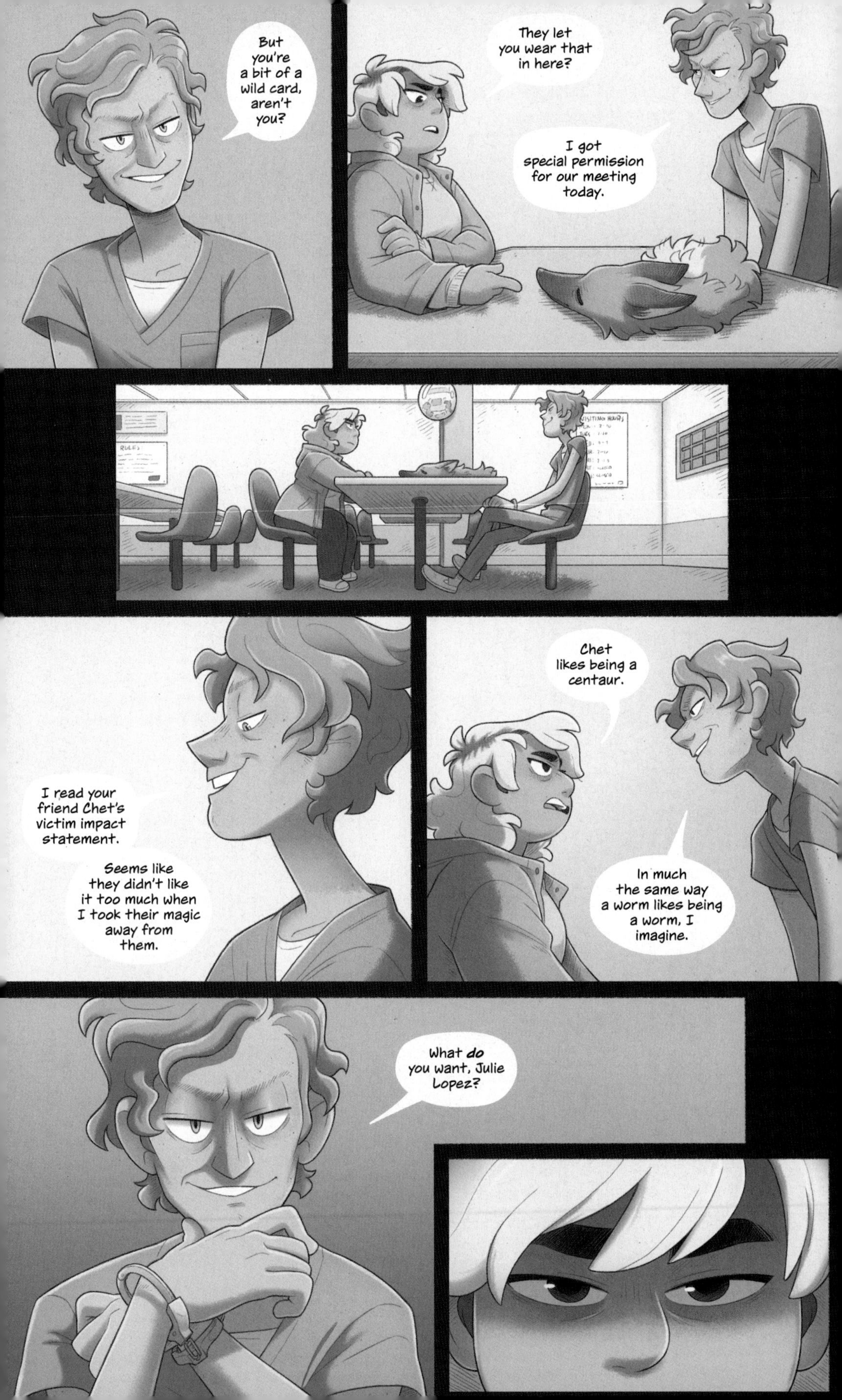
But you're a bit of a wild card, aren't you?
They let you wear that in here?
I got special permission for our meeting today.
I read your friend Chet's victim impact statement.
Seems like they didn't like it too much when I took their magic away from them.
Chet likes being a centaur.
In much the same way a worm likes being a worm, I imagine.
What *do* you want, Julie Lopez?

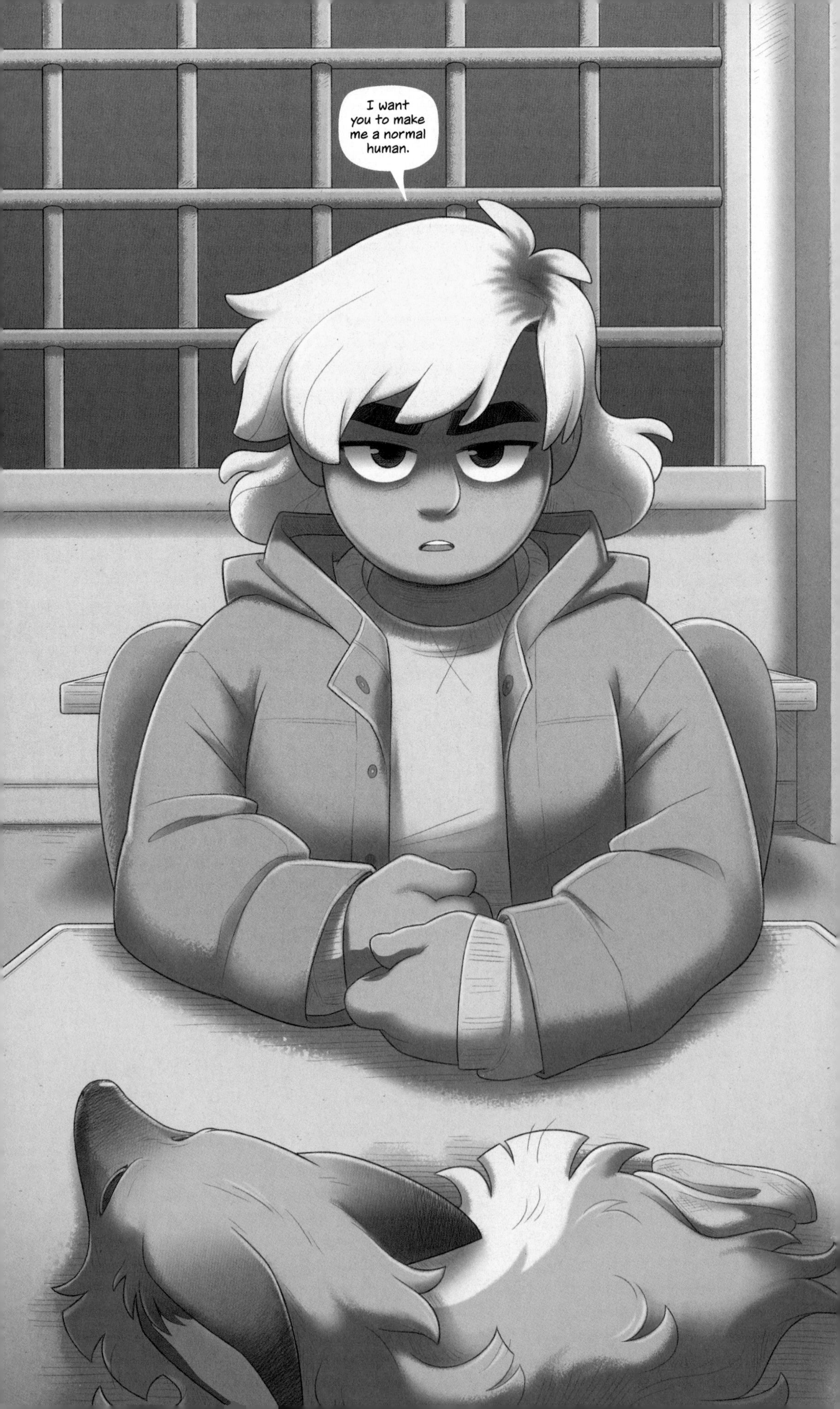
I want you to make me a normal human.

MESSAGES FROM THE MOON

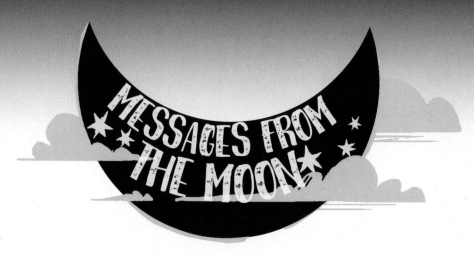

OOOOOF.

THIS IS SO MUCH, Y'ALL.

When Grace sent us the script for Volume 3, our first reaction was:

WHYYYYYY OMG WHYYYYYYYY

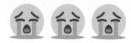

Then Grace just kind of laughed meanly at us. I think she likes drama. OMG, IS GRACE ACTUALLY KIT?!?! (She's not. I checked. She is totally a normal human, without any sign of mystical fox tails.)

Volume 3 of *Moonstruck* also introduces us to a new Pleasant Mountain Sisters artist, Claudia Aguirre! Claudia is a queer Mexican comic book artist and writer, and the co-founder of Boudika Comics with Eva Cabrera. She has drawn *Lost on Planet Earth* with Comixology Originals, *Hotel Dare* with Boom! Studios, *Firebrand*, with Legendary Comics, *Morning in America* with OniPress, and *Kim & Kim* with Black Mask. Check out more of her work at Boudikacomics.com!

We'll be back with Volume 4 soon - hmm, I wonder what kind of emotional torture Grace has in store for us next? I kinda can't wait to find out!

Shae Beagle
Grace Ellis
Laurenn McCubbin

SHAE SCRIBBLES

OMG, baby Julie!

We had a LOT of fun coming up with new characters and designs for this arc, including our first look at JULIE'S FAMILY! They are werewolves too, but maybe not as freaked out about it? We haven't seen them before this, since they don't live in Blitheton.

So mom, such dad.

Speaking of new characters... what do you all think of Kit? You may have figured out that she is a Kitsune, or a fox spirit. Kitsune are tricksters for sure, and they LIVE. FOR. DRAMA.

Hmmmm... I wonder what Kit wants with Julie?

Only the most ANCIENT of Kitsune end up with nine tails...

Along with new characters, there's a new location! Mermaid Lake, with its annual Spring festival for the Unfreezing seems like such a fascinating place.

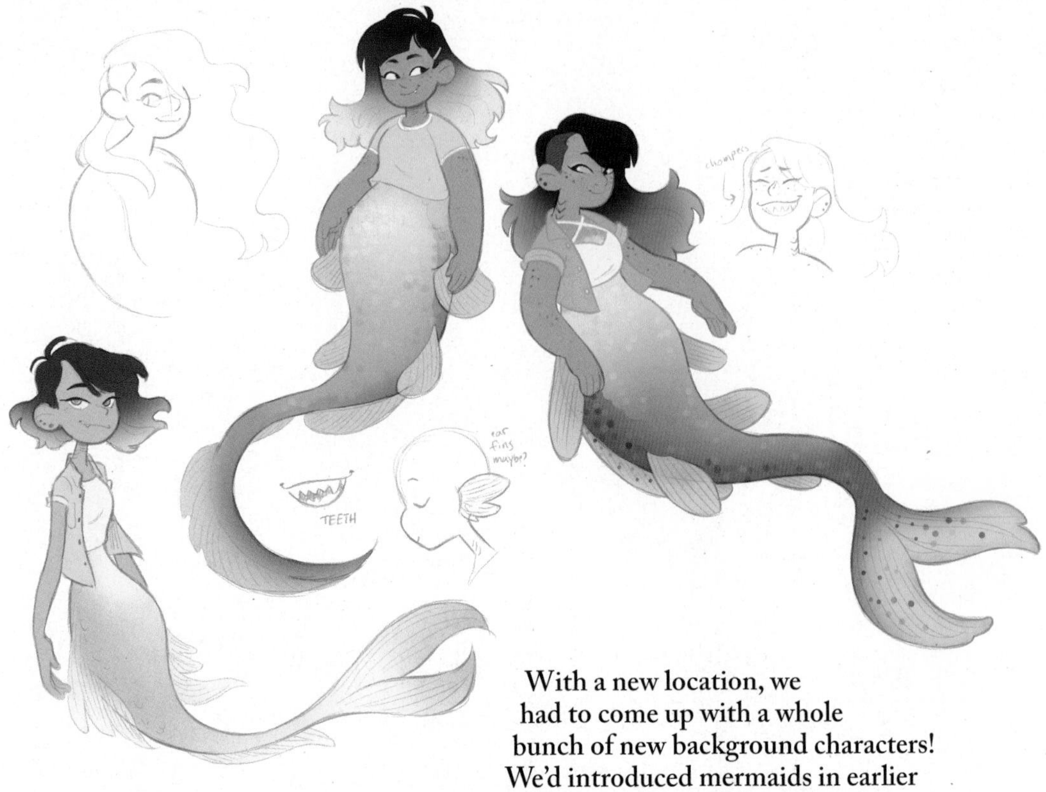
chompers
ear fins maybe?
TEETH

With a new location, we had to come up with a whole bunch of new background characters! We'd introduced mermaids in earlier volumes, but the ones who come from Mermaid Lake are different - they are lake mermaids! So Shae experimented with different lake fish for Skyla's tail.

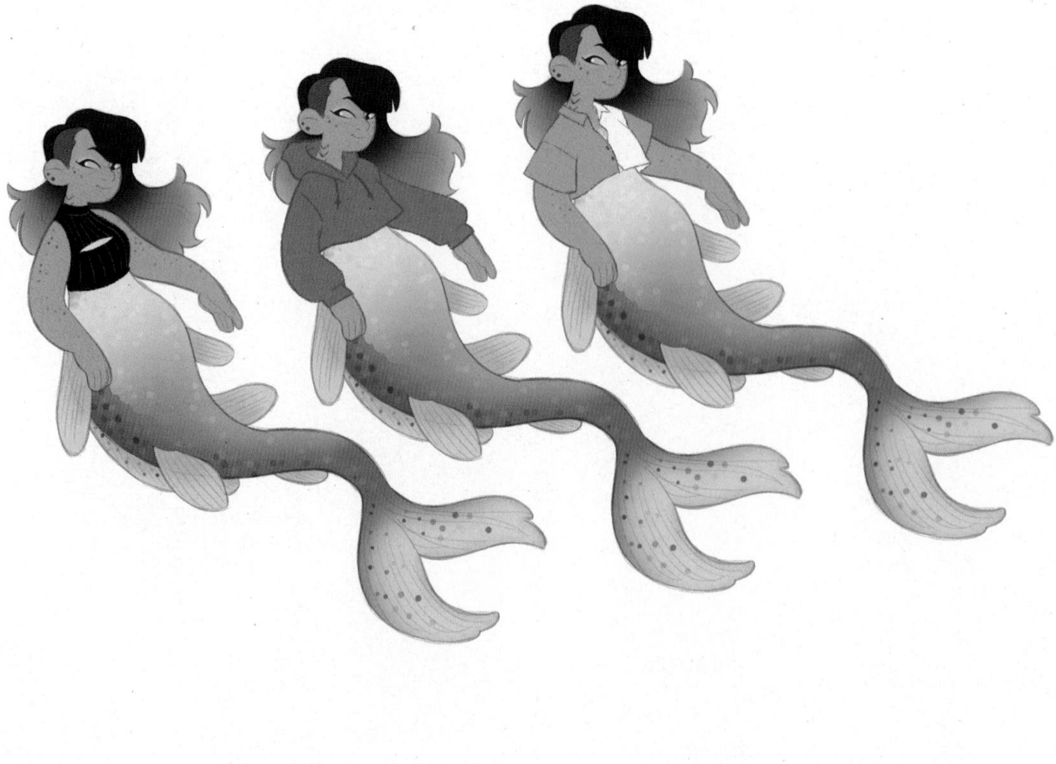

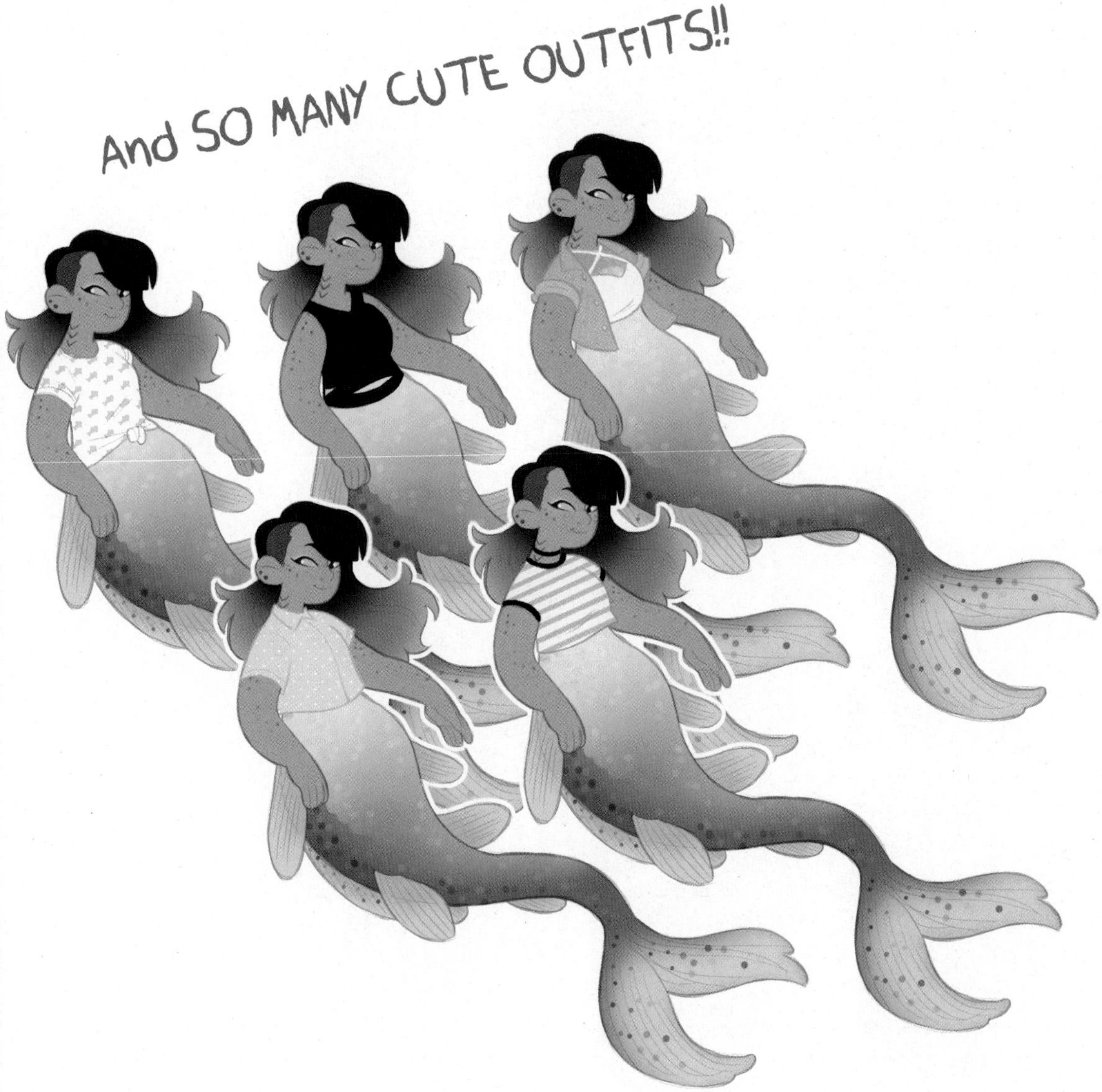
And SO MANY CUTE OUTFITS!!

Along with new characters and a new location, we had to think of a bunch of new background characters for Mermaid Lake. It was so fun looking at fairy tales and myths about lake creatures, like the Kushtaka or "lake otter men" from the Pacific Northwest, or the Kappa from Japan.

Lots of these folktales involved creatures who would pull people into lakes and drown them, like Kelpies, Jenny Greenteeth or the Grindylow. But... Shae made them look so *cute!*

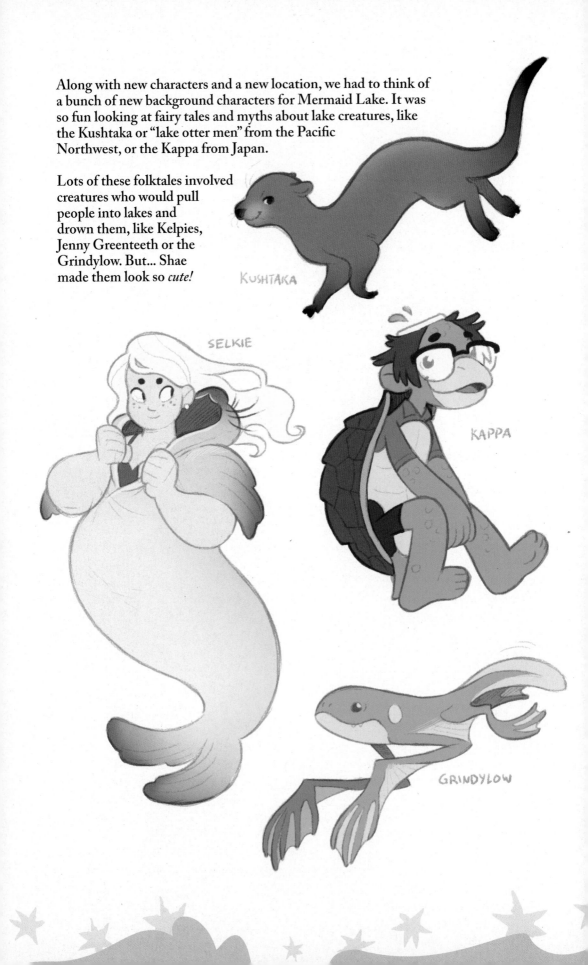

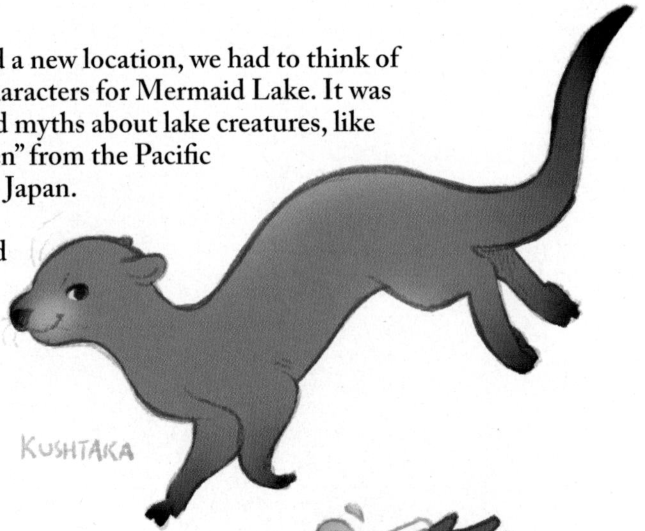
KUSHTAKA

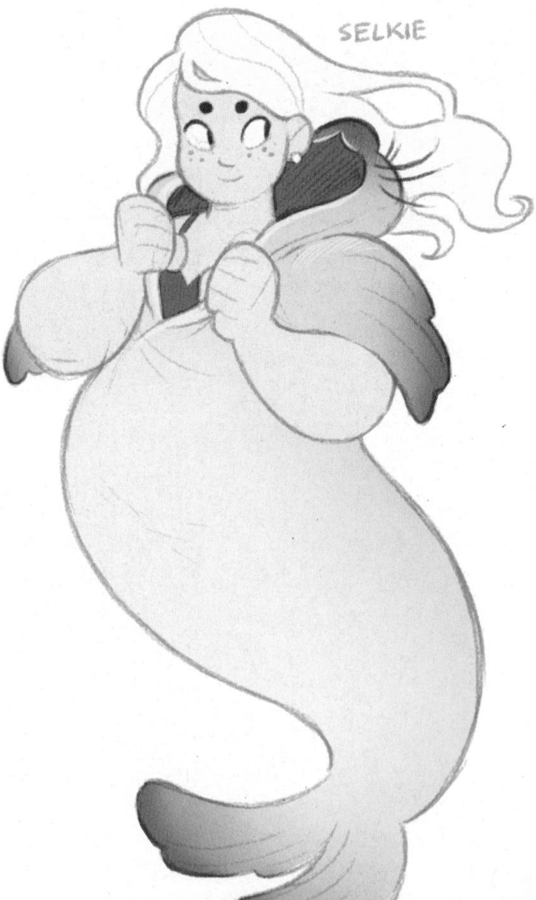
SELKIE

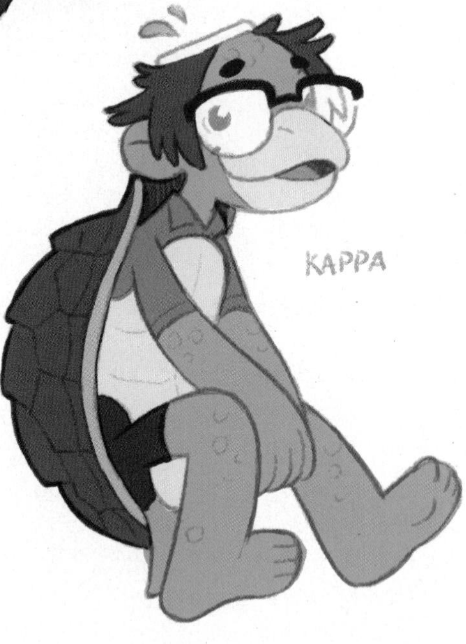
KAPPA

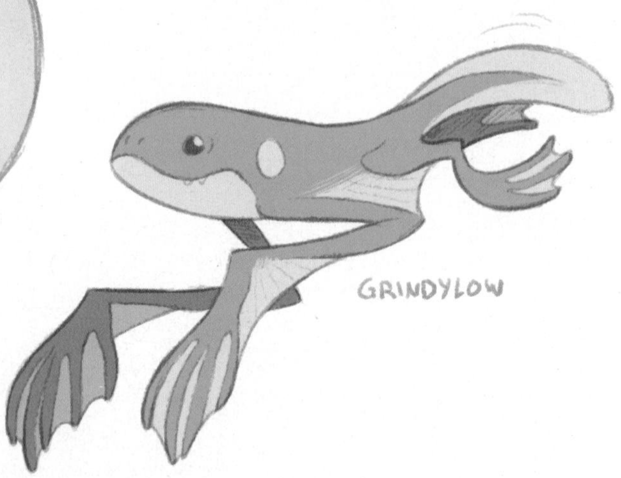
GRINDYLOW

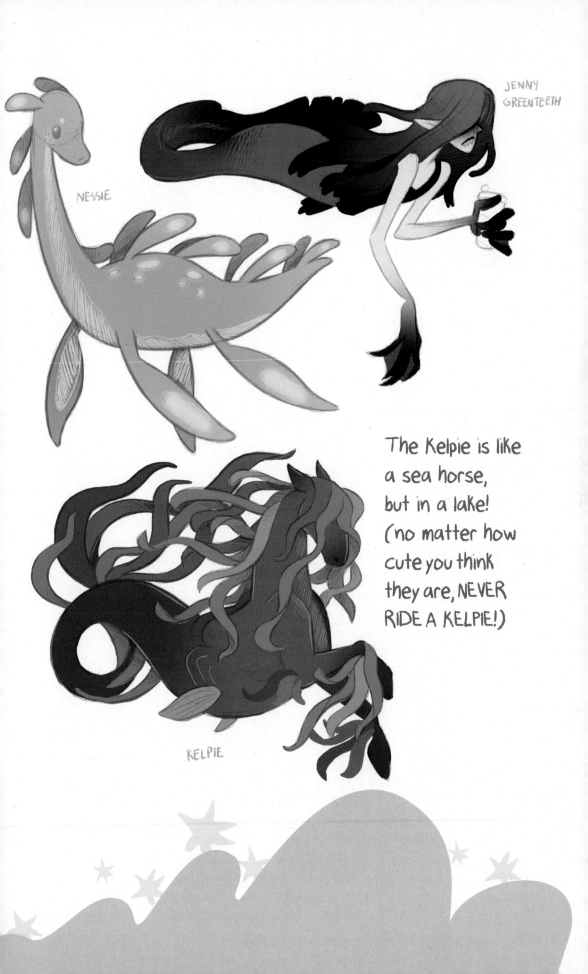

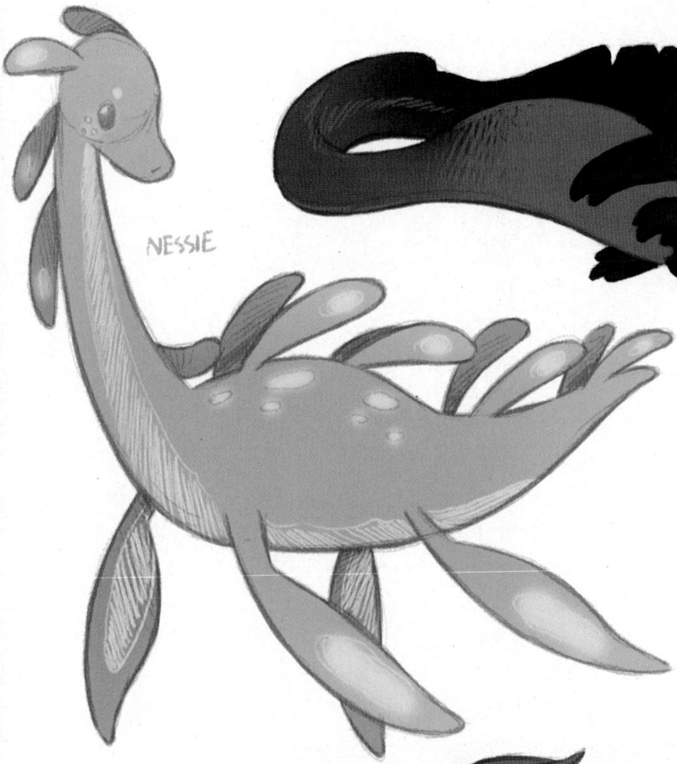
NESSIE

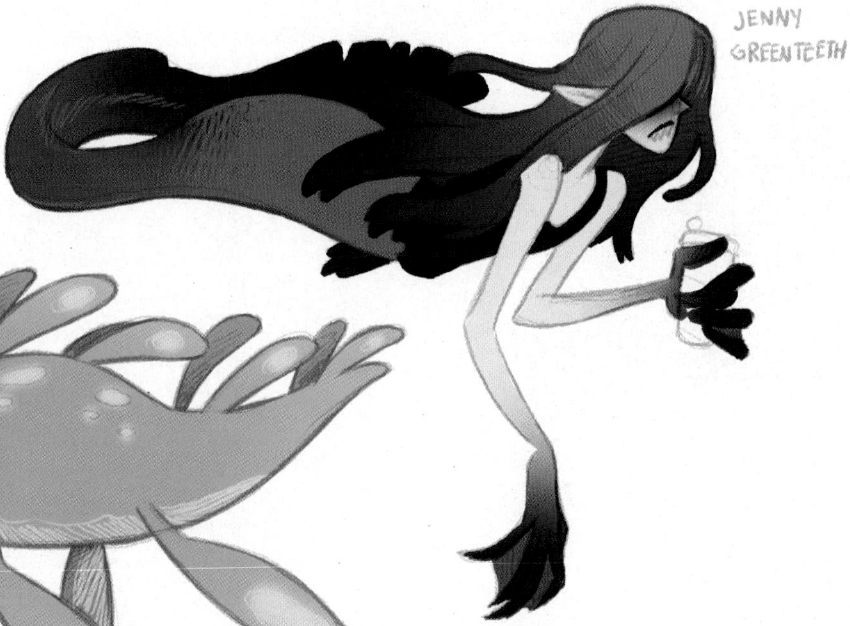
JENNY
GREENTEETH

The Kelpie is like a sea horse, but in a lake! (no matter how cute you think they are, NEVER RIDE A KELPIE!)

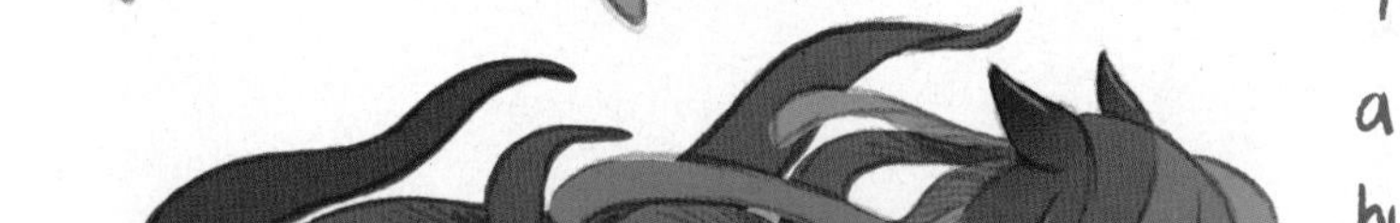
KELPIE

FAN ART

Do you have a favorite
Moonstruck character that
you'd like to draw for us?
We'd love to see it! Email us!
teammoonstruck@gmail.com

Blitheton State University Dean by Lauren Houser,
@lazuliarts on Instagram

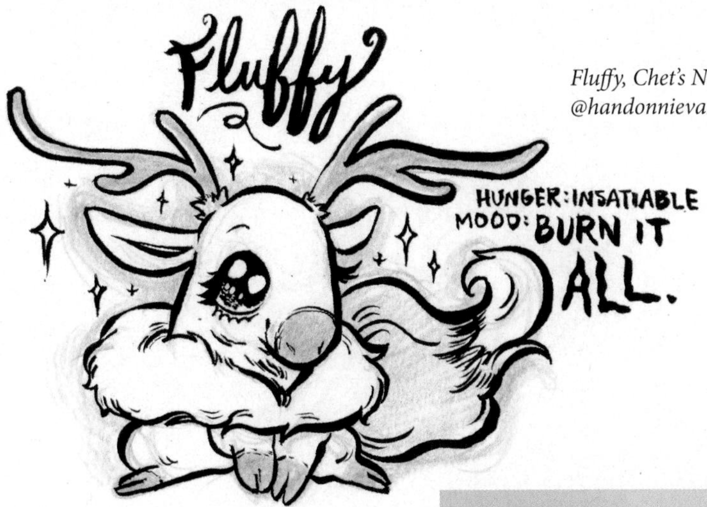
Fluffy
HUNGER: INSATIABLE
MOOD: BURN IT ALL.

Fluffy, Chet's Newpal by Han Donovan
@handonnievan on Instagram

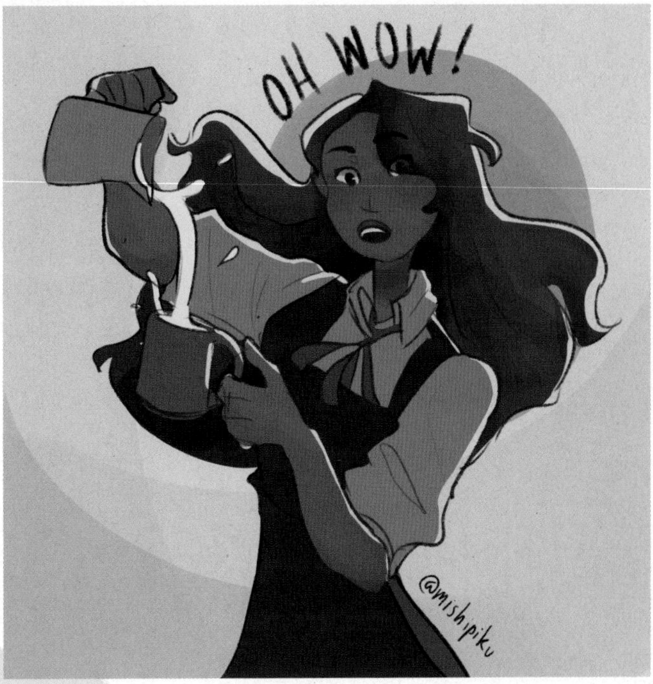
OH WOW!
@mishipiku

Cassandra by Schantelle Alonzo
@mishipiku on Instagram

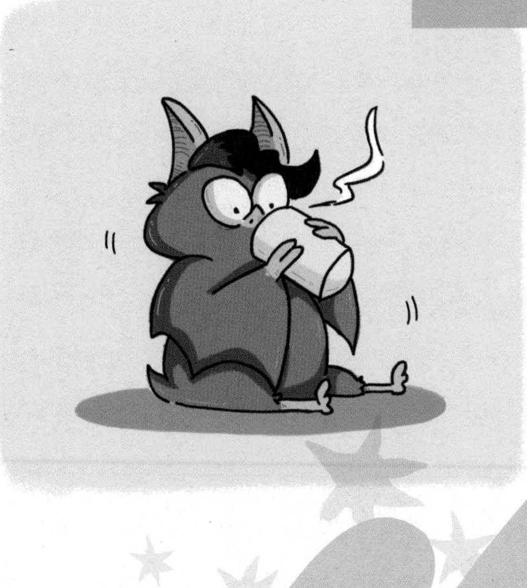

Bat! Mark! by Keely Hoffman
@blueinkmix on Instagram

Cassandra by Hannah Wheeler
@hannahwheelerart on Instagram

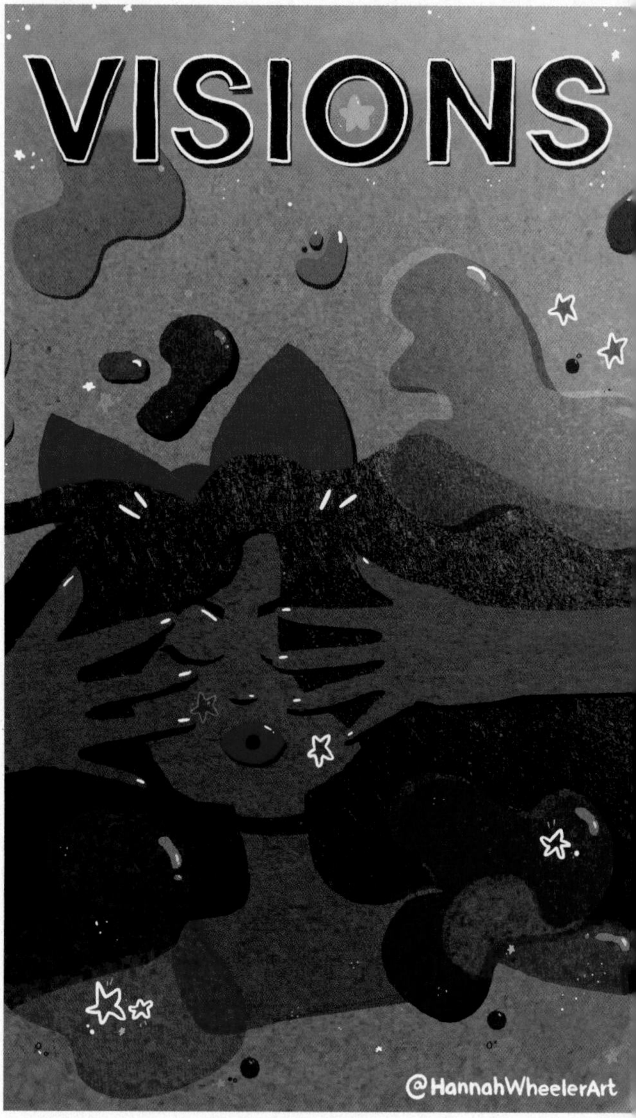
VISIONS
@HannahWheelerArt

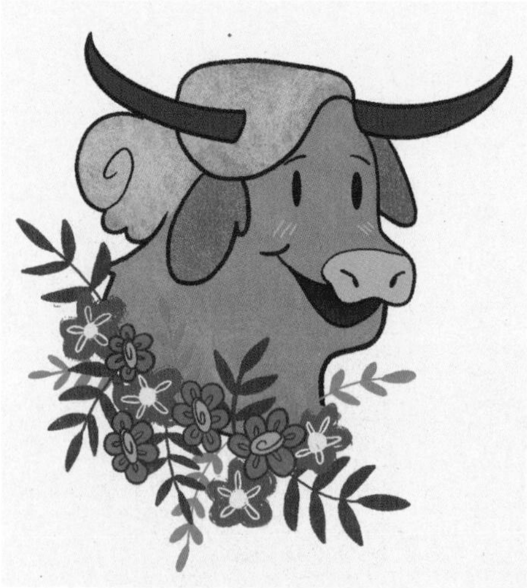

Manuel by Zoe Fox
@palelittlefox on Instagram

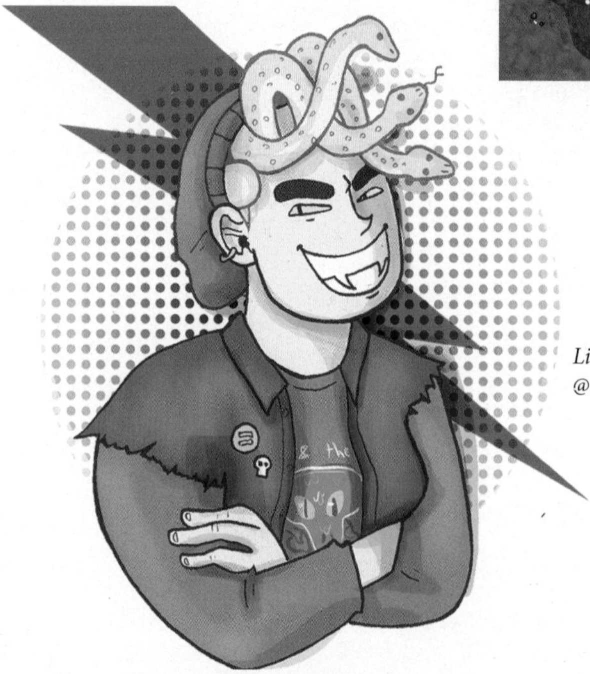

Lindi by Mickey Dyer
@mickeydyer on Instagram

Veronica by Lexi Ramos
@outraged_artist on Instagram

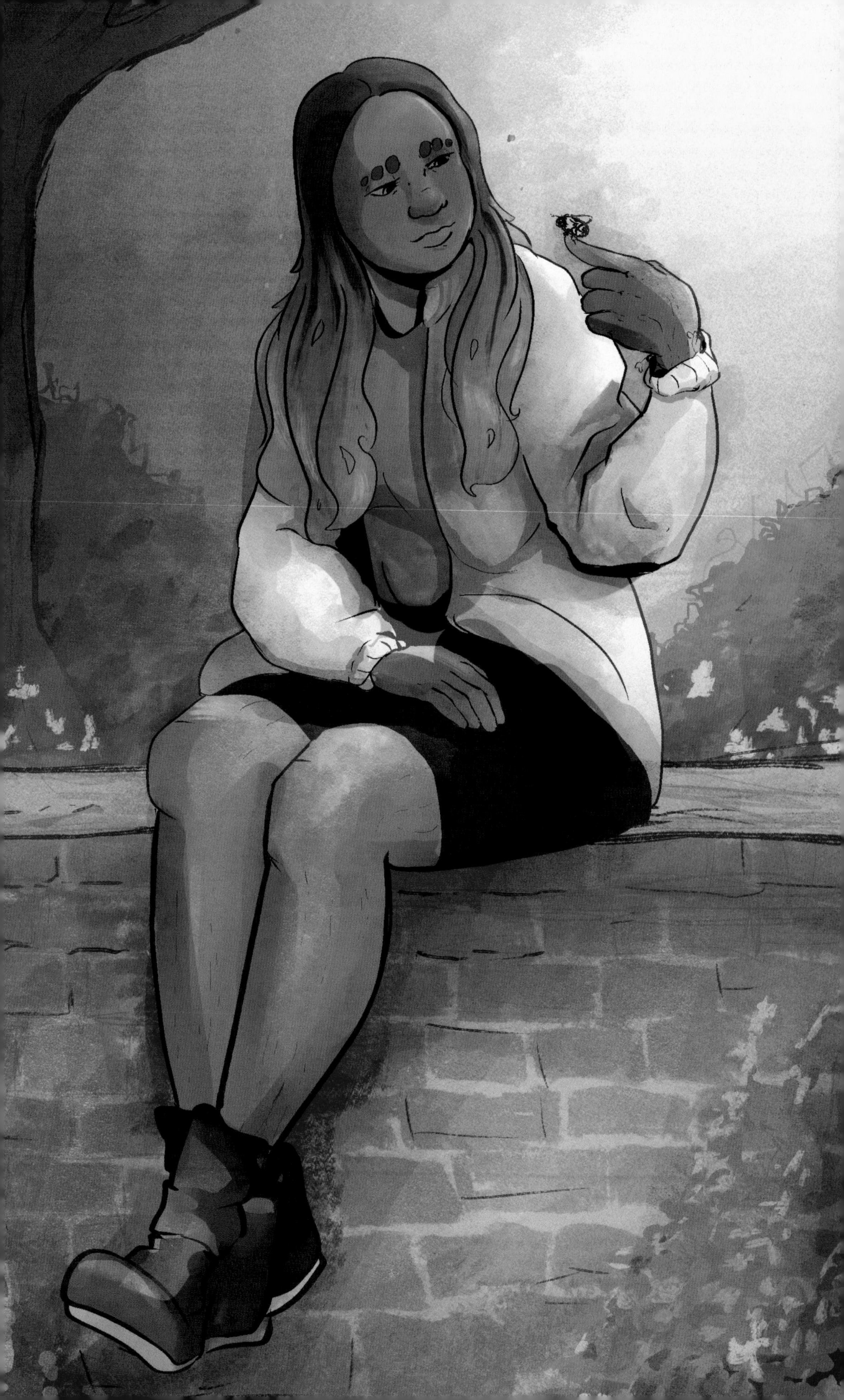

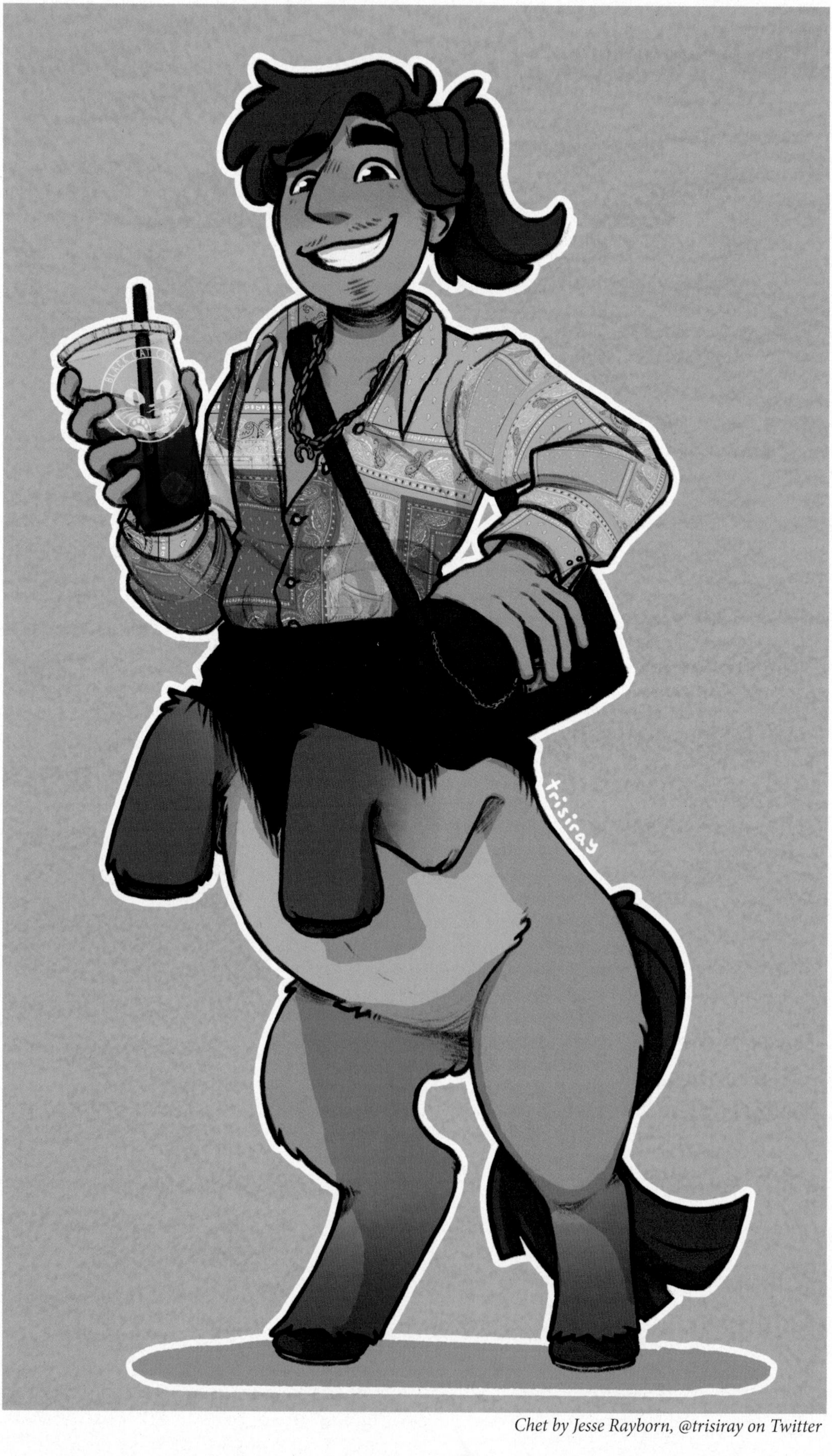
trisiray

Chet by Jesse Rayborn, @trisiray on Twitter

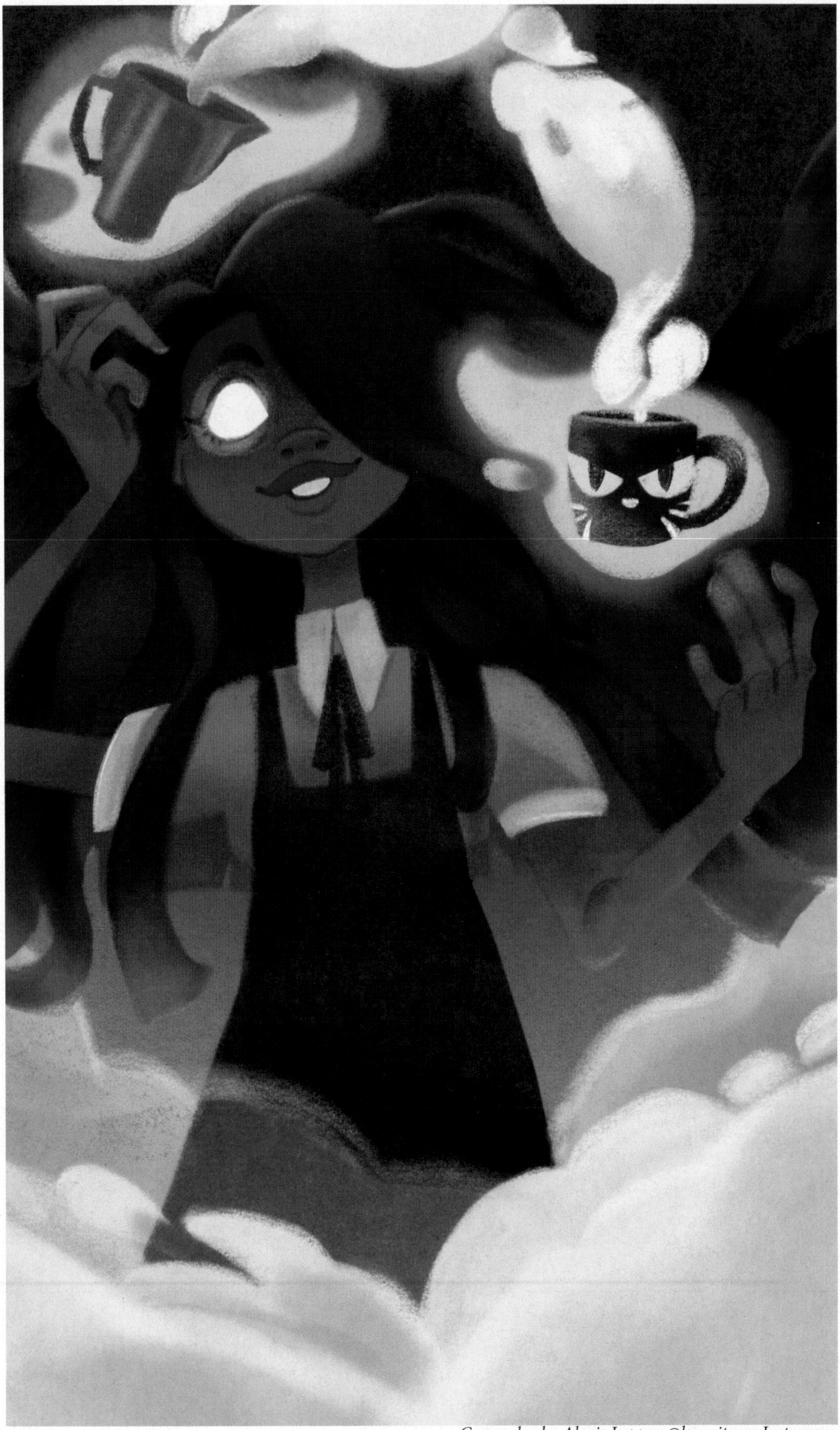

Cassandra by Alexis Lepper, @lexocity on Instagram

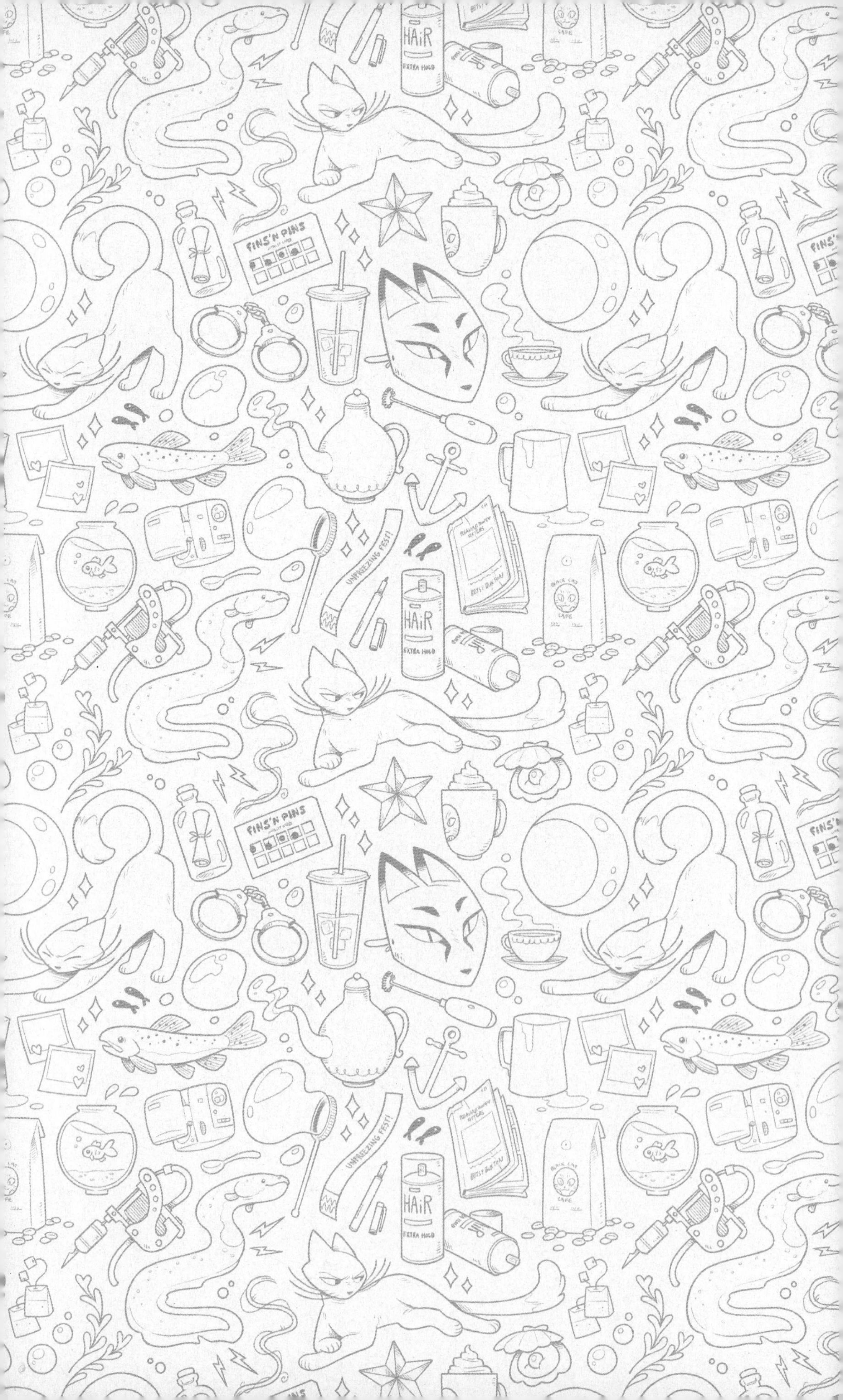
HAiR
EXTRA HOLD
FINS'N PINS
UNFREEZING FEST!